DANGEROUS RELATIONS

The Threat of Homosexuality

Bill Muehlenberg

Foreword by Janet Folger Porter

Melbourne

Published in 2014 by
CultureWatch Books, Melbourne, Australia.

Cover design: Panage Design,
PO Box 1208, Glen Waverley, Vic. 3150.

Dangerous Relations: The Threat of Homosexuality

Includes bibliographic references.

ISBN: 978-1500516031

Copyright 2014 by Bill Muehlenberg

All rights reserved. No part of this book may be reproduced or transmitted in any form or by any means, electronic or mechanical, including photocopying, recording or by any information storage and retrieval system, without prior permission in writing from the publisher.

Unless otherwise indicated, Scripture quotations are taken from the New International Version of the Bible. Copyright © 1973, 1978, 1984, by the International Bible Society.

Contents

Foreword v

Introduction ix

Chapter 1   The Homosexual War Against Freedom, Faith and Family 1

Any more evidence needed? 49

Case study 54

Chapter 2   How Families, Parenthood, and Identity Suffer 59

Gender mania 69

It's a brave new world 71

Chapter 3   What Slippery Slope? 73

Polyamory (group love/marriage) 74

SCOTUS and beyond 90

Paedophilia 94

The curious case of Kate 99

Incest 103

Bestiality 108

Objectamory 124

Conclusion 128

Chapter 4   Deconstructing the Family 131

The historicity and universality of the natural family 135

The family in history 138

Marriage the norm 142

Marriage is natural 145

Conclusion 153

Chapter 5   The Importance of Both Fathers and Mothers 157

The facts on fatherlessness 158

Economic difficulties 161

Educational performance 162

Criminal involvement 163
Involvement with drugs and alcohol 164
Sexual problems 164
Mental, emotional and physical well-being 165
Social costs 167
Child abuse 168
Conclusion 169
The importance of mothers 171
Children need both parents 176
Conclusion 178
Appendix 1   Homosexuality: A Select Bibliography 181
Appendix 2   One Man's Story 189
Appendix 3   One Woman's Story: A Life Redeemed 195
References and endnotes 201

Foreword

by Janet Folger Porter

In 2005 I wrote a book entitled *The Criminalization of Christianity*. In it I predicted the homosexual issue would be used to label, punish, silence, and criminalize people of faith. But my book was merely an introduction to what Bill Muehlenberg has discovered and documented since then in his compelling book, *Dangerous Relations: The Threat of Homosexuality*.

For those who think the homosexual agenda doesn't affect you, expect to have your eyes opened through the pages of this book. You don't care about the issue of homosexuality? I get that. But do you care about truth? How about freedom? The Gospel? As I wrote in *The Criminalization of Christianity*, if they can silence the truth, they *will* silence the Gospel. *Dangerous Relations* confirms this.

It is a well-documented, easy to understand warning to those lulled to sleep by the warm water about to reach the boiling point. It is later than you think, but there are still some freedoms left for us to use. The only way to keep our freedoms, however, is to use them *now*.

Yes, we have the right to remain silent, but if we use it very much longer, those may be the words we hear before we see the inside of a prison cell for the crime speaking the truth.

Pastor Jeff Kolodziej of Cornerstone Chapel in Medina Ohio is one of the people in our documentary on the same topic, *Light Wins: How to Overcome the Criminalization of Christianity*. In it he said, "The acid test for a formula or principle is: 'Does it bring life?' If homosexuals dominated the whole landscape, and we embraced that lifestyle as the norm, we would be *extinct*." God's design of natural marriage brings life (and life abundantly). The choice is clear: life or death.

Homosexual behaviour is one of the most dangerous practices out there. It is as dangerous as smoking, yet it is being taught to our children as if it is healthy and good. The government statistics (which are increasingly illegal to share) are irrefutable: homosexual behaviour brings with it rampant disease and early death. To love someone is to tell them the truth - to help them make the life-giving choice.

There are people trapped in homosexuality who need to know the truth. *Dangerous Relations* confirms the transforming power of a loving God by introducing you to the people you've been told do not exist - those who've been set free from homosexuality.

The primary reason that I, a pro-life activist, took notice of this issue is because it is being used to criminalize Christianity. For those who still don't believe it, Bill's book removes all doubt.

So what do we do about it? Read (beginning with this book). Speak. Act. Unite. An essential, but often overlooked, component to victory is unity. Bill's book inspired me to look beyond my own nation of America and join with our brothers and sisters throughout the world who are facing an even greater assault on their freedoms - they face outright persecution. You see, the homosexual lobby demands far more than tolerance. It now demands that we agree, teach, celebrate and subsidise its dangerous lie.

Compliance to that lie is now being enforced in schools, businesses, the church, the military, and the public square by our governments, courts, and international community.

If you feel overwhelmed by the stark reality of how far we've allowed evil to penetrate our culture, take a break and look up. Yes, it is later than we think, but God is bigger than we know and He's given us the way to get back on track - the four-point checklist found in 2 Chronicles 7:14: "If my people who are called by my name will humble themselves, and pray and seek my face, and turn from their wicked ways, then I will hear from heaven, and will forgive their sin and heal their land."

The first three words of God's promise are three of the most hopeful I know: "If *my people.*" That means we don't have to control the centres of power and influence, we don't even have to be a majority - all we need for God to heal us is for *God's people* to do what He says. If we do those four things, God will hear us, forgive us, and heal our land.

But turning from our wicked ways includes speaking the truth in love no matter what the cost. As Dietrich Bonhoeffer said before he was executed by the Nazis: "Silence in the face of evil is itself evil. God will not hold us guiltless. Not to speak is to speak. Not to act is to act." Silence and inaction in the face of this evil is not an option. So, take the information found in this book and shine truth into a dark world increasingly void of truth.

Dangerous Relations leaves no doubt as to the severity and urgency of the threat we face. Thank you Bill for your hard work and meticulous research to sound the alarm across the globe. The question that remains: what will we *do* in light of this unmistakable danger? Heed the warning, because there may not be another.

Janet (Folger) Porter is the Founder and President of Faith2Action, a U.S. network of pro-family groups and a pro-active arm of the pro-family movement. Janet hosts a 60 second daily radio commentary heard in 300 American markets, and produced a documentary film on marriage entitled *Light Wins: How to Overcome the Criminalization of Christianity.*

Introduction

In my 2011 book *Strained Relations: The Challenge of Homosexuality* I detailed just what is at stake with the rise of the militant homosexual agenda. In that volume – which is now in its fourth printing – I examined in detail the many myths put out by the activists ("It's all genetic," "Ten per cent of population is homosexual," etc.). I also warned of the various attacks on marriage and family, looked at their various strategies, and rebuffed the theological revisionists.

Little did I realise however how quickly all this would escalate, and how much worse things would become in such a very short period of time. Since writing my first volume the attacks on faith, freedom and family have especially taken off, with new horror stories appearing almost on a daily basis all around the Western world. And so too have the demands of other activist minority groups, emboldened as they are by the successes of the homosexual activists. Now all sorts of other fringe sexualities are being championed by various activist groups.

While my first volume covered just about all the bases in the homosexual debate, much more can always be said. This follow-up volume to *Strained Relations* will act as a supplement to what was presented there, and include new information and material to further round out my case.

Chapter One of *Dangerous Relations* looks at the many cases of homosexual intolerance of anyone and anything that dares to resist their radical and militant agenda. And I can say right now that as soon as this book goes to the printers, it will already be out of date in this area. There will be many dozens – perhaps hundreds – of new cases of anti-faith and anti-family bigotry which will have occurred in the short period of time needed to produce this book at the printers.

Chapter Two documents how families, parenthood and family identity all suffer as we allow the institutions of marriage and family to be redefined and recreated in the image of the activists. Children in particular suffer in this brave new world of social engineering.

Chapter Three offers several prime examples of the growing problem of the slippery slope. More and more activists are now very publicly and passionately pushing for paedophilia, polyamory, incest rights, and even bestiality, buoyed by the successes of the homosexual activists, and following on with the very same arguments and rationale.

Chapter Four provides some much-needed background information to head off some of the common criticisms made by the activists and their supporters. Specifically it will rebuff the silly notion that heterosexual marriage is just a recent invention, and that marriage has always been a wildly fluctuating and changing institution with no clear boundaries at all. Thus it takes on the oft-heard myth that the two-parent family is basically just an invention of the 1950s, and that families have – and can – come in any shape and size you want them to.

Chapter Five discusses the importance of fathers and mothers and demonstrates how both are absolutely vital for the optimal raising of children. Advocates for homosexual adoption rights need to let this data speak, and not allow emotional wants and desires to trump the wellbeing of children.

I conclude my book with three appendices. The first offers a recommended reading list for those who want to take these matters further. Then I feature two appendices containing the moving testimonies of a former homosexual and a former lesbian.

As stated, this book is built upon and follows from the wealth of information contained in my previous book. With over 700 footnotes, that volume properly laid the groundwork, and dealt with all the common criticisms and objections. I recommend that you obtain a copy of *Strained Relations* for a much more detailed and fuller account of all the various issues involved in the debate over homosexuality, the homosexual agenda, homosexual marriage, and so on.

These two volumes go together. With some 500 endnotes here, that makes for well over 1200 endnotes in total, and over 500 pages all up. Many other good books on this topic exist, but almost all are from America or England. There is nothing quite like these two volumes currently on offer in Australia, where I live; however the material here covers plenty of information, data and statistics from both Australia and overseas. My hope is that people from throughout the world find these books to be of great value and assistance.

CHAPTER 1

The Homosexual War Against Freedom, Faith and Family

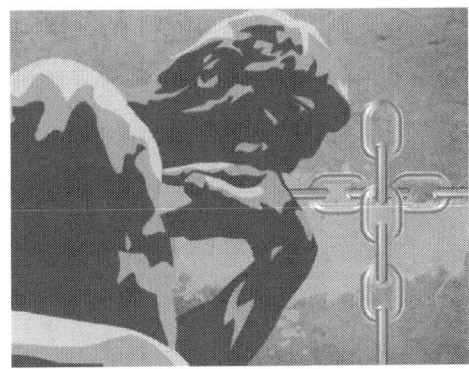

For years now I have been documenting the constant war which is being waged against those who value marriage and family, those who value freedom, and those who are people of faith. All three have been mercilessly hammered by a group of belligerent and antagonistic activists who will not stop until we all submit to their strident and stringent agenda.

And increasingly we find secular left governments which have jumped into bed with the activists, forcing all naysayers to comply with this new world order, or else face the consequences. Mark Steyn has recently penned a piece on this, and a few quotes are well worth sharing here. He certainly hits the nail on the head with this one:

"The bigger the Big Government, the smaller everything else: In Sweden, expressing a moral objection to homosexuality is illegal, even on religious grounds, even in church, and a pastor minded to cite the more robust verses of Leviticus would risk four years in jail. In Canada, the courts rule that Catholic schools must allow gay students to take their same-sex dates to the prom. The secular state's Bureau of Compliance is merciless to apostates to a degree even your fire-breathing imams might marvel at."[1]

And again: "Liberals take the same view as the proprietors of the Dar al-Islam: Once they hold this land, they hold it forever."[2] Exactly right. Big governments which have become subservient to radical activist agendas are a danger to all who value freedom and democracy.

We see both being whittled away time and time again. Our freedoms are taking a hammering, and new cases of homosexual bullying and intimidation appear daily. And the really bizarre thing is the activists keep insisting that special rights and marriage rights will not impact us. They keep telling us that nothing will change as they are granted all these special rights. Of course they are simply trying to lull to sleep a gullible public. They know full well that everything changes as they get various special rights.

There are plenty of examples to choose from here. Thus I offer just some recent examples of how the homosexual agenda is impacting – and/or soon will be – every one of us. I will only go back to 2011, and I will only offer a selection of examples. These are just the tip of the iceberg, but they very nicely demonstrate the war we are in, and how the other side will not rest until it has every one of us bowing in obeisance to its demands.

With so many examples to choose from, and so little space here, let me just offer the headline, date, and the opening paragraph or two of each recent news item. I will go back several years ago and move up to more recent times. In this period of just 34 months (January 2011 – October 2013), I document 165 examples of this growing war on faith, freedom and family. And as I said, these are just some of the cases that took place during this period, but not all.[3]

Here then is the evidence:

"Canadian Court: Marriage officials must marry homosexuals"
January 10, 2011
"The Saskatchewan Court of Appeal declared this morning that proposed legislative amendments that would have allowed Saskatchewan's marriage commissioners to refuse to perform same-sex 'marriages' on religious grounds are unconstitutional."[4]

"Quebec Human Rights Tribunal fines man $12,000 for 'homophobic' remarks"
January 17, 2011
"A Montreal man has been ordered to pay $12,000 to his homosexual neighbours for allegedly directing 'homophobic' remarks at them, by the Quebec Human Rights Tribunal. The homosexual couple has a history of pursuing lawsuits and complaints against neighbours."[5]

"Death threats against UK columnist for opposing homosexualist agenda"
February 2, 2011
"A prominent conservative UK columnist has said she received death threats after she criticized plans to insert homosexual materials into all subjects in the curriculum in Britain's schools. Writing in the *Daily Mail* this week, Melanie Phillips said that she had been expecting a reaction, 'which would amply bear out the truth of what I had written. The response, however, exceeded even my expectations'."[6]

"Gay couple files complaint against Christian B&B owners for refusing civil union ceremony"
March 7, 2011
"A homosexual man has filed human rights complaints against two bed and breakfasts in Illinois after they refused to let out their premises for a civil union ceremony between the man and his sexual partner."[7]

"Army: court-martial Chaplains for 'religious, conscience' objection to homosexuality"

March 24, 2011
"The U.S. Army has officially threatened military chaplains they must either embrace the new openly homosexual military, resign from service, or face court-martial for their 'religious, conscience' objections."[8]

"Mandated gay clubs in Catholic schools can't help students overcome homosexuality: Ontario gvmt"
April 8, 2011
"Ontario Catholic schools will not be permitted to use the support groups that are being mandated under the government's controversial equity and inclusive education strategy to counsel homosexual students to 'reform their sexuality.' The government revealed the unprecedented challenge to the province's publicly-funded Catholic education system in comments to *LifeSiteNews*."[9]

"Pro-marriage U.S. Olympic official forced to resign after criticism from gay activists"
May 10, 2011
"Just eight days after being named the U.S. chef de mission for the 2012 Olympic Games, Gold Medallist Peter Vidmar resigned his position after criticism from gay activists and athletes because of his support of true marriage. Vidmar, 49, received two Olympic gymnastics gold medals in 1984 in Los Angeles. He is chairman of the board of USA Gymnastics, has served on the President's Council for Physical Fitness, and is a prominent motivational speaker, among many other achievements."[10]

"Gay columnist: let's face it, we want to indoctrinate children"
May 18, 2011
"Queerty contributor Daniel Villarreal criticized the homosexual movement's knee-jerk reaction against accusations of meddling in public schools. Villarreal pointed to a recent National Organization for Marriage (NOM) ad launched in New York that points out how homosexual indoctrination has been introduced in Massachusetts and California schools. While gay activists usually deny that they want to indoctrinate children, said Villarreal, 'let's face it – that's a

lie. We want educators to teach future generations of children to accept queer sexuality. In fact, our very future depends on it,' he wrote."[11]

"Top sports anchor fired over beliefs on marriage"
June 23, 2011
"A former top sports anchor who revealed to *LifeSiteNews* Wednesday that he is filing a human rights complaint against Rogers Communications, after the company fired him for publicly backing true marriage, says his termination over his deeply-held religious beliefs affects all Canadians. 'My message to the millions of Canadians participating in social media is that "this can happen to you",' said Damian Goddard Thursday in an official statement. 'I was terminated 24 hours after expressing a widely-held opinion from my personal Twitter account – an opinion consistent with the teachings of the Catholic Church. And an opinion that is supposed to be protected by Canada's constitution'."[12]

"Genderless preschool bans 'him' and 'her'"
June 27, 2011
"At the Egalia preschool [in Sweden], staff avoid using words like 'him' or 'her' and address the 33 kids as 'friend' rather than girls and boys. From the colour and placement of toys to the choice of books, every detail has been carefully planned to make sure the children don't fall into gender stereotypes."[13]

"California passes bill mandating pro-gay teaching in schools, no parent opt-out"
July 6, 2011
"The bill prohibits any school material or instruction that reflects adversely on homosexuality, bisexuality or transgenderism, and prohibits parents from removing children from classes over offensive material."

"Florida High School removes Christian teacher for criticizing gay 'marriage' on Facebook"
August 18, 2011

"Mount Dora High School has removed a veteran social-studies teacher Gerald (Jerry) Buell from his classroom for Facebook comments critical of homosexual 'marriage'."[14]

"Tory MP calls for churches to be banned from holding marriages if they refuse gay couples"
September 2, 2011
"Mike Weatherley, the Conservative MP for Hove, has called for churches to be banned from holding marriages if they refuse to perform civil partnerships for gay couples. He says that the idea will bring more equality for gay couples."[15]

"Student's Homosexuality Comment Leads To Suspension"
September 21, 2011
"A Fort Worth high school student says he was suspended from school for expressing his Christian beliefs in class. His teacher, however, saw it differently, labelling the student's comments about homosexuality as bullying."[16]

"New York clerk faces lawsuit for refusing to sign same-sex 'marriage' license"
September 30, 2011
"Another town clerk in New York may lose her job for refusing to sign marriage licenses for same sex couples, the *New York Times* reports. Fifty-seven-year-old Rose Marie Belforti has been the town clerk in the small rural town of Ledyard, New York for ten years. When the state of New York legalized homosexual 'marriage' this past summer, Belforti decided that she could not reconcile signing same-sex marriage licenses with her Christian faith. Instead, she decided to delegate the task to a deputy, who would issue such licenses by appointment. Now, a lesbian couple is threatening to sue Belforti for discrimination."[17]

"Teacher under investigation for criticizing homosexuality on Facebook page"
October 17, 2011

"New Jersey school officials are investigating allegations that a teacher criticized homosexuality on her personal Facebook page. Special education teacher Viki Knox had posted complaints about a Union High School display recognizing October as Lesbian, Gay, Bisexual, and Transgender History month."[18]

"MPs vote to stop civil servants refusing to carry out gay weddings"
November 15, 2011
"[Dutch] MPs voted on Tuesday afternoon for a change in the law to prevent civil servants refusing to conduct gay marriages."[19]

"Lesbian couple mulls action against Christian wedding cake baker"
November 16, 2011
"An Iowa baker who politely declined to provide a wedding cake for two lesbians based on her Christian values may face legal action from the couple."[20]

"Gay rights activist calls for boycott of Salvation Army Christmas fundraiser"
November 28, 2011
"Gay rights activists who object to the Salvation Army's biblical stance on homosexuality are launching their annual call to shut down the organization's Christmas fundraiser."[21]

"Case of counselling student forced to undergo pro-homosexual 'sensitivity training' goes to court"
December 2, 2011
"After losing at a lower court, a counselling student at a public university in Georgia who was threatened with expulsion because she expressed discomfort with counselling homosexuals, is pleading her case before an Appeals Court this week. A legal complaint filed on behalf of Jennifer Keeton accuses Augusta State University of placing Keeton on academic probation after she refused to comply with faculty instructions that she must, in their words, 'alter her beliefs' on homosexuality and 'gender identity'."[22]

"Macy's fires woman for refusing 'transgender' man access to women's fitting room"
December 8, 2011
"A woman has been fired from a Macy's department store for denying a man dressed as a woman access to the women's fitting room. 'I had to either comply with Macy's or comply with God,' said Natalie Johnson."[23]

"All Ontario teachers will be forced to undergo 'diversity' training by 2013: minister"
December 22, 2011
"By 2013 prospective teachers in Ontario will be required to undergo focused training in 'sexual orientation' and 'gender diversity,' says a cabinet minister in Premier Dalton McGuinty's Liberal government."[24]

"Australian Open braced for anti-Margaret Court protest"
January 11, 2012
"Margaret Court, the most successful female grand-slam singles player in the history of the sport and the mother of the modern game, is facing the embarrassment of a demonstration against her powerful opposition to gay marriage being staged at the Australian Open next week on the court named in her honour."[25]

"Judge Rules Christian facility cannot ban same-sex civil union ceremony on its own premises"
January 13, 2012
"A New Jersey judge ruled against a Christian retreat house that refused to allow a same-sex civil union ceremony to be conducted on its premises, ruling the Constitution allows 'some intrusion into religious freedom to balance other important societal goals'."[26]

"Amsterdam chief rabbi suspended for gay stance"
January 18, 2012
"The Orthodox Jewish community of Amsterdam suspended its US-born chief rabbi on Tuesday for consigning a declaration which said homosexuality was a 'treatable' inclination. Rabbi Aryeh Ralbag

told *The Jerusalem Post* on Wednesday that he found it 'scandalous that a chief rabbi cannot state the Torah viewpoint for his community without being penalized'."[27]

"Attorney Says School Threatened, Punished Boy Who Opposed Gay Adoption"
January 24, 2012
"A 15-year-old Wisconsin boy who wrote an op-ed opposing gay adoptions was censored, threatened with suspension and called ignorant by the superintendent of the Shawano School District, according to an attorney representing the child."[28]

"Gay activists attack church over same-sex marriage message"
February 15, 2012
"Same Sex Marriage supporters attacked Wallsend, NSW Presbyterian Church last night in response to a message criticising same-sex marriage displayed on the building's outside notice board. The church on Nelson Street had updated its message board last week to read 'Even tradies know you need both male and female joints to make a marriage'. The front of the 1867 building, which recently received a $12,000 makeover, was defaced with messages such as 'sexuality is not a choice' and 'love thy neighbour not hate gays'."[29]

"All schools must teach about homosexuality, cabinet decides"
February 17, 2012
"All [Dutch] primary and secondary schools are to be required to provide pupils with information about homosexuality, ministers agreed at their Friday cabinet meeting. MPs from across the political spectrum had urged education minister Marja van Bijsterveldt to incorporate lessons about homosexuality in their core tasks last year. The minister had originally wanted to leave the issue up to schools themselves."[30]

"Criticize homosexuality in Sweden and go to jail: No problem for European rights court"
February 17, 2012

"Anyone challenging the homosexualist agenda in public in Sweden can be sent to prison, and the European Court of Human Rights (ECHR) has ruled that this does not constitute any violation of rights. In 2004, the Swedish government charged a group of pamphleteers with 'agitation against a national or ethnic group,' a crime that carries a maximum penalty of 2 years in prison."[31]

"Qld Labor candidate expelled after homophobic rant"
February 21, 2012
"Teenage Queensland ALP candidate Peter Watson has been expelled from the party after admitting to a series of anti-gay rants on the internet."[32]

"Brazilian government demands apology from televangelist for 'homophobia'"
February 21, 2012
"A Brazilian federal prosecutor is demanding that a televangelist retract certain statements he made in 2011 which the prosecutor says incited 'hatred' against homosexuals – a thinly veiled threat of future legal action."[33]

"14-year-old homeschooled girl receives death threats for defending marriage"
February 22, 2012
"A 14-year-old homeschooler who testified before the Maryland state senate against a bill redefining marriage has been the subject of cyberbullying, vicious name-calling, and death threats. Sarah Crank, 14, told the Maryland Senate Judicial Proceedings Committee last month she believes children need a mother and a father. 'I really feel bad for the kids who have two parents of the same gender,' she told the senators. 'Even though some kids think it's fine, they have no idea what kind of wonderful experiences they miss out on.' She continued, 'People say that they were born that way, but I've met really nice adults who did change. Today's my 14th birthday, and it would be the best birthday present ever if you would vote "no" on gay marriage,' she said."[34]

"Alberta readies to impose 'diversity' education on homeschoolers"
February 22, 2012
"Homeschooling groups are sounding the alarm this week as the Alberta government prepares to pass a bill that they say threatens to mandate 'diversity' education in the home."[35]

"Preacher's remarks spark USQ ban"
February 23, 2012
"A United States preacher has been banned from speaking at the University of Southern Queensland tonight due to disparaging comments he made about homosexuality. James Spinnati's visit was organised by the university's Multifaith Centre to make a presentation on Christology in Contemporary Times. But early yesterday Dr Spinnati's appearance was banned, with emails sent to all USQ staff advising of vice-chancellor Professor Jan Thomas' decision."[36]

"Stop Catholic schools from distributing 'homophobic' literature: leader of UK's largest union"
February 27, 2012
"The government is allowing 'homophobia' to be promoted in religious schools, in the form of a booklet distributed to students at some Catholic schools in Lancashire, says the UK's largest trades union. In a letter to Education Secretary Michael Gove in December, Brendan Barber, head of the powerful Trades Union Congress, (TUC), wrote, 'Schools now have a legal duty to challenge all forms of prejudice. Such literature undermines this completely'."[37]

"Christian vendor blocked from campus"
March 5, 2012
"Under mounting pressure from pro-'gay' activists, the student government at a university in Boston voted down a proposal to bring a Chick-fil-A franchise on campus. Under an onslaught of hostile criticism from Northeastern University students and faculty, the Student Government Association voted 31-5 not to allow Chick-fil-A to become a campus vendor in a food court that is being renovated. Among the critics claiming the company discriminates

against homosexuals was the university's LGBT advocacy group, NU Pride."[38]

"'Truth about homosexuality' pamphleteer arrested, threatened with committal to psychiatric ward"
March 8, 2012
"Bill Whatcott's controversial campaign to expose the harms of homosexuality has most recently resulted in him being detained by police and threatened with committal to a psychiatric hospital if he didn't stop distributing flyers at the university of Calgary and adjoining neighbourhoods. The activist had begun distributing 5000 pamphlets that criticize Alberta's new Education Act, and also contained photos of sexually transmitted disease infections common to those who engage in homosexual sex, when he was apprehended by Calgary police and put in jail. 'The police officer initially told me he was arresting me and detaining me under a Form 10 (Alberta Mental Health Act),' Whatcott wrote on his blog, 'and he told me he was going to have me committed to a psychiatric hospital.' Whatcott said that this was 'reminiscent of how Christian dissidents were treated in the old USSR'."[39]

"Christians Who Signed Petitions Investigated"
March 10, 2012
"A prosecutor has decided to pursue and possibly charge members of El Paso area churches who promoted petitions opposing the city administration's decision to implement benefits for same-sex partners even after voters decided not to allow that."[40]

"ABC presenter stood down for voicing Katter ad"
March 12, 2012
"An ABC radio presenter has been taken off the air after it was revealed she was the voice behind a controversial anti gay marriage television commercial produced for Katter's Australian Party."[41]

"Christian minister accused of 'crime against humanity' for homosexuality stance"
March 15, 2012

"Two years ago, Scott Lively, author of 'The Pink Swastika', addressed members of the Ugandan Parliament, which was considering a bill criminalizing homosexuality. Lively urged an emphasis on therapy rather than punishment, and, after the bill was released he opposed the death penalty provision. Now, on March 14th a lawsuit was filed in an American court alleging that Lively committed the 'Crime Against Humanity' by speaking against homosexuality in Uganda. The plaintiffs say that his address in Uganda is a cause of action in international law. The plaintiffs are the homosexualist organization Sexual Minorities Uganda (SMUG), and the law firm which filed the lawsuit, the Center for Constitutional Rights, a George Soros-funded Marxist group."[42]

"Lesbian with kids in Catholic school demands removal of Catechism quote on homosexuality"
March 16, 2012
"A self-proclaimed 'lesbian' whose two children attend a Catholic school near Peterborough, Ontario, is demanding that the Peterborough Catholic school board remove a Catechism quote dealing with homosexuality from a school pamphlet. Ann Michelle Tesluk has started an online petition to pressure the board to action and describes her activities as gearing to make the Catholic Church into an 'openly gay friendly church'."[43]

"Liberal outrage in Spain: Homosexual groups seek prosecution of bishop over sermon on homosexuality"
April 18, 2012
"Homosexual groups are seeking the prosecution of a Spanish bishop after he gave a sermon repeating the Catholic Church's teaching associating the gay lifestyle with the suffering of hell, and then an interview in which he endorsed psychological treatment for homosexual behaviour."[44]

"Kansas law would force churches to host same-sex 'weddings,' receptions"
April 24, 2012

"A proposed ordinance in one of the nation's most conservative states would force churches to rent their property out for same-sex 'weddings' and receptions. It would also force any public venue to allow people to use showers, restrooms, and locker-rooms based on their 'gender identity,' rather than their 'sex at birth'."[45]

"'Angry Queers' damage Driscoll's Portland church"
April 25, 2012
"A satellite church affiliated with controversial Seattle pastor Mark Driscoll was vandalized early Tuesday and a group calling itself the 'Angry Queers' has reportedly taken responsibility. Stained glass and other windows were broken at the Mars Hill Church."[46]

"Proposed Kansas Law Would Force Churches to Host Drag Queen Parties"
May 1, 2012
"On May 15, the city council of the small town, just northwest of Wichita, will vote on whether to add 'sexual orientation' and 'gender identity' to the list of other protected classes, such as race, age, and disability. If passed, this new law will destroy the 'free exercise of religion' in Hutchinson."[47]

"Nebraska football coach: I'd rather be fired than retract homosexuality remarks"
May 3, 2012
"University of Nebraska's assistant football coach, Ron Brown, who is facing censure and calls for his dismissal for publicly expressing his biblically-based views against the homosexual lifestyle, has stated that he'd rather be fired than retract his comments."[48]

"UK Catholic Schools Warned of Breaking Law in Opposing Gay Marriage"
May 9, 2012
"The government of Wales is moving against Catholic schools that are organizing students to protest a new government plan to back gay marriage in that country. The students at the Catholic schools were recently invited by their teachers to sign a petition against the

government's plans to legalize gay marriage. That drew the ire of some Welsh politicians. And government ministers in Britain are 'looking into' whether or not to issue a similar warning to schools in England."[49]

"California Considers Legislation Making it a Crime to Counsel Children Not to Be Homosexual"
May 9, 2012
"California Senate Bill 1172 would make it illegal for therapists, psychologists, counsellors and parents to engage in any kind of 'sexual orientation change efforts' against children 18 and younger. Violators could be subject to arrest, fines, possible jail time."[50]

"Victorian psychiatrist questioned over his stance on gay marriage"
May 13, 2012
"A psychiatrist lobbying against same-sex marriage must explain why he should retain his role on the board of the state's equal opportunity agency, critics say. Professor Kuruvilla George, who is Victoria's deputy chief psychiatrist, has signed a submission to a senate inquiry calling for a ban on same-sex marriage."[51]

"Christian Marriage Conference in UK Banned for Opposition to Gay Marriage"
May 14, 2012
"The organizers of a marriage conference in Britain have been told they can no longer hold the event on their regular hired premises because they support the biblical definition of marriage as between one man and one woman. The Law Society in England has revoked its permission for 'Christian Concern' to hold the conference on its premises saying that the event would breach its 'diversity policy' due to the Christian group's religious beliefs that there should be no redefinition of marriage to include same-sex couples."[52]

"Doctor quits equal rights board after same-sex row"
May 15, 2012
"A member of Victoria's Equal Opportunity and Human Rights Commission board has resigned after stirring controversy by signing

a petition opposing gay marriage. Professor Kuruvilla George is also the state's deputy chief psychiatrist and one of a group of 150 doctors who wrote to a Senate inquiry on marriage equality. The doctors' submission argued children with a mother and father were healthier than children with same-sex parents."[53]

"City in Kansas votes to outlaw discrimination against gays amid push to exempt churches"
May 15, 2012
"A city in Kansas, divided over a proposed ordinance that would bar organizations, including churches, from discriminating against same-sex couples, has backers saying gays deserve the protection as critics warn against the government going too far. The Hutchinson City Council voted 3-2 to add sexual orientation to the city's anti-discrimination ordinance, which covers churches, as well as employers, restaurants and other local businesses."[54]

"Boxing superstar Manny Pacquiao banned from shopping mall over gay 'marriage' remarks"
May 17, 2012
"World boxing superstar and Philippines congressman Manny Pacquiao has stated his opposition to Barack Obama's endorsement of same-sex 'marriage' and received a black eye for his trouble. During a May 12 interview with the *National Conservative Examiner* Pacquiao said the Bible is clear on homosexual activity and that with regard to marriage we must follow 'God's words first ... obey God's law first before considering the laws of man'."[55]

"N.J. teacher accused of anti-gay Facebook posts may retire to avoid charges"
May 17, 2012
"The Union Township High School teacher who created a firestorm last year after allegedly posting anti-gay comments on her Facebook page, wants to retire on a disability pension rather than face tenure charges."[56]

"UK Christian blogger under investigation by gov't ad authority for running pro-marriage ad"
May 18, 2012
"A prominent British Christian conservative blogger is under attack from a government agency, at the behest of a homosexualist activist group, for supporting the defence of traditional marriage."[57]

"NHS removes word 'Dad' from pregnancy handbook in case it offends same sex couples"
May 27, 2012
"The Health Service has removed the word 'dad' from a pregnancy handbook for fear of offending gay and lesbian parents. Officials decided to use the term 'partner' throughout the 200-page guide, titled *"Ready Steady Baby"*, after receiving a complaint that 'dad' was discriminating against same-sex couples."[58]

"'Dad' deleted from NHS baby guide – for sake of gay couples"
May 30, 2012
"'Dad' has been removed from a taxpayer-funded baby guide after a single complaint that same-sex couples were being excluded. The Scottish NHS guide, called "Ready Steady Baby", now features the word 'partner' instead of 'Dad'."[59]

"Court: Christians Can Be Ordered To Violate Beliefs"
June 5, 2012
"A ruling from Judge Tim L. Garcia in the New Mexico Court of Appeals says states can require Christians to violate their faith in order to do business, affirming a penalty of nearly $7,000 for a photographer who refused to take pictures at a lesbian 'commitment' ceremony in the state where same-sex 'marriage' was illegal."[60]

"Denmark forces churches to perform same-sex 'marriages'"
June 7, 2012
"The nation of Denmark has voted to force churches in the established Evangelical Lutheran Church to perform same-sex 'marriage' ceremonies inside their sanctuaries, although one-third of all the denomination's priests say they will not participate in such

rituals. Danish parliament voted by an overwhelming 85-24 margin to compel churches to carry out unions for same-sex couples that are identical to heterosexual marriage celebrations."[61]

"Cameron CANNOT protect Church against gay marriage laws (says his own Justice minister)"
June 13, 2012
"David Cameron's promise to protect churches from gay marriage laws could hit legal hurdles, a justice minister admitted yesterday. Crispin Blunt said it would be hard to guarantee that clergy would not face court challenges if they refused to preside over same-sex unions."[62]

"Angry response to Salvation Army's gay stance"
June 18, 2012
"Salvation Army's declaration that homosexuality is an unacceptable urge has provoked outrage in the gay community. Gay pop star Darren Hayes called for a boycott of the high-profile charity, a call backed by pro-gay lobbyists. The Salvos responded last night by pointing out they helped some of Australia's most marginalised and needy people, including gay and transgender ones."[63]

"First gay-marriage suit hits Catholic institution"
June 20, 2012
"A lesbian couple from Westchester yesterday filed the first suit against a Catholic institution for refusing to recognize New York's gay-marriage law."[64]

"Church groups suspended from school over homophobic leaflet"
June 28, 2012
"Three church groups have been suspended from preaching at a secondary school after a leaflet containing homophobic scripture was delivered to homes in Walthamstow. The anonymous leaflet, urging people to come to Wanstead High School in Redbridge Lane West on Sundays at 11am, quotes a version of a line of scripture from Corinthians 6:9 which refers to 'homosexual offenders'."[65]

"Schools could be forced to teach gay marriage"
July 2, 2012
"Secret Government emails reveal that schools could be forced to teach children about gay marriage if it becomes law. The emails between officials at the Home Office and Department for Education came to light following a Freedom of Information request. One official said the issue was a potential 'minefield' and wanted 'defensive lines to take' in case the press started asking questions."[66]

"Toronto school board promotes curriculum encouraging students to cross-dress"
July 5, 2012
"The Toronto District School Board is promoting a new curriculum guide encouraging students to cross dress. Lee Hicks, an elementary school teacher, artist, and 'trans activist' in Toronto wrote the 70-page long guide, called 'Both/And', for the school board. The guide targets students in kindergarten to grade 6, and uses art and discussion to talk about issues of 'identity' and 'inclusivity'."[67]

"Christian B&B owners ordered to pay gay couple $4,500 in damages"
July 19, 2012
"Christian owners of a bed and breakfast in British Columbia have been ordered to pay around $4,500 in damages after they refused to rent a room to a homosexual couple."[68]

"Mayor Menino on Chick-fil-A: Stuff it: Vows to block eatery over anti-gay attitude"
July 20, 2012
"Mayor Thomas M. Menino is vowing to block Chick-fil-A from bringing its Southern-fried fast-food empire to Boston – possibly to a popular tourist spot just steps from the Freedom Trail – after the family-owned firm's president suggested gay marriage is 'inviting God's judgment on our nation'."[69]

"Swedish high school student fails bio class for saying homosexuality 'abnormal'"

July 27, 2012
"A Swedish high-school student recently failed a biology class for saying that homosexuality is abnormal, according to Swedish national news-site, svt.se. The site reports that a grade 8 student at Nynäshamn High School in Stockholm County, Sweden, expressed the opinion that homosexuality was 'onormalt' – literally 'abnormal' – and, as a result, received a failing grade. When the student questioned the grade, the teacher reportedly replied that it was because of the student's opinions. The goal of the school's curriculum, the teacher said, was that students show respect for different sexual orientations, and the student's views did not correspond with that goal."[70]

"Activists Call for Boycott on Cake Shop After Owner Refuses to Bake Gay Wedding Cake"
July 30, 2012
"Move over Chick-fil-A. There's a new business getting heat for its stance on gay marriage. Masterpiece Cake Shop in Lakewood, Colorado, is facing critics who are calling for a boycott after it refused to make a cake for a same-sex couple."[71]

"Pastor's Sermon Defending Chick-fil-A Causes School to Consider Revoking Lease"
August 1, 2012
"Shortly after his sermon defending what God says about marriage and that homosexuality is a sin, Miami-Dade County school superintendent Alberto Carvalho announced that the school board was reviewing the church's lease to use the high school building for their services. Carvalho stated that the sermon 'appear to be contrary to school board policy, as well as the basic principles of humanity'."[72]

"Democrat admits, 'Attack on parental rights' is 'the whole point' of banning sex orientation therapy"
August 2, 2012
"The author of a California bill that would forbid minors from seeking therapy to overcome unwanted feelings of same-sex

attraction has admitted his intention was to undermine parental rights. 'The attack on parental rights is exactly the whole point of the bill, because we don't want to let parents harm their children,' said State Senator Ted Lieu, D-Torrance. Senate Bill 1172 would ban anyone under 18 from receiving reparative or sexual orientation conversion therapy, even if requested by the teens or their parents. The bill would label the treatment 'unprofessional conduct' and 'therapeutic deception'."[73]

"University suspends Chick-fil-A from campus"
August 9, 2012
"A liberal arts college in North Carolina has become the first in the nation to prevent Chick-fil-A from being served at campus events over the restaurant's indirect support of pro-family groups perceived by some as 'anti-gay'."[74]

"St Kilda's Milne fined over gay slur"
August 9, 2012
"St Kilda have fined their small forward Stephen Milne $3000 for making a homophobic remark against Collingwood's Harry O'Brien, even though there was no complaint from the Magpie."[75]

"Canadian Schools Teaching 8-Year-Olds There Are Six Genders Without Parental Permission"
August 10, 2012
"The Newly proposed, Ontario curriculum, which teaches six genders (male, female, transgendered, transsexual, two-spirited and inter-sexed) is being taught by teachers in Toronto schools and is confusing to our children."[76]

"Vermont Catholic couple pays $30,000 in dispute over hosting lesbian 'wedding' reception"
August 24, 2012
"The price of following your conscience in Vermont is $30,000. That's the amount a Roman Catholic family has agreed to pay over a disagreement about hosting a same-sex 'wedding' reception at its family inn."[77]

"Catholic college teacher suspended in gay marriage row"
August 29, 2012
"A teacher at a Catholic college in Whangarei [NZ] has been suspended and students allegedly threatened in a dispute with the principal over gay marriage. The bitter stand-off was prompted by comments from Pompellier College principal Richard Stanton in the school newsletter in which he lays out his objections to gay marriage under the heading 'keeping marriage sacred'."[78]

"Teachers 'face sack' for refusing to endorse gay marriage"
September 10, 2012
"Teachers who refuse to endorse gay marriage in the classroom could face the sack under controversial Government reforms, a legal expert has warned. Schools will be within their statutory rights to dismiss staff that wilfully fail to use stories or textbooks promoting same-sex weddings, it is claimed."[79]

"Ontario dad sues school board over no opt out classes on sex"
September 10, 2012
"A Hamilton-area Christian father is suing his children's public school board after they refused to allow him to withdraw his children from controversial lessons on sexuality. ... The Toronto District School Board has a formal policy forbidding withdrawals from its radical pro-homosexual curriculum and even of notifying parents in advance. Board chair Chris Bolton has insisted exemptions will 'not be condoned'."[80]

"Ontario Christian minister forced to conduct same-sex 'marriages' or get sacked"
September 11, 2012
"A Church of Christ minister who has been responsible for civic marriage ceremonies at Cambridge city hall for the past 15 years is facing the axe if she doesn't agree to perform same-sex 'marriages.' Rev. Jay Brown told *LifeSiteNews* that city council voted 8 to 1 Monday night on a motion, brought forward by Councillor Donna Reid, that Brown be forced to officiate at homosexual 'marriages' or they would issue a 'request for proposal' to find a replacement."[81]

"Franciscan U of Steubenville under investigation for teaching homosexuality as deviant"
September 11, 2012
"The national agency which grants accreditation to social work courses is questioning Franciscan University of Steubenville over a course which lists homosexuality as a deviant behaviour. Attention was drawn to the course by a group of Franciscan University alumni, identifying themselves as 'Franciscan Gay Alumni & Allies', who are demanding publicly that the university 'revise its course descriptions and to stop contributing the culture of hate and ignorance'."[82]

"Seminary professor fired for beliefs on homosexuality: complaint"
September 12, 2012
"A theological professor at an African-American Christian seminary has complained to federal anti-discrimination officials that he was fired based on his conservative views, particularly his stance against homosexuality."[83]

"No allowances for conscience in French 'gay marriage' bill: French Justice Minister"
September 12, 2012
"There will be no allowances made for conscientious or religious objection in upcoming French legislation instituting 'gay marriage,' the French minister of Justice, Christiane Taubira, revealed in an interview today."[84]

"Pro-family views cost ex-Marine a superintendent job in Berkeley"
September 19, 2012
"A former Marine's views about the sanctity of marriage have cost him a job as superintendent of schools in Berkeley, California. Dr Edmond Heatley, who is African-American, had already been selected as the final candidate and resigned his position as a superintendent in Georgia when news broke that in 2008 he supported Proposition 8, a pro-marriage state ballot initiative adopted by California voters that November."[85]

"[UK] Christian couple reveal how they have suffered a two-year campaign of death threats and abuse for refusing to let two gay men share a room in their B&B"
September 21, 2012
"It was the beginning of two-and-a-half years of hate mail, arson and death threats, obscene emails, filthy texts, bogus TripAdvisor and Google reviews, cancelled bookings."[86]

"France is set to ban the words 'mother' and 'father' from all official documents under controversial plans to legalise gay marriage"
September 24, 2012
"The move which has outraged Catholics means only the word 'parents' would be used in identical marriage ceremonies for all heterosexual and same-sex couples. The draft law states that 'marriage is a union of two people, of different or the same gender'. The words mother and father will be removed from the French civil code as the Government paves the way for same-sex marriage And it says all references to 'mothers and fathers' in the civil code – which enshrines French law – will be swapped for simply 'parents'."[87]

"Rupert Everett receives death threats over gay parenting comments"
September 29, 2012
"The openly homosexual star came under fire from campaign groups after he stated that children 'need a father and a mother', adding, '(I) can't think of anything worse than being brought up by two gay dads.' He subsequently clarified his remarks, insisting he is not 'against' same-sex couples having kids, but he has now revealed that he has since received a number of nasty messages. Everett tells British newspaper the Daily Telegraph, 'I've now had all this hate mail and there have been death threats, too... All the queens out there now have it in for me. I'm loathed by them. I'm having to take evasive action'."[88]

"University Punishes Staffer for Signing Marriage Petition"
October 15, 2012

"Conservatives and even some liberals across the nation are outraged after Gallaudet University suspended the school's chief diversity officer after she signed a petition in her church to put a gay marriage referendum on the ballot in Maryland. Angela McCaskill, a 23-year veteran of the university, was placed on paid leave as the university investigates her support for traditional marriage."[89]

"Being straight no longer normal, students taught"
October 17, 2012
"Students at 12 NSW high schools are being taught it is wrong and 'heterosexist' to regard heterosexuality as the norm for relationships. The 'Proud Schools' pilot program, implemented in 12 government schools in Sydney and the Hunter, is designed to stamp out 'homophobia, transphobia (fear of transsexuals) and heterosexism'. Teachers are given professional development to learn to identify and stamp out any instances of 'heterosexist' language in the playground, such as 'that's so gay'."[90]

"B&B Fined for Hurting Gay Couple's Feelings"
October 18, 2012
"Susanne Wilkinson, owner of the Swiss Bed and Breakfast, has been ordered to pay £3,600 in damages for hurting the feelings of a homosexual couple, Michael Black and John Morgan. Wilkinson says she was trying to uphold her sincere beliefs about marriage at the bed and breakfast in Cookham, Berkshire."[91]

"Lesbians Launch Discrimination Complaint Against NY Farm Owners for Refusing to Host Their Gay Wedding"
October 22, 2012
"Two New York women who say they were turned away from a potential wedding site because they are lesbians have filed a discrimination complaint."[92]

"Texas Pastor Jailed for Preaching at Pride Event Awaits Court Date"
October 31, 2012

"A pastor in Texas is awaiting his day in court following his arrest this month while preaching at a homosexual pride event. Pastor Joey Faust says that he and other members of his church, Kingdom Baptist Church in Venus, Texas, were physically blocked by police while attempting to share the Gospel of Jesus Christ with attendees of the Fort Worth 'Ride the Rainbow' pride parade."[93]

"Washington College OK's Exposure of Young Girls to
Transgender Male in Locker Room"
November 1, 2012
"College officials at Washington's Evergreen College gave approval to a transgender male to expose himself to young girls in the locker room. The college told the young girls to dress behind a curtain if they don't like it."[94]

"Last UK Catholic adoption agency loses final appeal over homosexual adoption"
November 2, 2012
"A Catholic charity that has provided adoption services since 1865 will no longer be able to offer that service while adhering to its moral principles. The UK's Upper Tribunal, the equivalent of the High Court in the administrative justice system, rejected an appeal by Catholic Care, the last Catholic adoption agency in the country, to change its constitution to exclude homosexuals from adopting children."[95]

"Judge: Parents have no right to know what homosexual activist taught their children in school"
November 10, 2012
"Parents and ratepayers in a Hamilton area school board will never know exactly what a homosexual activist told their children during a Gay-Straight Alliance assembly a year ago. The Information and Privacy Commissioner of Ontario upheld last week the decision of the Hamilton-Wentworth District School Board to 'deny access to the record' of the speech."[96]

"Middle Schoolers Subjected To Graphic Gay Indoctrination"
November 10, 2012
"Shortly before Maine became one of the first states to approve gay marriage at the ballot box, a school district in the state was ahead of the curve with a presentation of graphic gay sex acts. Promoted as part of the school's 'Diversity Day', 25 students in a middle school class were subjected to the filth by a group called Proud Rainbow Youth of Southern Maine. The reprehensible display included advising students about safe homosexual sex acts and suggesting the use of saran wrap during oral sex if a dental dam is not available. The mother of one 13-year-old upset by the presentation told the media that the PRYSM speaker also used profanity when spreading the gay-centric message."[97]

"A school district being sued for removing a book about a lesbian couple"
November 13, 2012
"*In Our Mothers' House*, a picture book about a lesbian couple raising three adopted children is stirring up some controversy in the state of Utah. The Associate Press reported on Tuesday that the American Civil Liberties Union of Utah has filed a lawsuit against the Davis School District, challenging a policy that limits access to the book. The lawsuit is challenging the elementary schools requirement that school students have a parent's permission to check out the book as unconstitutional."[98]

"Obama nominates black homosexual judge to 'ensure that the judiciary resembles the nation'"
November 15, 2012
"Obama appointed Judge William Thomas to the Southern District of Florida. Thomas has served on the Eleventh Judicial Circuit since 2005. 'Today's announcement...reflects the president's historic commitment to advancing a diverse judiciary that looks like America,' said Nancy Zirkin of The Leadership Conference on Civil and Human Rights. 'If confirmed, these nominees would bring more women, minorities, and openly gay judges to courts to better reflect the nation they serve'."[99]

"Primary school teachers 'could face sack' for refusing to promote gay marriage"
November 18, 2012
"Liz Truss, an [English] education minister, refused to rule out the possibility that teachers, even in faith schools, could face disciplinary action for objecting on grounds of conscience. Miss Truss said simply that it was impossible to know what the impact of the legislation would be at this stage."[100]

"San Francisco set to vote on ban on public nudity, except at 'gay pride' events
November 19, 2012
"The pendulum of the sexual revolution may be swinging slightly back toward sanity in San Francisco, as the city is set to vote on a new law that may bar public nudity – except at the city's gay pride march and other events covered by permit."[101]

"Newcastle blogger fined for vilifying homosexuals"
November 28, 2012
"A Newcastle blogger and taxi driver has been ordered to pay thousands of dollars in damages for vilifying homosexuals."[102]

"Commission Opposes T-Shirt Company's Refusal To Print 'Gay Pride' Message"
November 29, 2012
"A Kentucky commission has announced its support of a gay and lesbian group suing a T-shirt company owned by a Christian man who declined to print the group's shirts because the message, he said, violates his faith."[103]

"Ban children's books depicting traditional families: 'gender stereotyping' says EU report"
November 30, 2012
"The draft report 'on eliminating gender stereotypes in the EU,' tabled by a far-Left Dutch MEP, said school curriculum materials should stop depicting men and women in their 'traditional roles' of mothers and fathers. It said that such depictions are 'encouraging

more gender discrimination in different areas of society and all age groups'."[104]

"DOE Investigating School Over Bible and Homosexuality Comments"
December 1, 2012
"A federal investigation has begun in an Alabama school district after a Junior ROTC instructor allegedly expressed his belief that the Bible does not support the homosexual lifestyle during class."[105]

"Scottish parents 'cannot withdraw children from all gay marriage lessons'"
December 13, 2012
"Parents face being forced to allow their children to learn about gay marriage regardless of their religious beliefs, under Scottish ministers' plans to legalise the practice."[106]

"BBC 'should be bold in gay coverage'"
December 14, 2012
"The BBC has been urged to be 'more creative' and 'bolder' in how it represents lesbian, gay and bisexual (LGB) people across its output. The recommendation was made by experts contributing to a BBC review on its portrayal of LGB people. The report's contributors called on the corporation to feature more LGB people in its news and current affairs, sport and children's programming."[107]

"Wedding Vendor Opposed to Same Sex Marriage Shuts Down"
December 27, 2012
"A company in the wedding industry based in Annapolis, Maryland will close its doors, rather than face lawsuits for refusing to serve same-sex marriage couples."[108]

"Socialist politician says Spanish bishop should be 'muzzled'"
January 7, 2013
"A socialist government official in Andalusia, Spain, called for a local Catholic bishop to be 'muzzled' for arguing that men and women are both different and complementary. Bishop Demetrio

Fernandez of Cordoba should be silenced for levelling attacks against 'real and effective equality between men and women,' charged Miguel Angel Vazquez, a member of the Socialist Party and spokesman for the Andalusian provincial government."[109]

"French government warns Catholic schools to stay 'neutral' on homosexual 'marriage'"
January 7, 2013
"As French Catholics prepare to mobilize on January 13 for a national march against the creation of homosexual 'marriage,' the country's education minister is warning Catholic schools against participating, claiming that it could cause 'homophobia' against homosexual students. National Education Minister Vincent Peillon has written a letter to all of the country's 8,300 Catholic school principals, claiming that they have the responsibility to maintain 'neutrality' regarding the debate over homosexual 'marriage' in their institutions, according to reports by Le Monde and the French Press Agency."[110]

"Pastor Disinvited from Giving Inaugural Prayer Because of Sermon on Homosexuality"
January 10, 2013
"Louie Giglio, pastor of Passion City Church in Atlanta and founder of the Passion Conferences, an organization that brings college students together in prayer and worship, was selected by President Obama to deliver the benediction at his inaugural this month. He was disinvited, though, after it was discovered he had delivered a sermon about homosexuality in the mid-1990s."[111]

"'Gay' issue threatens plans for Christian law school"
January 22, 2013
"A Christian university in British Columbia wants to add a law school -- but the Council of Canadian Law Deans opposes it because the school would follow biblical principles on homosexuality. ... Even though the Council is opposing the move, Trinity Western University has communicated with lawyers, judges, and academics

who are not opposed. If it materializes, Trinity will be the first Christian law school in Canada."[112]

"Catholic adoption agency faces punishment for gay 'discrimination'"
January 23, 2013
"A Roman Catholic adoption agency faces being stripped of its charitable status after regulators ruled it is discriminating against gay couples. St Margaret's Children and Family Care Society in Glasgow was found to discriminate against homosexuals by giving higher priority to couples who have been married for at least two years."[113]

"The Oregon Department of Justice is looking into a complaint that a Gresham bakery refused to make a wedding cake for a same sex marriage"
February 2, 2012
"It started on Jan. 17 when a mother and daughter showed up at Sweet Cakes by Melissa looking for the perfect wedding cake. 'My first question is what's the wedding date,' said owner Aaron Klein. 'My next question is bride and groom's name ... the girl giggled a little bit and said it's two brides.' Klein apologized to the women and told them he and his wife do not make cakes for same-sex marriages. Klein said the women were disgusted and walked out."[114]

"Over 40,000 teachers 'face sack' over gay marriage"
February 4, 2013
"More than 40,000 [UK] teachers say they will probably refuse to teach about 'the importance of' same-sex marriage, according to a new poll. And 56 per cent of teachers believe any colleague who takes such a stance risks damaging their career. The survey has led to concerns that tens of thousands of teachers may face being sacked or disciplined over their views, because of how legislation is worded."[115]

"Canadian gvmt halts overseas funding to Christian group over beliefs on homosexuality"

February 11, 2013
"Canada's Conservative government has halted payments to a Christian group working to improve access to clean water in Uganda after a media report targeted the group's commitment to Christian sexual teaching."[116]

"Gay marriage: no opt-out for Christian registrars"
February 15, 2013
"Christian registrars will not be able to opt out of performing gay marriages if they object on grounds of belief, the [UK] Government's human rights watchdog has said. In guidance to MPs, the Equalities and Human Rights Commission (EHRC) said marriage registrars were public officials and so should expect to be 'required' to carry out the ceremonies."[117]

"AP caves into gay PC: 'His husband' and 'her wife' are now accepted stylebook terms"
February 21, 2013
"After overwrought pressure from the usual gay 'anti-defamation' lobbyists, the Associated Press has caved in and made another new statement approving the use of 'his husband' and 'her wife' in news stories, as if they've taken a stand for neutrality, instead of rewriting the gender dictionary. 'Victory!' was the headline on several gay websites as AP issued a new entry in its AP Stylebook Online, and is scheduled to appear in the 2013 print and mobile additions."[118]

"Canadian Supreme Court rules biblical speech opposing homosexual behaviour is a 'hate crime'"
February 28, 2013
"The Supreme Court of Canada has ruled that Biblical speech opposing homosexual behaviour, including in written form, is essentially a hate crime. On Wednesday, the court upheld the conviction of activist William Whatcott, who found himself in hot water after distributing flyers regarding the Bible's prohibitions against homosexuality throughout the Saskatoon and Regina neighbourhoods in 2001 and 2002."[119]

"Police chaplain dumped for opposing gay marriage"
March 1, 2013
"A police chaplain says he was removed from his post because he disagreed with gay marriage on his personal internet blog. Strathclyde Police said Revd Brian Ross can hold his beliefs in private, but publicly expressing them is a breach of their equality and diversity policy. Revd Ross, a retired Church of Scotland minister, has written to MPs explaining what happened to him."[120]

"Two 11-Year-Olds Receive Threats for Testifying Against Same-Sex Marriage"
March 31, 2013
"In the past two months, in attempts to offer an argument against same-sex marriage, two children have testified before their state legislators, countering other children who have been testifying for it. The two children testifying against it have either been crudely insulted or received death threats."[121]

"Homosexual Students Hope to Oust Catholic Chaplain from University Campus"
April 4, 2013
"Two homosexual students at George Washington University have announced a coordinated campaign to try to rid the campus of its Catholic chaplain, the *GW Hatchet*, the school's independent newspaper reports. Seniors Damian Legacy and Blake Bergen said they can no longer tolerate what they describe as Father Greg Shaffer's anti-homosexual and anti-abortion beliefs. They say they are upset that Fr. Shaffer counsels homosexual students to lead a celibate lifestyle. Fr. Shaffer has served as chaplain at George Washington University's Newman Centre for the past five years. Legacy and Bergen, who are in a homosexual relationship, have charged that Fr. Shaffer's beliefs have caused them psychological anguish."[122]

"US florist refused to serve gay couple"
April 10, 2013

"The attorney-general in the US state of Washington has filed a lawsuit against a florist who refused to provide flowers for the wedding of longtime gay customers, citing her religious opposition to same-sex marriage. The state's suit against Barronelle Stutzman of Richland, owner of Arlene's Flowers and Gifts, came just days after the attorney-general's office wrote to ask that Stutzman reconsider her position and agree to comply with the state's anti-discrimination laws."[123]

"Force 'gay marriage' on Northern Ireland through courts: Amnesty International"
Hilary White
April 10, 2013
"Amnesty International and a Northern Irish homosexualist campaign group, Rainbow Project, have announced plans to collaborate in an effort to create legalised gay 'marriage' in the province through the courts. The two groups have vowed to bring a human rights legal action against the Northern Ireland government 'on the basis of inferior treatment of same sex couples in Northern Ireland with regards to the right to marry and found a family'."[124]

"Supporting marriage may be offensive: Public school students need permission slips to hear Santorum"
April 11, 2013
"This week, controversy erupted at a public high school in Michigan after former presidential candidate Rick Santorum was disinvited from giving a speech to its students because he supports traditional marriage. The Young Americans for Freedom chapter at Grosse Pointe South Public High School invited the two-term U.S. Senator from Pennsylvania to give a speech on 'leadership' and secured school approval for the visit. But Grosse Pointe Public School System Superintendent Dr Thomas Harwood cancelled the speech on Monday because of Santorum's rejection of gay 'marriage,' according to *Breitbart.com*. After outcry from the group of teens who raised the $18,000 necessary to bring Santorum to their school, the district relented and will permit the speech to go forward. However, students will now need a signed permission slip

from their parents to hear from Santorum, implying his views are offensive or potentially harmful to young people."[125]

"Bill rescinds tax breaks for groups with Christian views on sexuality"
April 11, 2013
"The Youth Equality Act would deny tax-exempt status to any groups that affirm God's design for relationships. The bill was voted out of committee yesterday in California. Critics say SB 323 is meant to pressure the Boy Scouts into changing its policy regarding homosexuality. 'Although 13 people testified at Wednesday's hearing – including a man who, as a young Scout, was molested by an older Scout – the bill was passed without regard for its potential harm,' California Family Council CEO Ron Prentice said."[126]

"Gender-neutral terms possible for marriage forms"
April 13, 2013
"The words 'bride' and 'bridegroom' will disappear from official marriage forms if [the New Zealand] Parliament votes, as expected, on Wednesday to legalise same-sex marriages. A departmental briefing paper to the select committee that considered the bill said marriage forms would have to be changed if it passed. 'This includes, for example, changing the headings on the notice-of-intended-marriage form to allow for parties of the same sex (i.e. removing headings of bride and bridegroom),' the paper said. The bill would also replace the words 'husband' and 'wife' in 14 other acts with gender-neutral terms including 'spouse', 'married couple' and 'any two people (of any sex) who are married'."[127]

"Judge: Firing teacher who called homosexuality a sin reflects 'modern British values of tolerance'"
April 26, 2013
"In 2010, high school science teacher Robert Haye was dismissed from his position at Deptford Green School after he responded to questions from high school students aged 15-16 by saying that homosexual activity is a 'sin.' Teaching authorities subsequently banned him 'indefinitely' from teaching at any high school in the

country, a ban that was later endorsed by Education Secretary Michael Gove. A London High Court rejected Haye's appeal, saying that his comments were 'inappropriate' and that he was guilty of unacceptable professional conduct, the campaign group Christian Concern reported, noting that this is the first case of its kind. ... In his judgment, Mr Justice King said that teachers must present positive information on homosexuality 'to enable students to challenge derogatory stereotypes and prejudice,' and that this policy reflected 'modern British values of tolerance.' He said Haye's appeal was 'misconceived and must fail'."[128]

"Gay Activists Push for Gov't Officials to Drop Greg Laurie from National Day of Prayer Events"
April 29, 2013
"Homosexual activists are labelling evangelist Greg Laurie as the 'anti-gay California pastor' and are asking government officials to rescind Laurie's invitation to lead National Day of Prayer-related events in Washington, D.C. as the event's honorary chairman. The Human Rights Campaign, the largest lesbian, gay, bisexual, transgender (LGBT) advocacy group in America, contends that Laurie has a history of speaking out against LGBT Americans. And OutServe-SLDN, an association of actively serving LGBT military personnel, is calling on the Pentagon to remove the pastor from the agenda, citing 'his blatantly anti-LGBT message'."[129]

"Columbus Bishop risks jail defending Catholic school that fired teacher for coming out as lesbian"
May 3, 2013
"Columbus Bishop Frederick Campbell has weighed in publicly on the firing of a lesbian teacher from a diocesan high school, telling *the Columbus Dispatch* that Catholic schools have a 'fundamental responsibility' to make sure their teachers uphold the teachings of the faith."[130]

"Rohit Singh, Canadian Transgender Woman, Allegedly Denied Service At Bridal Boutique"
May 3, 2013

"A transgender Canadian woman is crying foul after allegedly being denied service at a bridal boutique. Of her experience at Jenny's Bridal Boutique in Saskatoon, Rohit Singh told CBC News both she and her husband were 'embarrassed,' and now plans to file a formal complaint with the Saskatchewan Human Rights Commission."[131]

"Homosexual rejected, heads to tribunal"
May 6, 2013
"A homosexual man is taking the Anglican Bishop of Auckland to the Human Rights Tribunal after being rejected for training as a priest. A hearing begins today following a complaint from the man, who says he feels discriminated against because of his sexuality."[132]

"Family First NZ faces deregistration"
May 6, 2013
"Family First NZ says it will be deregistered as a charity because of its views on gay marriage. National director of Family First Bob McCoskrie said the group has received notification the Charities Commission intends to deregister the organisation. He said the decision was highly politicised and showed groups that think differently to the politically correct view will be targeted."[133]

"Young Christians will be locked out of public professions by 'gay marriage', ministers warn"
May 20, 2013
"Young Christians will be shut out of all public professions, including teachers, doctors, nurses or any kind of public servant if the 'gay marriage' bill is passed, a group of religious leaders has warned the government. The ministers issued the warning in a letter to the *Daily Telegraph* on the same day that the government came to an agreement with opposition parties over amendments. The bill is expected to move past the committee stage and on to the House of Lords after two days of debate today and tomorrow. Should it be granted Royal Assent 'in its present form,' the 17 Christian ministers said, the bill will 'isolate hundreds of thousands of young students and workers across the country who hold a fuller view of marriage based on religion or a traditional view. These young people, from

teenagers to 30-year-olds, will suffer discrimination and face new risks to their careers, and futures'."[134]

"'You're not doing this in my home': lesbian bed ban sparks threats and abuse"
May 21, 2013
"The owners of a New Zealand guesthouse who refused to let a lesbian couple share a bed are standing firm despite threats. Karen and Michael Ruskin, of Pilgrim Planet Lodge, in central Whangarei, say they have received death threats and verbal abuse over their stance on homosexuality. But they say they will not have their beliefs silenced, even if it puts their business at risk."[135]

"Police investigate teacher who posted graphic gay sex brochures in 7-8 Toronto classroom"
May 31, 2013
"Toronto police are investigating a grade 7-8 teacher who was reinstated in his classroom this week after being put on 'home assignment' earlier this month for posting graphic sex brochures originally designed for gay bathhouses on his classroom walls. 'We are currently investigating this occurrence and we (are) gathering as much information as we can,' Det.-Const. Sean Cassidy said to *Sun News* yesterday. Wade Vroom, who teaches part-time at Delta Senior Alternative School, was sent home with pay earlier this month after school officials were notified about the explicit brochures on the walls of his classroom."[136]

"Colo. gay discrimination alleged over wedding cake"
June 6, 2013
"A gay couple is pursuing a discrimination complaint against a Colorado bakery, saying the business refused them a wedding cake to honour their Massachusetts ceremony, and alleging that the owners have a history of turning away same-sex couples. As more states move to legalize same-sex marriage and civil unions, the case highlights a growing tension between gay rights advocates and supporters of religious freedom."[137]

"Army soldier disciplined for serving Chick-Fil-A at promotion party"
June 6, 2013
"A U.S. Army serviceman has been reprimanded for serving Chick-fil-A sandwiches at a party celebrating his promotion to master sergeant. The unidentified soldier was investigated, reprimanded, threatened with judicial action, and given a bad efficiency report after sending invitations that read, 'In honour of my promotion and in honour of the Defence of Marriage Act, I'm serving Chick-fil-A sandwiches at my promotion party,' according to the Chaplain Alliance for Religious Liberty."[138]

"Court awards lesbian $170,000 after being fired from Catholic school for using IVF"
June 7, 2013
"[A] legal battle was won by a partnered lesbian who taught at two Catholic schools in the Archdiocese of Cincinnati. She was fired when it was learned that she became pregnant through the Church-condemned practice of in vitro fertilization, but she subsequently sued for discrimination. According to the Associated Press, a federal jury on June 3 awarded Christa Dias $171,000 after finding that the Archdiocese of Cincinnati discriminated against her by firing her in 2010. The schools were not held liable. Attorney Steven Goodin, who represents the archdiocese and the schools, had argued Dias was fired for violating her contract, which required her to comply with the teachings of the Roman Catholic Church. Dias is also in a lesbian relationship – something Goodin said Dias tried to keep secret from her employer because she knew the Church teaches against homosexual practice."[139]

"Boy, 3, taught about gay marriage in nursery"
June 11, 2013
"A three-year-old boy has been taught by his nursery carer that when he grows up he will be able to marry a boy or a girl. The boy's identity is being protected, but his parent wrote a letter to a local newspaper about the incident."[140]

"French mayor refuses to 'marry' homosexual couple: risks years in jail"
June 12, 2013
"The mayor of a small town in France's Basque region has announced his refusal to carry out a 'marriage' between two men who reside in his jurisdiction, becoming the first mayor to defy the country's new law that applies the name and rights of 'matrimony' to couples of the same sex. Jean-Michel Colo, a conservative who heads the town of Arcangues in the southern Basque region of Pyrenees-Atlantiques, faces the possibility of a prison sentence of up to five years and a fine of 75,000 euros (100,000 USD), according to French media sources. However, he appears to be unafraid of the consequences of his stand, telling the media that he will 'go all the way to the gallows' to oppose the law."[141]

"Scottish Catholic adoption agency threatened with closure over gay adoption"
June 12, 2013
"Another British Catholic adoption agency is being threatened with closure by the government for refusing to toe the government's line of support for the homosexualist political agenda. St. Margaret's Children and Family Care Society, associated with the Catholic archdiocese of Glasgow, has lost a ruling in its argument with the Scottish government's charity regulator, which is demanding the charity drop its policy of adopting only to mothers and fathers who have been married for at least two years."[142]

"Boston cops must defer to transgender crooks"
June 13, 2013
"Criminals just got more rights in the city of Boston – at least, those who identify as transgender. According to new regulations, officers of the Boston Police Department must use a transgender suspect's preferred first name, find out whether the person likes to be called 'he' or 'she,' allow him to choose whether male or female officers perform his frisking, and give any transgender inmate a private ride to and from court. New BPD rules say police must use the name anyone who is arrested prefers, 'even if the individual has not

received legal recognition of the adopted name.' Policemen must also 'respectfully ask the individual' when they are 'uncertain about which pronouns are appropriate.' All friskings will be performed by two members of the sex the transsexual chooses, if at all possible."[143]

"Professor Orders Students to Support Gay Rights"
June 18, 2013
"A Tennessee community college professor ordered her students to wear ribbons supporting gay rights and said those who believed in the traditional definition of marriage are just 'uneducated bigots' who 'attack homosexuals with hate,' according to a legal firm representing several of the students in the class. Students in a general psychology class at Columbia State Community College were directed by their professor to wear 'Rainbow Coalition' ribbons for an entire day and express their support for the homosexual community, said Travis Barham, an attorney with the Alliance Defending Freedom. Barham is calling for the college to punish Dr Linda Brunton and order her to apologize to the students whose constitutional rights he believes were violated, according to a letter he sent to the community college president. 'Dr Brunton essentially turned her General Psychology class into a semester-long clinic on the demands of the homosexual movement,' Barham said."[144]

"Teachers told 'watch what you say' on gay marriage"
June 25, 2013
"A union leader has told teachers that disagreeing with gay marriage could be like racism and carries a risk of disciplinary action. Scottish Secondary Teachers' Association acting general secretary, Alan McKenzie, said teachers who are against gay marriage should 'watch what they say at work'. 'If somebody made racist comments they'd be in danger of disciplinary action and it's no different from that,' he added. The remarks come as a nationalist MSP warned that teachers could be 'persecuted' if they criticise same-sex marriage. John Mason MSP said: 'I want to know if there will be protection

for employees, such as where a teacher says they disagree with same-sex marriage'."[145]

"University Fires Employee for Op-Ed Standing Against Gay Rights as Civil Rights"
July 2, 2013
"Alliance Defending Freedom and the Pacific Justice Institute have filed a brief with the U.S. Supreme Court that asks the court to review the case of a University of Toledo employee fired simply because she wrote an opinion column in her own personal name with a viewpoint that university officials didn't like. The university fired Crystal Dixon, who works in the school's Human Resources department, after she wrote a short op-ed responding to a local newspaper's editorial that compared the efforts of homosexual activists to the black civil rights movement of the 1950s and 60s. As an African-American, Dixon respectfully disagreed with the paper's editorial. She did not mention her job at the university. 'Universities should be the marketplace of ideas, not environments where officials dictate conformity to their own views even outside of the campus,' said Alliance Defending Freedom Senior Legal Counsel David Hacker."[146]

"Christian arrested for calling homosexuality a 'sin' warns of 'real-life thought police'"
July 4, 2013
"Tony Miano, 49, a former senior police officer from the US, was held for around six hours, had his fingerprints and DNA taken and was questioned about his faith, after delivering a sermon about 'sexual immorality' on a London street. Mr Miano, who served as a Deputy Sherriff in Los Angeles County, said his experience suggested that the term 'thought police' had become a reality in the UK. ... The father of three, who took early retirement from the police to become a full-time preacher two years ago, was detained after preaching outside a shopping centre in Wimbledon, south west London, on Monday. He was speaking from a passage from Thessalonians which mentions 'sexual immorality' and listed homosexuality alongside 'fornication' as examples what he believed

went against 'God's law.' A woman out shopping called the police to complain that she was offended, prompting two officers to be dispatched to arrest him."[147]

"Judge orders Ohio to recognize out-of-state gay 'marriage' despite state's marriage amendment"
July 23, 2013
"A U.S. district judge has ordered a clerk in the state of Ohio to recognize a same-sex 'marriage' conducted in another state, because the state's constitutional amendment defining marriages does 'likely violate the U.S. Constitution'."[148]

"Gay couple to sue church over gay marriage opt-out"
August 1, 2013
"Wealthy gay dad, Barrie Drewitt-Barlow, says he and his civil partner Tony will go to court to force churches to host gay weddings. He told the *Essex Chronicle* that he will take legal action because 'I am still not getting what I want'.
A Government Bill legalising gay marriage passed Parliament recently but it included measures to protect churches from being forced to perform same-sex weddings. Mr Drewitt-Barlow said: 'The only way forward for us now is to make a challenge in the courts against the church'."[149]

"Scottish man fined $62,000 for 'homophobic' Twitter message"
August 9, 2013
"The Court of Session in Edinburgh has fined a Scottish man £40,000 ($62,020 U.S.) in damages after he sent a message on Twitter calling a lesbian same-sex 'marriage' advocate 'a danger to children.' Lesbian Jaye Richards-Hill sued David Shuttleton, an antiques dealer from Barrhead, near Glasgow, for defamation because of his remarks about her homosexual activism."[150]

"Chaplain Assistant Facing Punishment for Calling Homosexuality a Sin on Facebook"
August 9, 2013

"Last month a chaplain in Alaska was ordered to remove a religious column he had written because it supposedly offended atheists at his Air Force base. Now a young soldier says she was reprimanded for a Facebook post about homosexuality. A female Army chaplain's assistant told *Fox News Radio* host Todd Starnes she was accused of creating a 'hostile and antagonistic' environment after writing a message on her personal Facebook page in which she called homosexuality a sin. ... The chaplain's assistant, who believes individuals within her unit reported her, was ordered to the commander's office the next day and was told she must either remove the post or face a reduction in rank and pay."[151]

"Business owners threatened, face legal action for refusing to rent facility for gay 'wedding'"
August 12, 2013
"A Christian couple is facing a state complaint, business cancellations, and vulgar, harassing, and threatening e-mail messages after refusing to rent out a business facility for a gay 'wedding.' Dick and Betty Odgaard said they could not in good conscience allow a homosexual couple to use their business, the Görtz Haus Gallery, to conduct the ceremony itself. ... As the story of their denial broke, frightening messages began filling up the Odgaard's inbox, the couple says. 'F--k you, f--k your God, f--k your religion,' said one message from an angry gay rights activist. The same writer enlarged upon his thoughts, adding, 'You are mean, rude, selfish, mother f---er racist sons of b---hes from hell'."[152]

"War on Christianity? Airman allegedly relieved of duty for opposing gay marriage"
August 16, 2013
"Is the Air Force waging a war on Christianity? Senior Master Sgt. Phillip Monk, a 19-year veteran of the Air Force and an evangelical Christian, says he was relieved of his duties after disagreeing with his openly gay commander who wanted to severely punish an instructor who had expressed religious objections to homosexuality, Todd Starnes reported at Fox News Wednesday. 'I was relieved of my position because I don't agree with my commander's position

on gay marriage,' he told Fox News. 'We've been told that if you publicly say that homosexuality is wrong, you are in violation of Air Force policy'."[153]

"Judge allows lawsuit against pastor for opposing homosexuality"
August 23, 2013
"A U.S. judge is allowing a lawsuit by a Ugandan homosexual group charging an Evangelical pastor with a 'crime against humanity.' The American pastor is accused of violating international law for speaking against homosexuality and discussing legislation with Ugandan leaders. Scott Lively, an attorney and author, runs the Holy Grounds coffee house in Massachusetts where coffee and Bibles are free and Sunday church services minister to homeless people, drug addicts and others. In 2009, he was invited to speak at a conference in Uganda where he said the goal of the homosexual movement is 'to defeat the marriage-based society and replace it with a culture of sexual promiscuity'."[154]

"Christian bakers who refused cake order for gay wedding forced to close shop"
September 2, 2013
"A husband-and-wife bakery shop team in Oregon were forced to close their shop doors and move to cheaper digs – their home – after gay-rights activists hounded them and drove away contract business because they refused for Christian reasons to bake for a same-sex wedding. Aaron and Melissa Klein own and operate Sweet Cakes by Melissa. In the past few months, they've faced heated scrutiny – some in the form of physical threats – from those in the gay-rights crowd who decried their May refusal to bake for a lesbian couple who wanted to marry. The Kleins cited their Christian beliefs of traditional marriage when they turned down that business gig, *The Blaze* reported. But the lesbian couple filed a complaint with the state, accusing the shop owners of discrimination. Since, they've been hounded by vicious telephone calls and emails."[155]

"One complaint, Facebook campaign force restaurant owners to take down 'anti-gay' newspaper clipping"

September 3, 2013
"A restaurant owner in the Eastern Ontario town of Bancroft has been forced to remove a newspaper clipping that had been on a bulletin board for over ten years because of one complaint that resulted in a Facebook campaign to organize a protest at the privately owned business. The old *Toronto Star* clipping featuring the words 'God made Adam and Eve, not Adam and Steve' has been pinned to the bulletin board of the Eagle's Nest Restaurant and Bakery for a decade, according to owners Sadie and Doug Creighton. The clipping stirred no controversy until a lesbian couple new to the community complained that they were offended by it."[156]

"Fox Sports football announcer fired over 2011 remarks on homosexuality"
September 9, 2013
"Thou shalt not refer to homosexuality as 'a choice' – at least not if you ever want to work for Fox Sports. That's the lesson announcer Craig James learned this week when he was fired from his job covering college football after just one appearance, because of remarks he made on the campaign trail during his unsuccessful run for U.S. Senate back in 2011."[157]

"Air Force Sergeant claims he was fired for refusing to endorse gay 'marriage': faces court martial"
September 10, 2013
"An Air Force sergeant who filed a discrimination complaint with the U.S. military claiming he was fired by his lesbian commander for refusing to make a statement of support for same-sex 'marriage' may now face prosecution for taking his accusations public. Senior Master Sergeant Phillip Monk was relieved of his duties as first sergeant at Lackland Air Force Base in San Antonio in August after two separate confrontations with an openly homosexual superior officer, Major Elisa Valenzeula."[158]

"Transgender man wins complaint against bridal shop for not letting him try on wedding dress"
September 19, 2013

"The Saskatchewan Human Rights Commission announced that a mediated settlement has been reached between the owner of a Saskatoon bridal shop and a man who presents himself as a woman. Rohit Singh, a student from India who came to Canada in 2010, filed a complaint against Jenny's Bridal Boutique after the owner of the shop refused to allow him access to the women's changing room. When Singh selected a dress and wanted to try it on, shop owner Jenny Correia refused him, saying "I don't allow men to wear dresses in my store.' Singh retorted, 'I'm not a man, I'm a transgender and my sex-change procedure is going on,' according to media reports of the incident that happened on April 21. The owner believed allowing a man to try on dresses would make female customers in the shop uncomfortable."[159]

"Gay activists launch complaint against teacher who included homosexuality on list of possible sins"
September 23, 2013
"Days after the Italian lower house passed the country's 'anti-homophobia' law, the country's leading homosexualist lobby group, Arcigay, appears to be testing the legal waters. Together with The Omphalos Association and Arcilesbica Perugia, Arcigay has launched a complaint, called a 'denunzia,' of 'homophobia' that they allege was committed during a religious education class at the Liceo Classico Mariotti, a university preparatory high school, in the Umbrian town of Perugia."[160]

"Washington state judge faces formal reprimand for refusing to officiate same-sex 'weddings'"
October 8, 2013
"A Washington state judge has been officially reprimanded by the Judicial Conduct Commission after refusing to officiate same-sex weddings for what he said were 'philosophical and religious reasons.' Thurston County Superior Court Judge Gary Tabor first came under scrutiny by the Commission after Washington voters approved a measure late last year authorizing same-sex 'marriage' in the state. Immediately prior to the law's taking effect, in a private meeting between judges and court personnel, Tabor had expressed

discomfort with the idea of officiating gay nuptials. One of the attendees later leaked his comments to the press, which reported them widely."[161]

"US Army defines Christian ministry as 'domestic hate group'"
October 14, 2013
"Several dozen U.S. Army active duty and reserve troops were told last week that the American Family Association, a well-respected Christian ministry, should be classified as a domestic hate group because the group advocates for traditional family values. The briefing was held at Camp Shelby in Mississippi and listed the AFA alongside domestic hate groups like the Ku Klux Klan, Neo-Nazis, the Black Panthers and the Nation of Islam."[162]

"Katter Party candidate Tess Corbett ordered to apologise over election comments"
October 16, 2013
"An unsuccessful candidate in the September [Australian] federal election has been ordered to make a public apology over comments she made about homosexuals earlier this year. Tess Corbett was a Katter Party candidate for the Federal seat of Wannon, in western Victoria, when she made the comments to the *Hamilton Spectator* newspaper."[163]

"Mayors cannot refuse to 'marry' homosexual couples: French Constitutional Court"
October 22, 2013
"French mayors and members of municipal councils in charge of registering civil status will not be allowed to invoke a right to conscientious objection to justify their refusal to celebrate same sex "marriages," the French Constitutional Court decided last Friday. Two groups of mayors had brought the issue before the Court. But the court's decision now puts an end to their hopes of finding a loophole to guarantee that elected civil rights officers who object to same sex "marriage" will have their conscience rights respected."[164]

Any more evidence needed?

So are you convinced yet? These are just some of the many examples from around the Western world which have occurred in the past several years. Many more could be mentioned. And one of the prime pieces of evidence is what has happened in the American state of Massachusetts. Since they legalised homosexual marriage in 2004, all hell has broken out. This is all very nicely documented in a very important paper which every single one of us should read and become familiar with.[165]

The article begins with these words: "Anyone who thinks that same-sex 'marriage' is a benign eccentricity which won't affect the average person should consider what it has done in Massachusetts. It's become a hammer to force the acceptance and normalization of homosexuality on everyone. And this train is moving fast. What has happened so far is only the beginning."[166]

It ends this way: "Homosexual 'marriage' hangs over society like a hammer with the force of law. And it's only just begun. ... This is about putting the legal stamp of approval on homosexuality and imposing it with force throughout the various social and political institutions of a society that would never accept it otherwise. To the rest of America: You've been forewarned."[167]

Or consider the situation in Canada. As Michael Coren reports, "it's estimated that, in less than five years, there have been between 200 and 300 proceedings – in courts, human-rights commissions, and employment boards – against critics and opponents of same-sex marriage. And this estimate doesn't take into account the casual dismissals that surely have occurred."[168]

He concludes his eye-opening article this way: "The Canadian litany of pain, firings, and social and political polarization and extremism is extraordinary and lamentable, and we haven't even begun to experience the mid- and long-term results of this mammoth social experiment. I seldom say it, but for goodness' sake learn something from Canada."[169]

Another important article on this has recently appeared, and it is also a real eye-opener. Law professor Bradley Miller assesses the damage which has taken place in Canada during the past decade, and is not optimistic of things turning around any time soon.

He focuses on three key areas: "Anyone interested in assessing the impact of same-sex marriage on public life should investigate the outcomes in three spheres: first, human rights (including impacts on freedom of speech, parental rights in public education, and the autonomy of religious institutions); second, further developments in what sorts of relationships political society will be willing to recognize as a marriage (e.g., polygamy); and third, the social practice of marriage."[170]

His piece, along with Coren's, should forever put to rest the deliberate deception put forward by the activists that special rights for homosexuals – including homosexual marriage – will not change anything or impact adversely on any of us. The truth is, everything changes, and we all are impacted.

Clearly a full-blown war has been declared against faith, freedom and family, and it is coming from the homosexual activists and their supporters in the courts, the workplace, and in almost all sections of society. At very real risk are such tremendous social goods as marriage and family; freedom of religion; freedom of speech; freedom of conscience; and liberty and democracy.

Those who think that special rights for homosexuals – including the right to marriage – can be granted with everything remaining the same are just kidding themselves. Everything changes, as I have just documented. A recent article by Princeton University's McCormick Professor of Jurisprudence Robert George highlights the folly of thinking compromise can be achieved here. He is worth quoting at length:

"The fundamental error made by some supporters of conjugal marriage was and is, I believe, to imagine that a grand bargain could be struck with their opponents: 'We will accept the legal redefinition of marriage; you will respect our right to act on our consciences without penalty, discrimination, or civil disabilities of any type. Same-sex partners will get marriage licenses, but no one will be forced for any reason to recognize those marriages or suffer discrimination or disabilities for declining to recognize them.' There was never any hope of such a bargain being accepted.

"Perhaps parts of such a bargain would be accepted by liberal forces temporarily for strategic or tactical reasons, as part of the political project of getting marriage redefined; but guarantees of religious liberty and non-discrimination for people who cannot in conscience accept same-sex marriage could then be eroded and eventually removed. After all, 'full equality' requires that no quarter be given to the 'bigots' who want to engage in 'discrimination' (people with a 'separate but equal' mindset) in the name of their retrograde religious beliefs. 'Dignitarian' harm must be opposed as resolutely as more palpable forms of harm. ...

"The lesson, it seems to me, for those of us who believe that the conjugal conception of marriage is true and good, and who wish to protect the rights of our faithful and of our institutions to honour that belief in carrying out their vocations and missions, is that there is no alternative to winning the battle in the public square over the legal definition of marriage. The 'grand bargain' is an illusion we should dismiss from our minds."[171]

And Matthew J. Franck also weighs into what is at stake here. In a lengthy article he clearly demonstrates that when homosexual marriage rights are granted, that of necessity will dampen religious rights and diminish freedom. He is also worth quoting at length:

"Churches and other religious organizations are major employers. They operate schools, universities, hospitals, hospices, and clinics; social service agencies, retirement homes, eldercare and childcare facilities, food pantries, and soup kitchens; and other charitable ministries of every kind. They employ teachers, doctors, nurses, psychologists, counsellors and clinicians, caregivers, food-service workers, housekeeping and grounds staff, even pool lifeguards. These religious ministries typically present themselves as equal opportunity employers, and they mean it. Can they continue to do so in the redefined-marriage legal regime? If a church ministry hires someone in a same-sex marriage, or employs someone who enters such a marriage; or if it declines to hire such a person, or treats him or her adversely if already employed – in any of these scenarios there is trouble ahead, if federal, state, or local employment law considers it wrongful discrimination to treat persons in same-sex marriages differently from men and women in marriages.

"The 'ministerial exception' to employment discrimination law, affirmed 9-0 by the Supreme Court in the *Hosanna-Tabor* case in January 2012, will be no protection at all, since there is no way to shoehorn all these roles and functions into that exceptions category, no matter how broadly 'minister' is defined. But to date, there is no state that has seen fit to accommodate the religious conscience even of avowedly religious ministries in this respect, let alone the consciences of religious persons doing business in the for-profit and nonprofit sectors. Or consider public accommodations law, which can cover equal access to healthcare services, marriage and family counselling, daycare, adoption services, as well as religious schools and universities that are open to taking students of every faith or none at all. Churches and other religious bodies are among the largest providers of health, social service, and educational opportunities, but they understandably consider themselves obliged to provide them in keeping with the moral dictates of their faith."[172]

Education too will be in jeopardy: "And on the subject of universities and schools, consider the matter of the accreditation of higher-ed programs and whole institutions, and the control of curriculum in primary and secondary education. Already we can see individual degree programs compelled by accrediting bodies, in fields such as counselling, to conform themselves to the transformed understanding of marriage and sexuality, as some religiously dissenting students have discovered to their cost. Whole colleges and universities are themselves accredited by regional private accrediting associations – and the accreditors are in turn accredited by the US Department of Education, and recognized by the DOE as authoritative regarding which institutions grant valid degrees and enrol students eligible for federal aid of various kinds. If and when the regional accreditors and the DOE decide that the norm of 'respect' for same-sex marriage must pervade higher education, which religious colleges and universities will keep standing firm in the winds that will blow?"[173]

He concludes, "The transformation of the law to redefine the meaning of marriage will be bad for marriage, bad for children, and very bad indeed for those people of faith who want to maintain their faith's teaching on marriage, in their religious institutions and in their work. The preservation of meaningful religious liberty, it turns out, is inseparable from the preservation, in our legal order, of the truth about marriage. They stand or fall together."[174]

If homosexuals were once the object of intolerance, the exact opposite is now the case. The oppressed have become the oppressor, and those who dare to stand in their way had better watch out. As Michael Brown writes, "Today, those who have come out of the closet are trying to put their ideological opponents into the closet; those preaching tolerance have become the most intolerant; those calling for inclusion are now the most exclusionary; those celebrating diversity demand absolute uniformity."[175]

Freedom of speech, freedom of conscience, and freedom of religion are all under major threat as special rights for homosexuals are being extended across the globe. The push for homosexual marriage is especially resulting in the global erosion of freedom and democracy. Do not believe the rhetoric of the activists: when they are granted special rights, everything changes, and we are all adversely impacted.

Case study

Just as I was finalising this book for print, a case in the US state of Arizona was making the headlines. It involved a bill that would have granted some freedom of conscience to those who do not want to become complicit in the homosexual agenda – specifically, homosexual marriage. Arizona Senate Bill 1062 which was passed by the legislature in February 2014 has just been vetoed by the Governor Jan Brewer (as of the time of this writing).

The bill would have allowed certain groups to not have to provide services for events they object to for religious reasons. The secular left and the mainstream media really went quite ballistic about this one, claiming it would legalise discrimination and the like. But the bill's defenders said that "the bill does not allow businesses to deny service to someone at an establishment such as a restaurant or coffee shop. The law looks to protect those with religious objections from being compelled to participate in or use their creative expression in circumstances that violate their conscience. Since there is no current law on the issue in the state, lawmakers hope to preempt situations such as bakers and photographers facing legal action for not working a same-sex wedding, as has occurred in neighbouring states."[176]

Four helpful commentaries on this bill appeared just before the veto took place, and they each have thoughtful insights which are well worth sharing here. Religious commentator Albert Mohler said in part: "Christian automobile dealers can sell cars to persons of various sexual orientations and behaviours without violating conscience. The same is true for insurance agents and building contractors. But the cases of pressing concern have to do with forcing Christians to participate in same-sex weddings – and this is another matter altogether.

"Photographers, makers of artistic wedding cakes, and florists are now told that they must participate in same-sex wedding ceremonies, and this is a direct violation of their religiously-based conviction that they should lend no active support of a same-sex wedding. Based upon their biblical convictions, they do not believe that a same-sex wedding can be legitimate in any Christian perspective and that their active participation can only be read as a forced endorsement of what they believe to be fundamentally wrong and sinful. They remember the words of the Apostle Paul when he indicted both those who commit sin and those 'who give approval to those who practice them.' [Romans 1:32]. ...

"But the advocates of same-sex marriage are not friendly to the idea of toleration. One prominent gay rights lawyer predicted just this kind of controversy almost a decade ago when she admitted that violations of conscience would be inevitable as same-sex marriage is legalized. Chai Feldblum, then a professor at the Yale Law School, also admitted that her acknowledgement of a violated conscience might be 'cold comfort' to those whose consciences are violated."[177]

Blogger Matt Walsh in a piece entitled "Yes, of course a business owner should have the right to refuse service to gay people," said this about the Arizona bill: "The legislation simply solidifies a business owner's right to act according to his or her religious beliefs (I say 'further solidifies' because the First Amendment already covers this ground pretty thoroughly). 'News' outlets like CNN, engaging in blatant editorializing (surprise!), refer to it as 'the anti-gay bill,' because part of religious freedom is the right to not participate in activities which you find mortally sinful.

"It's not that business owners want to 'refuse service' to gays simply because they're gay; it's that some business owners – particularly people who work in the wedding industry – don't want to be forced to employ their talents in service of something that defies their deeply held religious convictions.

"This shouldn't be an issue, but it is, because some gays in some states have specifically and maliciously targeted religious florists, bakers, and photographers, so that they can put these innocent people in a compromising position, and then run to the media and the courts when – GASP! – Christians decide to follow the dictates of Christianity."

He concludes, "I can't force a Jewish deli to provide me with non kosher meat. I can't force a gay sign company to print me 'Homosexual sex is a sin' banners (I'd probably be sued just for making the request). I can't force a Muslim caterer to serve pork. I can't force a pro-choice business to buy ad space on my website. I can't force a Baptist sculptor to carve me a statue of the Virgin Mary.

"I can't force a private citizen to involve himself in a thing which he finds abhorrent, objectionable, or sinful. And you know what? *I would never try.* Maybe that's what separates liberty lovers from liberals. For all their talk about 'minding your business' and 'this doesn't concern you' and 'live and let live,' theirs is truly an ideology of compulsion. The free speech and expression of other citizens must be tamed by the whip of their lobbying, legislating, and litigating.

"It is, of course, ridiculous to insist that any man or woman has a 'right' to have a cake baked or t-shirt printed. It's equally ridiculous to put the desire and convenience of the would-be cake consumer and t-shirt wearer above the First Amendment rights of the cake maker and t-shirt printer. But this is tyranny. It doesn't have to make sense."[178]

Gary DeMar echoes these thoughts, saying: "What if a print-shop owner holds to a 'pro-choice' view on abortion and a pro-life group comes in and wants shirts and signs made that read 'Babies are Murdered Here' to use in front of an abortion clinic? Should the owner of the shop be forced to make the shirts and signs?
What if a print-shop owner who is homosexual gets an order for shirts and signs that are to read 'God Hates Fags'? Should the owner be forced to fill the order under penalty of law?

Should a supporter of PETA who owns a print shop be forced to make signs and shirts that read 'PETA: People Eating Tasty Animals'?
Should a baker be forced to supply cakes to a KKK-themed wedding or birthday party?
Should an atheist who owns a print shop be forced to print signs and shirts that read 'All Atheists are Going to Hell'?
Should a printer be forced to print shirts and signs that read 'Hitler Was Right'?
Should a photographer be forced to film and photograph a wedding that has a 'White Power' or KKK theme?
I suspect that the vast majority of people in America would sympathize with these business owners who were asked to do something contrary to their beliefs that is an advocacy position against those beliefs. ...

"The above examples would not be prohibited by law. Same-sex sex has special protection under the law. Laws have been written that say a business cannot refuse to support the behaviour of people who engage in same-sex relationships and marriage. This is tyranny of the highest order. The First Amendment was drafted to protect speech, popular or not. My view of unpopular speech and someone else's view of unpopular speech are equally protected."[179]

Finally, Ryan Anderson says this: "Part of the genius of the American system of government is our commitment to protecting the liberty and First Amendment freedoms of all citizens while respecting their equality before the law. The government protects the freedom of citizens to seek the truth about God and worship according to their conscience, and to live out their convictions in public life. Likewise, citizens are free to form contracts and other associations according to their own values.

"While the government must treat everyone equally, private actors are left free to make reasonable judgments and distinctions – including reasonable moral judgments and distinctions – in their economic activities. Not every florist need provide wedding arrangements for every ceremony. Not every photographer need capture every first kiss.

"Competitive markets can best harmonize a range of values that citizens hold. And there is no need for government to try to force every photographer and every florist to service every marriage-related event. Freedom is a two way street. And it requires allowing others to do or not do things that we might choose differently for ourselves."[180]

But it has all been a one way street here, with the homosexual militants demanding full subservience, while those with differing views are deprived of their basic liberties. This is a terrific way to destroy freedom and democracy. And it is happening right under our very nose.

CHAPTER 2

How Families, Parenthood and Identity Suffer

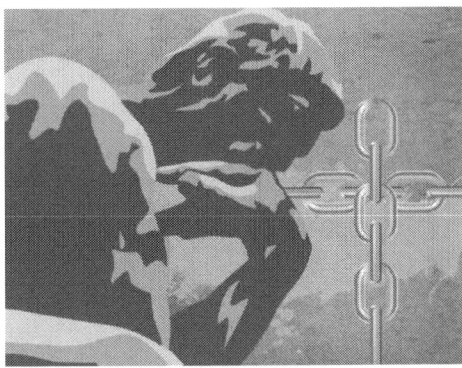

Make no mistake about it: there is a real war going on. And at risk are some of our oldest and most important social institutions. Marriage, family, and even the very concept of mothers and fathers are now all under threat. The homosexual activists are intent on remaking all these precious social goods into their own distorted image.

The legislative and judicial assaults on marriage and family are far reaching indeed. The push for special rights for homosexuals, including marriage and adoption rights, of necessity means the destruction of the family in general, and motherhood and fatherhood in particular. Gendered parenthood, as has always been understood, is the latest casualty in this ongoing assault on children, parents, marriage, family and society by the militants. This tragically means leaving children especially in a state of bewilderment and identity crisis.

The homosexual activists and their judicial supporters are happy to destroy all family as we know it in order to force-feed their social engineering agenda onto us all, whether we like it or not. It appears that they will not rest till the very foundation of society is gutted and transformed into a sexual no-man's land where families and parents have been replaced by whatever kinky combo can be dreamed up.

To please the militants our completely befuddled leaders are happy to smash the oldest and most important of social institutions. Everything must go in order to allow this tiny minority group to get full social recognition and approval. Never mind that so many – probably even most – homosexuals don't even want marriage; it seems our cowardly governments are bending over backwards to give them anything they want.

But in their ongoing push for special rights, they are causing untold damage to our oldest and most venerable institutions. Marriage and family are taking a hammering, as is the very notion of parenthood. We have many examples of this occurring, and it is frightening just how much at jeopardy the very notion of parenthood is. So let's examine how these changes are taking place around the world.

One such example of moral perversion and family suicide comes from France. As they move ahead with homosexual marriage, they of course must ensure that everything else falls into line. Thus mums and dads must forever be squashed, and left on the ash heap of history.

Here is how one news report covers this madness: "France is set to ban the words 'mother' and 'father' from all official documents under controversial plans to legalise gay marriage. The move which has outraged Catholics means only the word 'parents' would be used in identical marriage ceremonies for all heterosexual and same-sex couples.

"The draft law states that 'marriage is a union of two people, of different or the same gender'. And it says all references to 'mothers and fathers' in the civil code – which enshrines French law – will be swapped for simply 'parents'. The law would also give equal adoption rights to homosexual and heterosexual couples.

"Justice Minister Christiane Taubira told France's Catholic newspaper *La Croix*: 'Who is to say that a heterosexual couple will bring a child up better than a homosexual couple, that they will guarantee the best conditions for the child's development? What is certain is that the interest of the child is a major preoccupation for the government.'

"The head of the French Catholic Church Cardinal Philippe Barbarin warned followers last week that gay marriage could lead to legalised incest and polygamy in society. He told the Christian's RFC radio station: 'Gay marriage would herald a complete breakdown in society. 'This could have innumerable consequences. Afterward they will want to create couples with three or four members. And after that, perhaps one day the taboo of incest will fail'."[1]

This of course is not the first time such madness has occurred. All over the Western world governments are caving in to the radical agendas of the militants as they seek to blitzkrieg all before them. Let me just offer a handful of other examples of this.

For example the UK has decided mothers and fathers no longer exist, at least as far as passports are concerned. Here is how the story has been covered: "From December, gay parents applying for passports for their children will not have to list themselves as 'mother' and 'father'. The Identity and Passport Service said the amendments would be made to accommodate gay and lesbian parents applying for passports on behalf of the children.

"Currently, they must fill in details in boxes marked 'mother' and 'father', despite being the same gender. When the changes come into force, they can fill in boxes marked 'parent 1' and 'parent 2'. A spokesman for the Identity and Passport Service told the *Daily Mail*: 'IPS is planning to amend the application form and associated guidance to deal with same-sex parents applying for a passport on behalf of a child. Currently, the application form provides the relevant boxes of "mother" and "father" to be completed. The new form to be introduced by December 2011 will in addition provide for "parent 1" and "parent 2"'.".[2]

And it gets even worse there. A recent article demonstrates that social engineering must always be preceded by verbal engineering: A man can be a 'wife' and a woman can be a 'husband,' the UK government has decided, overruling the *Oxford English Dictionary* and effectively putting an end to the traditional meanings of the words for marriage partners. The move has been denounced as the vocabulary of 'cloud cuckoo land' and 'gobbledegook' by critics who believe that the terms 'husband' and 'wife' should have their traditional meanings preserved." The article continues:

> Updated explanatory notes in *The Marriage (Same Sex Couples) Bill* being considered by the government is causing it to have to redefine the two terms, "clarifying" what it means. "'Husband' here will include a man or a woman in a same sex marriage, as well as a man married to a woman. In a similar way, "wife" will include a woman married to another woman or a man married to a man," says the new footnote. However, the traditional male-only meaning of husband and female-only understanding of wife could return in some cases – to "ensure that gender-specific terms such as 'husband' keep their gender-specific effect." "The term 'husband' will in future legislation include a man who is married to another man (but not a woman in a marriage with another woman); and 'wife' will include a woman who is married to another woman (but not a man married to another man) unless specific alternative provision is made," declares the drafted legislation. Critics stated that they had anticipated the legal confusion the government would run into while trying to eliminate 'gender specific' terms, which have to be introduced as the UK tries to establish gay marriage laws, meaning marriage terms will be 'outdated.' "We always knew the government would tie itself in knots trying to redefine marriage, and this shows what a ridiculous mess they've created," a spokesperson

for the Coalition for Marriage, which campaigns against the change, told the *Telegraph*. "This mangling of the English language shows what happens when politicians meddle with marriage. They're in cloud cuckoo land," they said.[3]

In the US we have had similar moves with passports. As one write-up explains: "Obama's State Dept. Removes Mother, Father From Passports". A news item says this: "In what seems to be a diplomatic effort at extreme political correctness and a nod to gay rights groups, the Obama administration is removing the words 'mother' and 'father' from U.S. passport applications and replacing them with 'gender neutral' terminology. Mom and dad will now be referred to rather coldly as 'parent one' and 'parent two.'

"Conservative Christian groups are outraged over the decision. 'Only in the topsy-turvy world of left-wing political correctness could it be considered an "improvement" for a birth-related document to provide less information about the circumstances of that birth,' Family Research Council president Tony Perkins wrote in a statement to Fox News Radio. 'This is clearly designed to advance the causes of same-sex "marriage" and homosexual parenting without statutory authority, and violates the spirit if not the letter of the Defence of Marriage Act.'

"'The words in the old form were "mother" and "father",' Brenda Sprague, deputy assistant Secretary of State for Passport Services, confirmed Fox News. 'They are now "parent one" and "parent two".' A statement on the State Department website noted: 'These improvements are being made to provide a gender neutral description of a child's parents and in recognition of different types of families.' The statement didn't note if it was for child applications only."[4]

In another capitulation to political correctness and the homosexual lobby, the US government has also decided to delete the words "mother" and "father" from their student aid forms. In a press release we find this:

Today the U.S. Department of Education announced that beginning with the 2014-2015 federal student aid form, the Department will – for the first time – collect income and other information from a dependent student's legal parents regardless of the parents' marital status or gender, if those parents live together. The 2014-2015 Free Application for Federal Student Aid, or FAFSA, will provide a new option for dependent applicants to describe their parents' marital status as "unmarried and both parents living together." Additionally, where appropriate, the new FAFSA form will also use terms like "Parent 1 (father/mother/stepparent)" and "Parent 2 (father/mother/stepparent)" instead of gender-specific terms like "mother" and "father".[5]

And in the US state of Washington we find another case of governments selling out on parents. Consider this headline: "US: Words 'husband' and 'wife' axed from marriage certificates". The story opens as follows: "The health department in the US state of Washington is to remove the words 'husband' and 'wife' from marriage and divorce certificates, after same-sex marriage was approved in a recent referendum. The state began changing the legal document wording before the public vote even happened, according to a spokesman. Tim Church, from the health department, said spaces once reserved for a 'bride' and 'groom' will become more gender-neutral. He said: 'We are proposing a change where it will say something like "Spouse A" and "Spouse B". The law comes into effect on 6 December."[6]

Also, in the US state of Florida we had this incredible judgment: "Florida judge OKs 3-parent family: two lesbians and a homosexual man". The story begins: "In what could become a landmark decision, a Florida judge has ruled that a 23-month-old girl can have three people listed on her birth certificate as her parents. Miami-Dade Circuit Court Judge Antonio Marin approved a settlement between a lesbian couple, Maria Italiano and Cher Filippazzo, who were legally 'married' in Connecticut, and Massimiliano Gerina, a homosexual who donated sperm for Italiano to become pregnant."[7]

Perhaps most of interest, Gerina's lawyer, Karyn J. Begin, said this: "We're creating entirely new concepts of families".[8] That's for sure.

To America's north, the Canadian province of Ontario has also moved in this frightening direction. As one news item reports, having introduced and passed its

> same-sex 'marriage' Bill 171, the Ontario government has advanced a revolutionary change in the way all laws and government programs and institutions refer to marriage and married persons. Everything referring to spouses must now be gender neutral. No longer can a married couple be referred to as "husband and wife" or "man and woman". The terms "Widow" and "widower" are also struck from government statutes. Attorney General Michael Bryant stated, on introducing the bill, "Currently, the statutes offend the Charter of Rights and Freedoms". Bryant continued, "The bill removes references to gender and gender-specific language from Ontario definitions of spousal terms and uses one term, 'spouse', to include opposite-sex couples and same-sex couples who are married or who live together in conjugal relationships outside of marriage."[9]

But not to be outdone, consider this craziness from Sweden. In at least one preschool there they have actually banned the words 'him' and 'her'. Says one report: "The taxpayer-funded preschool which opened last year in the liberal Sodermalm district of Stockholm for kids aged one to six is among the most radical examples of Sweden's efforts to engineer equality between the sexes from childhood onward. Breaking down gender roles is a core mission in the national curriculum for preschools, underpinned by the theory that even in highly egalitarian-minded Sweden, society gives boys an unfair edge. To even things out, many preschools have hired 'gender pedagogues' to help staff identify language and behaviour that risk reinforcing stereotypes."[10]

As I wrote at the time: "Can you believe this absolute insanity? Now Swedish preschools have gender cops roaming the halls, ready to drag away little Bjorn or little Hilda into re-education camps for daring to live out the gender they were born with. Today – in some parts of Sweden at least – it seems it is a crime to be a boy or a girl.

"It appears that the only evil in Sweden is to actually allow boys to be boys and girls to be girls. The destruction of marriage is fine. The war against the family is just peachy. The radical feminist agenda is neato, and the push of the social engineering homosexuals is fine and dandy.

"But dare to have a child remain true to his or her – sorry, to its – gender, and then you are asking for trouble – big time. Perhaps soon they will outlaw all gender differences. Maybe they will force men to breastfeed their babies and force women to have vasectomies."[11]

Other parts of Europe are also witnessing this erosion of families and parenthood. In Spain, which legalised homosexual marriage in 2005, they have taken the next step of declaring that mothers and father no longer exist. As one report states, "Despite opposition from the Church and pro-family groups, the government has continually turned a deaf ear to the needs of traditional families, in favour of fringe politics. The argument, according to the Socialists, is that the family has changed with the times, and so has marriage. In the end, legislation was approved not only allowing homosexual couples to marry, but to also adopt children.

> Ironically, the Socialist government claims that although it pushed through legislation to benefit a small minority of the population – and in the process changed the definition of marriage – that this could in no way be construed as an attack on the traditional family. Indeed, the government claims that it is in truth pro-family. So now, jump fast forward to last Friday. That's when the Spanish government announced a ministerial order that new births would have to be registered at the State Civil Registries in the Family Book under the headings of Parent (progenitor) A, and Parent (progenitor) B. In other words, the terms "Father" and "Mother" were to be no longer used.[12]

Another example of this has recently occurred in Scotland. Once again the relentless push of the activists has resulted in more deconstruction of parenting and parenthood. Consider how one news report begins: "The words 'mother' and 'father' will be dropped from Scottish matrimonial law under First Minister Alex Salmond's plans to redefine marriage. Official consultation documents which accompany the Scottish Government's draft Bill spell out the changes to terminology. Where current matrimonial law refers to 'mother' and 'father', the Scottish Government plans for legislation to use the gender–neutral term 'parent'."[13]

Fortunately not everyone there was thrilled with the idea. The former leader of the Scottish National Party, Gordon Wilson, said: "The politically correct elite are going mad. They are going far beyond what people envisage." And Norman Wells of the Family Education Trust put it this way:

"The Scottish Government's plan to introduce a new lexicon for family relationships shows just how far its proposals to redefine marriage extend. It is engaging in a linguistic revolution to accommodate the wishes of a tiny minority of same-sex couples who want their relationships to be recognised as a marriage. Under these proposals, marriage is not so much being extended to same-sex couples as being taken over by them."[14]

And the Italians – or at least some of them – also seem to hate the idea of a mother and father, and find even the use of the words to be horribly 'stereotypical' and offensive. Here is how one report covers the story:

> The municipal government of the city of Venice, Italy has passed a law banning the terms "mother" and "father on forms parents must fill out to gain a place for their children at publicly funded day care and kindergartens. The "civil rights and anti-discrimination" policy was introduced by city councillor Camilla Seibezzi, who said that such changes to language are a fundamental objective to combat stereotypes. "The [linguistic]

construction forms a category of thought, a daily practice," she said. The newspaper, Corriere del Veneto, reports that the terms will be replaced by "parent 1" and "parent 2". The change has not been popular, however, and Seibezzi has lodged a complaint with police against comments posted to a social media platform that she says were threatening.[15]

Even a tiny place like Prince Edward Island is not immune from this politically correct social engineering. As one article elaborates, "Prince Edward Island's Conservative government is amending the province's marriage laws to remove all references to husband and wife in favour of the gender-neutral 'spouse,' to come in line with the new federal law granting same-sex 'marriage.' 'We're following the lead of the federal government on this,' claimed Health Minister Chester Gillan, according to a CP report. 'We didn't have a lot of pressure from the public, actually, but this was necessary. We had to do this'."[16]

Sadly Australia is not immune from all this idiocy. Consider just two recent examples. One Melbourne headline said this: "Gay school guide: Teachers' manual rejects 'mum' and 'dad'." Victorian schools are being advised to dump the words "mother" and "father" by a new teachers' manual that promotes the cause of same-sex parents.

A booklet called "Learn to Include" and a "Teacher's Manual" advises: "Use inclusive spoken and written language (e.g., 'parent' or carer' rather than 'mother' and 'father'; 'dominant' or 'widespread' rather than 'normal') whenever possible."

At the time I wrote this: "This teachers' manual also urges schools to put up posters of homosexuals and lesbians, and also not use gender-specific toys. Children as young as five are also urged to act out homosexual scenarios. The teachers' manual is meant for students from Prep to Level 3, and is already in use in dozens of Victorian schools."[17]

And from New South Wales we find this headline: "'Father' to go from birth certificates". The story goes as follows: "A controversial new bill that will remove the word 'father' from birth certificates to recognise lesbian couples who have children through IVF will be put before NSW Parliament. Fifty laws across NSW covering the Local Government Act, Industrial Relations Act and the constitution will be amended to include new parental presumption protection for female same-sex couples.

"The bill equates the position of a lesbian partner of a woman who has a child after becoming pregnant by a fertilisation procedure, other than sexual intercourse, with the position of a married woman's husband. Lesbian parents will see expressions such as 'birth mother' replace 'mother' and 'both parents' to replace 'the father and the mother' on birth certificates."[18]

Gender mania

In addition to declaring war on male and female, mother and father, men and women, now the activists are telling us that gender is almost infinite in number. Of course the radicals have been telling us for years that gender is merely a social construct, and there are as many genders as one might have moods in a day, but now it is becoming formalised and officialised.

Government and schools and other institutions seem to be rushing in here to find as many genders as they can. The initial acronym LGB (Lesbian, Gay, Bisexual) just keeps on expanding, and soon we will run out of letters in the alphabet. Using numbers would help, since then we would basically be limitless in the number of genders we can dream up. In Germany things are rather modest – at least for now. As one news report states: "A new law in Germany will allow parents to select a "third gender" on the birth certificate of their child, should the child want to identify with a certain gender in the future. Germany is the first country in Europe to pass this type of legislation."[19]

Our universities are certainly getting into all this big time. Throughout the Western world universities are pulling genders out of a hat on a regular basis. The examples are mounting up, but let me just examine of couple of them. Consider what is taking place in a school in the US state of Washington:

> A community college in Washington State has stopped asking applicants if they are male or female, reports KIRO radio in Seattle. In place of that simple query, Bellevue College has two convoluted questions about gender identity and sexual orientation. The application form lists no fewer than seven possibilities for "gender identity" and seven more for "sexual orientation." For the question, "What is your sexual orientation?" the answer choices are: bisexual, gay, lesbian, queer, straight/heterosexual, other and "prefer not to answer." For the question, "What is your gender identity?" the answer choices are: feminine, masculine, androgynous, gender neutral, transgender, other and "prefer not to answer." According to *the Daily Caller's* math, then, that's almost 50 distinct possibilities – none of which are just your basic, garden-variety male or female. Colin Donovan, the LGBTQ Centre adviser at the public, taxpayer-funded school, told KIRO radio that the school is collecting the data in an effort to cater to the few students who say they don't fit traditional definitions of gender and sexuality.[20]

Also consider this recent report on what one Colorado college is now offering:

> Colleges often boast that they offer students more choices. Colorado College, located in Colorado Springs, lists five separate options for gender on its job applications and numerous other documents. The listed categories are male, female, transgender, decline to answer, or "queer." Ironically, the term – intended to be a positive and affirming choice for the LGBT community – was discovered by a gay job-seeker. "I couldn't believe it. I thought I was going to have a stroke," John Kichi of Pennsylvania told the *Denver Post*. "If them including it on

applications isn't against the law, it should be." Denver Fox station KDVR reported that Kichi has filed a complaint with Colorado Attorney General John Suthers. The school has protested that the term "queer" is now embraced as its own separate gender identity. Colorado College's office of Minority and International Students – which includes an office for "LGBTQIA+" students – states that the newest sexual self-identity is "an umbrella term describing people who have a non-normative gender identity, sexual orientation, or sexual anatomy" and "includes lesbians, gay men, bisexual people, asexual people, transgender people, intersex people, etc."[21]

So basic human biology must now give way to political correctness and the radical sexual revolutionaries and anarchists.

It's a brave new world

These are just some of the cases of family and gender vandalism which are occurring of late to placate the social engineers. Never mind that mothers and fathers need to be eradicated in the process. Godless Communist regimes could go only so far in destroying marriage and family, but it looks like our new secular humanist regimes are succeeding where even the Marxists failed. That's some 'victory'.

And it is not just those who can be called members of the religious right who are appalled at all this. Consider the thoughts of UK columnist Brendan O'Neill. He recently penned a piece entitled, "How the gay-marriage campaign has unleashed a bureaucratic assault on people's identities". In it he is not reserved in expressing his contempt for this PC madness:

> Anyone who thinks the introduction of gay marriage will give rise to a new era of liberty and choice should look at the Canadian experience. There, the passing of the 2005 Civil Marriage Act, which allows same-sex unions, unleashed a

phenomenal amount of state meddling in families and relationships. Most notably, the state utterly overhauled the traditional language of the family, airbrushing from official documents terms such as "husband" and "wife" and even "mother" and "father". The Orwellian obliteration of such longstanding identities, which mean a great deal to many people, demonstrates that modern politicians are more than happy to ride roughshod over the majority in their desperate pursuit of some PC political points.[22]

He examines how this is working out there, and then concludes as follows:

Such tinkering with lingo, the replacement of words that have real depth and meaning for millions of people with bureaucratic terms that no normal person uses, reveals the social-engineering instinct that lies behind the gay-marriage campaign. Because this is not simply about elevating gay relationships, as we are so often told – more importantly, it is about demoting and devaluing traditional relationships, as built on marriage as it was once understood. Who in their right mind introduces their husband or wife as their "spouse"? What normal woman describes herself as "Parent 1" to her children rather than "mother"? No one does. The emergence of such vapid terminology on the back of the gay-marriage bandwagon shows that traditional identities will be trounced in the name of allowing political elites to look cool by backing gay marriage. What message does it send to people who define themselves as husbands, wives, mothers or fathers when those ancient terms, so packed with moral purchase, are overnight replaced by bureaucratic BS? It doesn't matter, it seems. Those people and their identities count for little in the face of David Cameron's desire to look both caring and daring as he gives his blessing to gay marriage.[23]

Quite right. So who says granting special rights to homosexual couples will not change anything?

CHAPTER 3

What Slippery Slope?

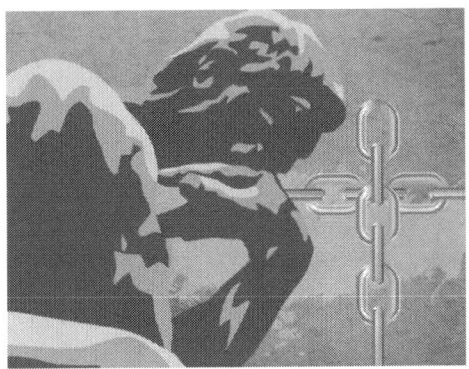

Granting special rights to homosexuals seems to be a never-ending affair: just as soon as some are granted, more are demanded. The list of demands seems to be an endless list. The big push in much of the West is for homosexual marriage. But we know that this push will most certainly not stop there – it will open the door to all sorts of other sexualities to be legalised and normalised, and all sorts of other "marriage" rights. The truth is, a Pandora's Box has been opened here, and a real slippery slope is now in play.

But let me stop here and say this: I have had people tell me I can't use the slippery slope argument, that it is not sound philosophically or logically. Let me reply in this fashion: at this point I am not at all interested in mere philosophy or theory – I am interested in reality. And the reality is this: the slippery slope is already occurring right before our very eyes. Every day we see more examples of it occurring. So those who take umbrage at my use of the term can feel free to just think of something else when they see it – maybe such terms as:

-the domino effect
-the knock-on effect

-the open door effect
-the ripple effect

I am happy to use any one of these terms if you prefer. But the slope is certainly here, and it is certainly slippery. So in terms of logical fallacies, we can agree that x may not of necessity always lead to y. But as I say, I am not interested in just theoretical mental exercises here, but what in fact is actually happening. The ripple effect of homosexual marriage is now fully evident for anyone with eyes – and without ideological blinders – to see. There are four main areas we can clearly see the knock-on effect taking place here:
-Polyamory (group love/marriage)
-Paedophilia
-Bestiality
-Incest

Let me look much more closely at each one in turn. In every case we see not only an increase in these activities and much more public and vocal demand for them, but a leading justification of it is that if homosexual marriage has been allowed, then why can we not have real "marriage equality" and allow all these things to occur as well?

Polyamory (group love/marriage)

As I have already documented in my previous book, *Strained Relations*, the push for group love and group marriage is now moving along in top gear.[1] There are countless groups which are now deadly serious in their calls for the complete recognition and legalisation of group marriage. And they are all riding on the coat-tails of the homosexual marriage activists.

In fact they are offering us exactly the very same arguments. And they are fully logical to do so. Once we accept the sham arguments of the militant homosexual lobby, then we must, to be consistent, embrace the arguments of the other sexual militants. Thus if the homosexual lobby says that gender is irrelevant to marriage, then the poly crowd can rightly claim that number is irrelevant to marriage. Both claim that marriage is simply about "love" – whatever that means – and as long as adults are consenting, any and all combinations and permutations should be given full steam ahead.

Indeed, every single lame argument that was used to make the case for homosexual marriage is now being used by the polyamorists as well. And why not? They are in complete agreement on this. They both sing from the same song sheet. We now know all the standard arguments being proffered:

-love is all that matters
-keep the state out of the bedroom
-why are we being denied our rights?
-as long as adults are consenting, what business is it to anyone else?
-marriage equality is what we want
-love is not bigoted
-why should religion prevent us from our love?
-it is time to end all unjust discrimination
-love knows no bounds
-only bigots will want to block our love
-marriage should be for everyone
-we're here, we're queer, so get used to it
-we're poly, we're jolly, so get used to it

On and on it goes: the identical weak arguments; the identical bloated rhetoric; the identical illogic; the identical attempts to redefine marriage out of existence. And it is happening all over the place now. An entire book on its own could be filled with all those making these arguments. There is far too much material here to choose from, so let me offer just a select few examples.

One of the clearest examples of a slippery slope in action has just occurred in New Zealand. Within days of that country passing homosexual marriage legislation, other activist groups came out of the woodwork demanding their "rights" as well. Ever since that nation legalised homosexual marriage on April 17, 2013, the rot has begun to set in. In no time the polyamorists were out loud and proud, rightly asking, 'when will we get our marriage equality?' This is how one New Zealand media outlet began the story:

> A group is calling for the government to consider legalising multi-partner marriages. The group set up a Facebook page just before the Marriage Amendment Bill passed through Parliament last week, legalising gay marriage. "A statement on the page described multi-partner – or polyamorous – marriage as 'responsible, adult, committed non-monogamy,' and said all committed loving relationships between adults regardless of number should be respected and given legal acknowledgement. "Some Australian Greens have now got a lobby group going, there are several MPs around the world coming out as poly and poly-friendly and it seems the time is right to at least bring it to the attention of the New Zealand public and New Zealand parliament," the group said. "This will be a long-term project but with the rest of the world getting on the bandwagon legal multiple partner marriages/unions may one day be accepted."[2]

Or consider this recent example. A writer for the *Slate* makes an unashamed case for polygamy and polyamory. Jillian Keenan's piece is entitled "Legalize Polygamy! No. I am not kidding" and begins as follows:

> Recently, Tony Perkins of the Family Research Council reintroduced a tired refrain: Legalized gay marriage could lead to other legal forms of marriage disaster, such as polygamy. Rick Santorum, Bill O'Reilly, and other social conservatives have made similar claims. It's hardly a new prediction – we've been hearing it for years. *Gay marriage is a slippery slope! A gateway drug! If we legalize it, then what's next? Legalized polygamy?* We can only hope. Yes, really. While the Supreme Court and the rest of us are all focused on the human right of marriage equality, let's not forget that the fight doesn't end with same-sex marriage. We need to legalize polygamy, too. Legalized polygamy in the United States is the constitutional,

feminist, and sex-positive choice. More importantly, it would actually help protect, empower, and strengthen women, children, and families.

She looks at a number of objections to polygamy and then ends her piece this way:

Finally, prohibiting polygamy on "feminist" grounds – that these marriages are inherently degrading to the women involved – is misguided. The case for polygamy is, in fact, a feminist one and shows women the respect we deserve. Here's the thing: As women, we really can make our own choices. We just might choose things people don't like. If a woman wants to marry a man, that's great. If she wants to marry another woman, that's great too. If she wants to marry a hipster, well – I suppose that's the price of freedom. And if she wants to marry a man with three other wives, that's *her damn choice.*

We have a tendency to dismiss or marginalize people we don't understand. We see women in polygamous marriages and assume they are victims. "They grew up in an unhealthy environment," we say. "They didn't really choose polygamy; they were just born into it." Without question, that is sometimes true. But it's also true of many (too many) monogamous marriages. Plenty of women, polygamous or otherwise, are born into unhealthy environments that they repeat later in life. There's no difference. All marriages deserve access to the support and resources they need to build happy, healthy lives, regardless of how many partners are involved. Arguments about whether a woman's consensual sexual and romantic choices are "healthy" should have no bearing on the legal process. And while polygamy remains illegal, women who choose this lifestyle don't have access to the protections and benefits that legal marriage provides.

As a feminist, it's easy and intuitive to support women who choose education, independence, and careers. It's not as intuitive to support women who choose values and lifestyles that seem outdated or even sexist, but those women deserve our respect just as much as any others. It's condescending, not supportive, to minimize them as mere "victims" without considering the possibility that some of them have simply made a different choice.

The definition of marriage is plastic. Just like heterosexual marriage is no better or worse than homosexual marriage, marriage between two consenting adults is not inherently more or less "correct" than marriage among three (or four, or six) consenting adults. Though polygamists are a minority – a tiny minority, in fact – freedom has no value unless it extends to even the smallest and most marginalized groups among us. So let's fight for marriage equality until it extends to every same-sex couple in the United States – and then let's keep fighting. We're not done yet.[3]

There we have it again: "the definition of marriage is plastic;" "marriage equality;" and "we're not done yet". And where have we heard all this before? Oh yeah, this is the very thing the homosexual activists have been saying for decades now. No wonder it so nicely flows off the tongue of other sexual anarchists. The groundwork has already been well and truly laid.

This is not just theoretical of course. It is already happening. Consider this Australian headline: "Identical twins in relationship with same man". The article says this: "A Perth man who is in a relationship with two identical twin sisters says he would marry both women if it were legal. Marc Glasby, who will appear on SBS current affairs program *Insight* tonight, was married to his wife Belle for 30 years before falling in love with her sister Dorothy."

The piece continues:

However, despite falling for her twin Mr Glasby still loved Belle and the trio entered into a polyamorous relationship. "The relationship has not been without its hiccups, not least of all due to sibling rivalry that exists between sisters," Mr Glasby said. Dorothy agreed the start of the relationship had been unusual. "When I first came into the relationship there was a lot of guilt of course... looking at what the Bible says," Dorothy said. But her sister Belle said after time the relationship became a source of strength for the trio. "Our love keeps the three of us strong," she said. Marc said he feels unfortunate to live in a society that doesn't accept marriage to multiple partners, blaming religion for the taboo. "If I had the option I would most certainly be legally married to both girls, as they are both, in every respect except on paper, my wives," Mr Glasby said. "As far as I'm concerned Dorothy's my wife as much as Belle."[4]

Staying in Australia for a moment, did you know that we already have dedicated lobby groups pushing for this? As but one example, consider the Polyamory Action Lobby (PAL). This is what they say on their homepage:

> PAL is about LOVE (and lot's [sic] of it). We exist to campaign for the rights and cultural recognition of polyamorous and non-monogamous relationships in Australia. Poly love is equal love, and deserves the same legal rights and cultural recognition as monogamous love. We believe all Australians in loving, consenting relationships deserve the right to be married (regardless of the number of partners involved). We also challenge negative community stereotypes of poly relationships – and seek to build cultural recognition and understanding of our lifestyles. Over the last year we have seen politicians on the right compare the lifestyles of Australian's [sic] who practice poly-love and non-monogamy to those of paedophiles and beastialists. We have seen politicians on the left buckle to this pressure, sidelining the rights of the polyamorous community in their campaign for marriage equality. Polyamory is not a niche phenomenon – it is a lifestyle and sexual identity that exists throughout mainstream society and the LGBTIQ community. We

will not allow our elected representatives to ignore us any longer.[5]

One write-up about them says this: "The Polyamory Action Lobby's key operatives and founders are Greensparty up-and-comers Brigitte Garozzo/McFadden (the convenor of the Sydney Uni Greensparty), Timothy Scriven, an 'anarcho-revolutionary libertarian socialist' who describes himself on Facebook as 'an active member of the Greens on Campus' and Kieran Adair who wrote on *New Matilda* that he is 'a Green'."[6]

And there you may have thought that the greenies were just about trees. It appears that they are far kinkier than that. 'But this is just a fringe group' you say. OK, so is *Scientific American* just a fringe group periodical? Check out their recent article: "New Sexual Revolution: Polyamory May Be Good for You". No I am not making this up. The article says, "Two-by-two isn't the only way to go through life. In fact, an estimated 4 to 5 percent of Americans are looking outside their relationship for love and sex – with their partner's full permission." It continues:

"These consensually nonmonogamous relationships, as they're called, don't conform to the cultural norm of a handholding couple in love for life. They come in a dizzying array of forms, from occasional 'swinging' and open relationships to long-term commitments among multiple people. Now, social scientists embarking on brand-new research into these types of relationships are finding that they may challenge the ways we think of jealousy, commitment and love. They may even change monogamy for the better."[7]

It certainly seems that the mainstream media is increasingly happy to run with their stories as well. It seems almost daily we have these human interest stories of all sorts of whacky and wild sexual combos which the media is keen to portray as perfectly normal and acceptable. Consider this recent story about "My two husbands". It begins:

What Slippery Slope?

> My family is very ordinary to me. We eat dinner together. We gather in the living room and watch movies. Last weekend, we went on a camping trip and sat around the campfire making s'mores, the grown-ups enjoying a few beers while my 9-year-old daughter challenged us with endless rounds of 'would you rather?' It all feels so wonderfully mundane that sometimes I have to remind myself that most people view us as strange at best, depraved at worst. I'm polyamorous, which means I believe you can love multiple partners at the same time. I'm in a relationship with my husband of nearly 17 years, and my boyfriend, with whom I celebrated my second anniversary in May. (In polyamorous lingo, our relationship is known as a "V"; I'm the "hinge" of the V and my two partners are the vertices.) People often say our lives sound complicated, but the truth is, we're quite harmonious. We often joke that we'd make incredibly boring subjects for reality TV.[8]

Yep, oh so ho-hum and matter-of-fact. At least that is what this threesome and a morally numb media wants to suggest. But wait, there's more:

> When I learned about polyamorous relationships, I knew that's what I wanted. My husband wasn't so sure, though. It sounded fine for other people, but just not him. And it still seemed unrealistic to me, so I never pressed the issue. When I returned to school to finish my bachelor's degree in my late 20s, I became friends with a man who changed my mind about all that. He believed in polyamory, too, and we had long conversations about it together: how it could work, how it was truly possible.

> One night, I sat down with my husband and spilled everything. I told him that being polyamorous was a part of who I am, and I asked if he would at least do some research and give it serious consideration before dismissing the idea. He understood that I never would have asked this if it hadn't been extremely important. That conversation could have ended our marriage. But instead, our journey into non-monogamy began.

> One of the biggest hurdles in non-monogamy – probably *the* hurdle – is jealousy. My husband was an incredibly jealous person back then, but he began to question its usefulness and purpose. Jealousy is born from a fear of losing a partner; if you believe that love and intimacy can be shared, and are not diminished by sharing, then that fear loses a lot of its power. It was liberating for my husband to step outside of the box that saw everyone else as some kind of threat.[9]

Yes, if we can just get rid of jealousy and other out-dated moral suasions, we can all just swing. Learn how to repress those pesky moral constraints and just get on with, well, anything. And one more thing: all this must be legalised as well: "When my daughter talks about same-sex marriage or polyamorous relationships, she always looks perplexed and says, 'I don't understand why anyone is angry about people being in love and not hurting anyone.' And I long for a world where everyone is able to see it so simply."[10]

Yep, and why not? If we can gut marriage of its fundamental gender requirements, then we might as well slash and burn its fundamental requirements about number as well. In the postmodern world of sexual anarchy and revolution, anything goes.

Then there's a recent piece in the *Huffington Post* entitled "'Monogamish': Two Is Company, but Is Three Really a Crowd?" continues the drum-beating for group sex and group love. At least the author nicely spills the beans about homosexual 'faithfulness': "When I think about dating and relationships, especially when talking with friends, I tend to come to the same conclusion: Monogamy isn't possible. I feel that in the gay world, no matter how committed a couple appears to be, or how beautiful their life together looks, or even how perfect they seem, there always seems to be the threat of infidelity lurking in the background. Countless dinner parties, nights at bars, Pride events and everything in between suggest one thing to me, over and over again: Most men don't really seem interested in sticking with just one person."

What Slippery Slope?

After offering "arguments" and "research" as to why monogamy is just not a goer, he says this:

> All this can be, and probably is, worrisome to marriage equality advocates as they fight for access to the traditional options that heterosexual folks enjoy. But should we see 'monogamish' relationships as a threat to marriage? I think not. If people are actually happier when they're able to openly and frankly discuss their desires, their passions and what they need from each other, even if that means another partner a few nights a month, wouldn't that help marriages remain strong? It's often said that half of all marriages end in divorce, so the sanctity of marriage is being threatened even without help from the gays. I would argue that marriage is in great need of an intervention or, at the very least, a slight readjustment of what we expect from it, because clearly the way society approaches it now is not working. By expanding our understanding of how a couple can operate together, and maybe throwing away that old saying, 'two's company, but three's a crowd,' maybe we can actually make ourselves happier and have longer, healthier relationships, even if they are 'monogamish'.[11]

Of course, when our side says that homosexuals are not exactly known for their love of monogamy, we are shouted down as "homophobes" and "bigots". So just what exactly does that make this homosexual writer? Is he a bigot as well, and mired in homophobia?

Finally, have a look at this article which looks at the scene in the US:

> Los Angeles, California: *ABC News* recently aired a segment about a woman involved in what is called a polyamorous relationship – living with multiple boyfriends or girlfriends under one roof. The woman, identified as Jaiya, began by living with her boyfriend Jon. However, because Jaiya wanted to have children and Jon didn't, he suggested that she bring someone else into the picture that would conceive with her. Therefore, Jaiya

brought home Ian, and the two had a little boy together. Both Ian and Jon are raising the child, and Jon quit his job to stay home with him. "I'm looking for what helps me to be the best human that I can possibly be," Jaiya told reporters. "I stopped searching for 'the one.' I can have the one, and I can also have the one, and the one and the one."

Jaiya works as a professional sexologist, giving sexual advice to others. She admits to having sexual relations with both men, and states that while Jon now wants other children, she does not. "There's a part of me that wants to go back to 'That was MY girlfriend'," Jon said. However, according to the ABC report, Jon is now looking for a second girlfriend, and Ian already has another relationship on the side. Jaiya said that the family structure has taken a lot of new forms in recent years, so she does not see a problem with living with two boyfriends. "What is the modern family today?" she asked. "We've got step-moms and step-dads; we've got gay parents raising children… The family today is a different thing than what it was years ago."[12]

And again, the academics, activists and other heavyweights are all proudly calling for this. It is not just nutter fringe groups, but mainstream academics, key homosexual leaders, and other elites who are fully behind it all. In addition to the piece in *Scientific American* mentioned above, consider this recent example of a New York professor.

During a law school debate on April 15, New York University professor of social and cultural analysis Judith Stacey argued against the nuclear family and monogamous relationships, and for decriminalizing polygamy. The debate, sponsored by the conservative Federalist Society and between Ms Stacey and the conservative Heritage Foundation's Ryan T. Anderson, was on "the defence of marriage." Among Ms Stacey's wicked smart musings: "I say why should there be marriage at all;" "What should limit it to two and why should it be monogamous? Nothing in view gives the state that particular interest;" and "So I would agree that we should get rid of the sexual family, there's no reason in the contemporary world to base our relationships necessarily on sex." On the subject of holding down many wives, Ms Stacey said, "I'm not arguing for those other forms, though I do in my book argue for the decriminalization of polygamy – which I think is a deeply hypocritical stance, and we can get into that if you want – but it's not because I advocate polygamy." Polygamy is an ancient tradition...[13]

We also have the prestigious *BBC* weighing in on the push for polyamory as well. Indeed, it recently aired a documentary, "Monogamy and the Rules of Love". As a supplement, they had a large article on all this in their *BBC Magazine*. The story begins, "Charlie is talking excitedly about a first date she went on the night before. Next to her on the sofa is her husband of six years, Tom. And on the other side of him is Sarah, who's been in a relationship with Tom for the last five years. Sarah's fiancée, Chris, is in the kitchen making a cup of tea. The two women are also in a full-blown relationship, while the two men are just good friends. Together, they make a polyamorous family and share a house in Sheffield. 'We're planning to grow old together,' says Charlie."[14]

Yep, it's all so very normal. It is just one big happy household. On and on the story goes:

> "I feel safe and secure, with the ability to trust and grow, with Tom, Sarah and Chris," says Charlie. "It is from the base and security of the three of them that I face the world and the challenges the day brings." "The way I see it, it's only a problem if I feel like one of my partners is spending more time with all their other partners than with me," says Sarah. "It just leads to people feeling hurt." A shared Google calendar is the answer. "We mostly use it for keeping track of date nights," says Charlie. "The couple who is on a date gets first pick of what film goes on the TV and it helps keep track of who's in what bedroom." Sarah chips in. "So, for example, I have a weekly date night with

> Charlie. It's us snuggling up, us with the TV, us going to bed together and all that kind of business."[15]

The article concludes, "Tom is cautiously optimistic that polyamory will become 'average and everyday. Anyone who is expecting some massive social change overnight is terribly mistaken, but it will happen.' In the meantime, the four of them are planning an unofficial ceremony to mark their commitment to each other. 'Sometimes people just write the relationship off as a lazy way of getting more sex than you normally would. There are easier ways,' says Tom wryly. They all agree managing a multi-partner relationship can be exhausting. 'But we don't have a choice. We're in love with each other,' they chime."[16]

Since I have not seen the doco in question, let me draw upon the commentary of another group: "Monogamy is out of fashion and polyamorous relationships, involving multiple partners, could become the norm, a controversial BBC investigation has said. *BBC Radio 4* documentary, Monogamy and the Rules of Love featured a number of interviews with people in polyamorous relationships, which are intimate relationships between three or more people at the same time. Presenter Jo Fidgen questioned whether there is still room for sexual fidelity in a 'society where choice is everything'. She suggested that the 'taboo' surrounding intimate multi-partner relationships could disappear within the next ten years."[17]

It continues:

> Miss Fidgen said: "We don't see any contradiction in loving more than one friend. No-one asks us to only love one of our children. Why shouldn't it be any different with romantic love?" In June a group of polyamorists in Canada called for the same legal status as other relationships, following the group's first national convention in Canada. Canada redefined marriage in 2005 and saw a major legal case involving polygamy in 2011. The Canadian Polyamory Advocacy Association intervened in the case and now says it wants to see polyamorous relationships

What Slippery Slope?

treated on the same legal footing as others. In May polyamorous supporters in New Zealand started calling for legal recognition just weeks after same-sex marriage was legalised in the country. In March the politician who masterminded the gay marriage campaign in Holland said that "group marriage" was now being discussed in the country.[18]

Still in the UK, the leftist *Guardian* also recently weighed into the topic with this opinion piece:

> Non-monogamy is nothing new. Recent research suggests that alongside the stubborn population of adulterers, 15 to 28% of heterosexual couples and about 50% of bisexuals and gay men have some sort of "non-traditional" arrangement. This week the BBC Radio 4 documentary Monogamy and the Rules of Love tapped into a growing curiosity about polyamory, the formal practice of having multiple romantic partners at one time. For many people, though, polyamory isn't curious at all – it's just another way of organising life, love and whose turn it is to make the tea.
>
> It may be hard for the conservative old guard to fathom, but for a long time lots of people have quietly been getting on with non-monogamous relationships. During the recent debates around the legalisation of gay marriage, Tory critics warned that the next, unthinkable step would be multiple marriage. I can't be the only one who wondered if that'd be such a bad idea. Some of the sweetest couples I know, including many with healthy, happy children, are not couples at all, but triples or even quadruples – but the public conversation about open non-monogamy is still stuck on horrified confusion.[19]

And here we see the radicals' first rule of thumb come to the fore: verbal engineering must always precede social engineering. Radically change the vocabulary and then you can much more easily radically change society. Works every time. In this case, dump scary terms like "group sex" and "polygamy," and try winners like this instead: "non-monogamy". Yep, that is a good one. That will suck in a lot of gullible folks. Our columnist continues:

> Personally, I started practising non-monogamy in my early 20s as a statement against the tyranny of the heterosexual couple form and the patriarchal nuclear family – but then again, I did a lot of silly things for similar reasons in my early 20s. If you'd asked 21-year-old me why precisely I was hanging half-naked out of a fourth-floor window on Holloway Road, I'd probably also have answered "as a statement against the tyranny of the heterosexual couple form". Nowadays, from the wise and serious vantage point of my mid-20s, I practice non-monogamy because it works for me. It doesn't work for everyone, and I might not choose it forever. I've been in various polyamorous relationships, some delightful, some less so.[20]

She finishes: "Polyamorists and monogamists alike fall prey to the delusion that their rules are the only proper way to organise relationships, and if we could all just stick those rules, no one would ever have to get their heart broken ever again. If only it were so simple. The truth is that there is no magic set of rules for love, sex and home economics that works for everyone – and that's why it's so important that there are other options out there. *Radio 4* predicted that monogamy would lose its 'moral monopoly' within 10 years. Bring it on, I say."[21]

So the push continues. And as I documented in my previous book on homosexuality, *Strained Relations*, plenty of homosexual activists themselves want to see the definition of marriage blown wide open.[22] They do not have in mind what we have in mind when they talk about marriage, and many of them admit they want to see an end to marriage altogether.

Another recent example of this comes from Russian author and journalist Masha Gessen. In May 2012 the annual Sydney Writers' Festival was held. It included a panel discussion by homosexual authors, including Gessen. Her remarks about how marriage must change are revealing, even if consistent with what so many other homosexual activists have been saying. This is what she had to say:

> It's a no-brainer that we should have the right to marry, but I also think equally that it's a no-brainer that the institution of marriage should not exist [*cheers from the audience*]. That causes my brain some trouble. And part of why it causes me trouble is because fighting for gay marriage generally involves lying about what we are going to do with marriage when we get there – because we lie that the institution of marriage is not going to change, and that is a lie. The institution of marriage is going to change, and it should change. And again, I don't think it should exist. And I don't like taking part in creating fictions about my life. That's sort of not what I had in mind when I came out thirty years ago. I have three kids who have five parents, more or less, and I don't see why they shouldn't have five parents legally.... [After my divorce,] I met my new partner, and she had just had a baby, and that baby's biological father is my brother, and my daughter's biological father is a man who lives in Russia, and my adopted son also considers him his father. So the five parents break down into two groups of three.... And really, I would like to live in a legal system that is capable of reflecting that reality. And I don't think that's compatible with the institution of marriage.[23]

That marriage will radically change is of course clear, as I have been documenting all along. But notice her candid admission: "fighting for gay marriage generally involves lying about what we are going to do with marriage when we get there – because we lie that the institution of marriage is not going to change, and that is a lie." Yep, nothing like admitting that to be fully open with the public on how they plan to destroy marriage and family would make their case too hard to make, so they must lie to sneak their sinister agendas through. At least she spilled the beans here.

SCOTUS and beyond

Each passing day brings us more examples of the slippery slope in action, especially in regard to polyamory. Consider what happened when the Supreme Court of the United States handed down its decision on marriage late in June 2013. The SCOTUS decision helped pave the way for even more marriage destabilisation, especially in its attack on the Defence of Marriage Act. Because of this, the polyamorists came out of the closet in droves. They demanded – quite logically – that if homosexual marriage is a goer, then there is no reason why group marriage cannot be legalised as well.

One article on this written just before the Court decision offers some revealing quotes: "Anita Wagner Illig, a longtime polyamory community spokesperson who operates the group Practical Polyamory, is unsure of the direct impact of a ruling that would legalize same-sex marriage nationwide. Until recently, she noted, 'the polyamory community has expressed little desire for legal marriage,' but now more options seem possible in the future. 'We polyamorists are grateful to our [LGBT] brothers and sisters for blazing the marriage equality trail,' Illig said.

"Illig believes there is indeed a 'slippery slope' toward legal recognition for polygamy if the court rules in favour of nationwide same-sex marriage, an argument typically invoked by anti-gay marriage advocates. 'A favourable outcome for marriage equality is a favourable outcome for multi-partner marriage, because the opposition cannot argue lack of precedent for legalizing marriage for other forms of non-traditional relationships,' she said."[24]

George Washington University law professor Jonathan Turley, who is representing a polygamist family, said this: "There is no reason that the decision should impact polygamy and particularly the Brown case in Utah. Polygamists are where homosexual couples were before 2003 and the Lawrence [v. Texas] decision" – a case striking down laws against homosexual relations."[25]

Another article quotes more excited polyamorists: "Anne Wilde, a vocal advocate for polygamist rights who practiced the lifestyle herself until her husband died in 2003, praised the court's decision as a sign that society's stringent attachment to traditional 'family values' is evolving. 'I was very glad… The nuclear family, with a dad and a mom and two or three kids, is not the majority anymore,' said Wilde. 'Now it's grandparents taking care of kids, single parents, gay parents. I think people are more and more understanding that as consenting adults, we should be able to raise a family however we choose.' 'We're very happy with it,' said Joe Darger, a Utah-based polygamist who has three wives. 'I think [the court] has taken a step in correcting some inequality, and that's certainly something that's going to trickle down and impact us.'

"Noting that the court found the Defence of Marriage Act unconstitutional because the law denied marriage rights to a specific class of people, Darger said, 'Our very existence has been classified as criminal… and I think the government needs to now recognize that we have a right to live free as much as anyone else'."

Wilde can see the clear logic in all this, and the clear slippery slope in action: "I'm not a fortune-teller, but it seems like if more people are accepting of gay marriage, it would follow that polygamist marriage wouldn't be criticized quite so much."[26]

In yet another article appearing soon after the SCOTUS decision, a Boston College Law School professor has admitted that incest and polygamy are the next logical developments. Let me quote from part of this article:

> "You know those opponents of marriage equality who said government approval of same-sex marriage might erode bans on polygamous and incestuous marriages?" asks the professor, Kent Greenfield. "They're right." In a piece at the website of *The*

American Prospect, the Catholic law school prof then goes on to challenge gay marriage supporters to differentiate totally acceptable gay and lesbian marriages from various forms of communal marriage and sibling love. "The left is in this bind in part because our arguments for expanding the marriage right to same-sex couples have been so compelling," Greenfield brags proudly. "Marriage, we've said, is about defining one's own family and consecrating a union based on love. We've voiced these arguments in constitutional terms, using claims arising from the doctrines of 'fundamental rights' and equal protection." After a discussion of the famous sodomy case, *Lawrence v. Texas*, which waxes poetically about the "right to define one's own concept of existence," Greenfield then pops the question: under such a legal rubric, "why can't people in polyamorous relationships claim that right as well?" ... "We can admit our arguments in favour of marriage equality inexorably lead us to a broader battle in favour of allowing people to define their marriages, and their families, by their own lights," he concludes.[27]

Even the *Economist* magazine, which is in favour of homosexual marriage, had an article on this recently, and yes they too used the term "slippery slope" at the very outset. "Now that the federal government recognises the marriages of same-sex couples from enlightened states, what's next? Polygamy? Well, polygamists are hopeful. And it does stand to reason. DOMA was struck down in no small part because it picks out a certain class of people and, by denying them recognition of their marriages, denies their families equal freedom and dignity.

"Can it be denied that polygamous families, whose marital arrangements are *illegal,* much less unrecognised, are denied equal liberty and are made to suffer the indignity active discrimination? Joe Darger, a Utahn with three wives, has said, 'Our very existence has been classified as criminal... and I think the government needs to now recognize that we have a right to live free as much as anyone else'."[28]

In the article, Matt K. Lewis of the *Daily Caller* asks: "What's magical about the number two?" Quite right. Once you jettison gender in the marriage equation, why not abandon number as well? Indeed, why even worry about other things such as age?

The *Economist* piece concludes with a hearty endorsement of polyamory: "Same-sex-marriage activists have wisely sought to separate themselves from advocates of even more exotic marital arrangements. However, as Mr Lewis suggests, the idea that marriage is an inherently heterosexual institution is less plausible than the idea that it is inherently exclusive to couples. If a man can love a man, a woman can love a woman *and* a man. And if they all love each other... well, what's the problem? Refraining from criminalising families based on such unusual patterns of sentiment is less than the least we can do.

"If the state lacks a legitimate rationale for imposing on Americans a heterosexual definition of marriage, it seems pretty likely that it likewise lacks a legitimate rationale for imposing on Americans a monogamous definition of marriage. Conservatives have worried that same-sex marriage would somehow entail the ruination of the family as the foundation of society, but we have seen only the flowering of family values among same-sex households, the domestication of the gays. Whatever our fears about polyamorous marriage, I suspect we'll find them similarly ill-founded. For one thing, what could be more family-friendly than four moms and six dads?"[29]

When mainstream journals like the *Economist* start talking this way, then you know we have a slippery slope in action. The militant homosexuals can keep pretending it does not exist, but as I have just documented here, and in so many other articles, the slope is most certainly alive and well.

So, what was it that we said years ago about the slippery slope? What was that we said about how the homosexual assault on marriage and family would not end there, but would open the door to any and every weird sexual combo – more options available than at Baskin-Robbins? They only offer 31 flavours of ice cream, but it seems the sky is the limit with the new sexual wrecking crews now on the prowl. The sexual liberationists want complete open slather on all things sexual. Never mind if they destroy society in the process. Hey, at least they will be "free" – or so they think. They will be as free as the prodigal son, who had the whole pigsty to himself.

Paedophilia

Those who want to see normalised sexual relations with children have also been much more vocal of late. Of course they have long been making these demands, and they have had a long relationship with the homosexual rights movement as I have documented elsewhere.[30]

In fact, the homosexual activists have long called for the lowering of the age of consent – or abolishing it altogether. Sadly they are not alone in all this. Just recently a leading legal eagle in the UK called for the age to be dropped to 13, to stop the 'persecution of old men'! Yes, that is what she actually said. As a newspaper report says:

> A senior human rights barrister has sparked a storm of outrage after calling for the age of consent to be lowered to 13 in order to prevent the 'persecution of old men'. Barbara Hewson made the controversial suggestion in an article for the online magazine 'Spiked'. In the column, Hewson, who is a barrister at Hardwicke in London, stated that the move was necessary in the wake of the Savile scandal. She refers to Operation Yewtree as the 'Savile Inquisition' and describes its inquiry as reminiscent of Soviet-era Russia. She goes on to suggest some of the offences investigated were 'low level misdemeanours'.[31]

Fortunately not everyone took kindly to the idea:

Peter Watt, Director of the NSPCC helpline said: "These outdated and simply ill-informed views would be shocking to hear from anyone but to hear them from a highly experienced barrister simply beggars belief. Stuart Hall has pleaded guilty to abusing children as young as 9 years-old, we think most people would agree that crimes of this nature are incredibly serious. Thankfully the law, and most people, are very clear on this matter. To minimise and trivialise the impact of these offences for victims in this way is all but denying that they have in fact suffered abuse at all. Any suggestion of lowering the age of consent could put more young people at risk from those who prey on vulnerable young people."[32]

This is certainly of very great concern – although perhaps it is not too surprising. And worse yet, there are now many "experts" who are arguing that paedophilia is an innate predisposition and orientation, just like is claimed about homosexuality. A number of illustrations of this can be provided here. Take for example this ominous headline: "Some homosexual activist groups a 'dream' to paedophiles". The piece begins as follows:

Two psychologists testified before a parliamentary session on a bill related to sexual assault on children that paedophilia is a "sexual orientation" just like homosexuality or heterosexuality. Lifesitenews reported on the testimony at a parliamentary session in Canada regarding a bill intended to increase mandatory minimum sentences on child sex offenders for particular crimes. Dr Vernon Quinsey and Dr Hubert Van Gijseghem were testifying on how offenders responded to treatment. Van Gijseghem, psychologist and retired professor of the University of Montreal, said, "Paedophiles are not simply people who commit a small offense from time to time but rather are grappling with what is equivalent to a sexual orientation just like another individual may be grappling with heterosexuality or even homosexuality." He went on to say, "True paedophiles have an exclusive preference for children, which is the same as having a sexual orientation. You cannot change this person's sexual orientation. He may, however, remain abstinent."[33]

We find here the same line used for homosexuals: this is an orientation from which no change is possible. And just as groups like the American Psychiatric Association (APA) were hounded by the militants to change their stance on homosexuality, so too the paedophile activists are trying to do the same thing.

Consider the words of Matt Barber who attended a pro-paedophilia conference in Baltimore in August 2011. In an article by Jeremy Kryn we get to hear from Barber and what he experienced: "As a former law enforcement officer I've dealt with situations involving suicide, homicide and other violence. That said, I've never felt the level of spiritual oppression and evil that I felt in that room."

He continues, "These mental health 'professionals,' and self-described paedophile and 'gay' activists were inexplicably able to cavalierly discuss, in an almost dismissive way, the idea of child rape. They used flowery, euphemistic psychobabble to give quasi-scientific cover to a discussion about the worst kind of perversion." Kryn describes the conference:

> The organization B4U-ACT sponsored the event in Baltimore last week, which was attended by pro-paedophile activists and mental health professionals. The conference examined the ways in which 'minor-attracted persons' could be involved in a revision of the American Psychological Association (APA) classification of paedophilia. Conference panellists included Fred Berlin of the Johns Hopkins University School of Medicine, Renee Sorentino of Harvard Medical School, John Sadler of the University of Texas Southwestern Medical Centre, and John Breslow of the London School of Economics and Political Science. Speakers addressed the around 50 individuals in attendance on themes ranging from the notion that paedophiles are "unfairly stigmatized and demonized" by society to the idea that "children are not inherently unable to consent" to sex with an adult. Also

discussed were arguments that an *adult's* desire to have sex with children is "normative" and that the APA's Diagnostic and Statistical Manual of Mental Disorders (DSM) ignores the fact that paedophiles "have feelings of love and romance for children" in the same way adult heterosexuals and homosexuals have romantic feelings for one another.[34]

Just as homosexual activists successfully bullied and intimidated the American Psychiatric Association in 1973 to pull homosexuality off its list, so too the paedophiles are seeking to do the same thing. And it is likely that they will succeed. After all, they can use all the handy arguments already used so successfully by the homosexual activists.

Kryn cites Law Professor Judith Reisman: "I go into detail on this in my last book, *Sexual Sabotage*. Following Alfred Kinsey 'sexologists' began to occupy our schools, so that educated professionals have largely been trained to be a form of sexual anarchists.

"Although the stupidity of advocating harmless amoral sexuality overwhelms us daily, our arrogant 'educated' populations say morality has no place in our sexual lives. Just as AIDS is a natural outgrowth of amoral sexual education and media, so too is child sexual abuse. We are breeding a new human character and child sexual abuse is increasingly part of that character."[35]

Another alarming piece entitled "Many researchers taking a different view of paedophilia" in the *Los Angeles Times* also notes how so many of our sexperts are arguing that paedophilia is an unchangeable condition. It begins with a "case study" of a man who claims his desires for children are intrinsic to who he is. It then says this:

> In the laboratory, researchers are coming to the same conclusion. Like many forms of sexual deviance, paedophilia once was thought to stem from psychological influences early in life. Now, many experts view it as a sexual orientation as immutable as

heterosexuality or homosexuality. It is a deep-rooted predisposition – limited almost entirely to men – that becomes clear during puberty and does not change. The best estimates are that between 1% and 5% of men are paedophiles, meaning that they have a dominant attraction to prepubescent children.[36]

Once again we see this as a mere "sexual orientation" which we are meant to simply accept. And the real worry here is this: in numerous places laws are being enacted which makes it a criminal offence to "discriminate" against anyone based on their "sexual orientation". So the obvious concern here is this: if paedophilia is just another sexual orientation, must we now accept, embrace and promote it like we now must do with homosexuality?

And this is no hollow concern. Consider a pro-homosexual bill in California which is based on this very way of thinking. This is what one report says about the proposed law:

> California Congresswoman, Rep. Jackie Speier CA (D), wants to federalize a state law to prohibit counselling to change a person's sexual orientation. Under the bill's language, a mental health counsellor could be sanctioned if there was an attempt to get a gay individual to change his or her behaviour or speak negatively about their behaviour as it relates to sexuality. The bill calls on states to prohibit efforts to change a minor's sexual orientation, even if the minor requests it, saying that doing so is "dangerous and harmful." The text of the legislation doesn't specifically ban "gay" conversion therapy. Instead, it prohibits attempts to change a person's sexual orientation.

> "'Sexual orientation change efforts' means any practices by mental health providers that seek to change an individual's sexual orientation," the bill says. In regards to California state law SB 1172, which was initiated to ban conversion therapy in California, there were questions regarding the text of the bill. "This language is so broad and vague, it arguably could include all forms of sexual orientation, including paedophilia," said Brad

Dacus, president of the Pacific Justice Institute. "It's not just the orientation that is protected – the conduct associated with the orientation is protected as well." It also means that, if paedophilia is a sexual orientation, that discrimination laws also apply to paedophiles. That means you cannot block a paedophile from being a preschool teacher or any other high-risk occupation.[37]

But thanks to the homosexual activists, we now are having a very hard time saying no to any of this. Indeed, we know things will not stop there. Soon every conceivable "sexual orientation" imaginable will be argued for and publically championed – and eventually legalised. You see, there is still so much sexual inequality and injustice which needs to be dealt with. Welcome to the brave new world, or should I say, the big bad ugly world of sexual insanity.

The curious case of Kate

Here is a recent story you likely did not hear much about in the mainstream media. And if you did, you would have gotten a rather one-sided slant on all this. How many of you know about Kaitlyn Hunt? Nope, didn't think you would. However, a few of you may have heard something about a "Free Kate" movement.

So what is all this about, and why should Kate be freed? Well, the story is quite straight forward – except to the homosexual activists and a pro-homosexual MSM who are trying to pretend it isn't. Kate is an 18-year-old lesbian who was caught out having a sexual affair with a child – a 14-year-old girl.

Now that is illegal in the state of Florida, where this sordid event occurred. So we have here a clear case of paedophilia: adults having sex with children. That should be the end of the story, except that the homosexual activists have turned Kate into a poster girl – and even a victim – for their cause.

They can find absolutely nothing wrong with this, and are bending over backwards to justify it to the world. Just imagine if a man was found to have had sexual relations with a 14-year-old girl: he would be in jail by now and the whole world would think justice had been served.

But because this is a lesbian affair, the media as a whole and a homosexuality-drenched West is having trouble finding anything wrong with this. Thus we have yet another clear indication that the granting of special rights to homosexuals simply opens the door to every other sort of sexual perversion – in this case paedophilia.

Once again it is only the alternative media which has been reporting this case, and doing so free of the pro-homosexual bias. One writer who has been closely following this story, attempting to accurately present the facts on the case, is Robert Stacy McCain.

He has now penned a number of important articles on this deviant case, with his first entitled "Liberals Now Arguing for a Lesbian's Right to Have Sex With a 14-Year-Old Girl". He points out how the secular left – the cheer squad for all things homosexual – are throwing up all the usual sick defences: "but it's consensual," "equality," and so on.

Kate's own mother has come out wholeheartedly defending the actions of her daughter. She "says that the parents of the 14-year-old who pressed charges are 'out to destroy my daughter [because] they feel like my daughter "made" their daughter gay,' and these 'bigoted, religious' parents 'see being gay as a sin and wrong, and they blame my daughter.'

"See? You deviant weirdos thought *Jailbait Lesbian School Girls* was just a popular DVD title, but now it's a civil right. And the only people who disagree are bigoted religious zealots – including the authorities in Indian River County, Florida: 'If this was an 18-year-old male and that was a 14-year-old girl, it would have been prosecuted the same way," Indian River County Sheriff Deryl Loar said during a Monday news conference. ...

"'The idea is to protect people in that vulnerable group from people who are older, 18 and above,' said Bruce Colton, state attorney for Florida's 19th circuit, which includes Indian River County and other parts of the Treasure Coast. '...The statute specifically says that consent is not a defence.'

"Colton said this case exemplifies the purpose of the current law and added he would not support any effort to make consensual relationships among peers legal. 'There's a big maturity difference between them,' he said. 'You're talking the difference between a senior in high school and a freshman in high school. That's what the law is designed to protect'."[38]

He begins a follow-up article this way: "In January, Rush Limbaugh warned that there was 'an effort under way to normalize paedophilia,' and was ridiculed by liberals (including CNN's Soledad O'Brien) for saying so. But now liberals have joined a crusade that, if successful, would effectively legalize sex with 14-year-olds in Florida."

He continues, "Using the slogan 'Stop the Hate, Free Kate' (the Twitter hashtag is #FreeKate) this social-media campaign has attracted the support of liberals including Chris Hayes of *MSNBC*, *Daily Kos, Think Progress* and the gay-rights group Equality Florida. Undoubtedly, part of the appeal of the case is that Hunt is a petite attractive green-eyed blonde. One critic wondered on Twitter how long activists have 'been waiting for a properly photogenic poster child of the correct gender to come along?'

"Portraying Hunt as the victim of prejudice, her supporters claim she was only prosecuted because she is homosexual and because the parents of the unnamed 14-year-old are 'bigoted religious zealots,' as Hunt's mother said in a poorly written Facebook post.

The apparent public-relations strategy was described by Matthew Philbin of Newsbusters: 'If you can play the gay card, you immediately trigger knee-jerk support from the liberal media and homosexual activists anxious to topple any and all rules regarding sex.'

"None of Hunt's supporters seem to care about the possible consequences of issuing what Philbin calls a 'Get Out of Jail Free' card to their teenage lesbian hero-victim. Some have deliberately falsified the narrative of Hunt's crime, claiming that the sexual relationship began when she was 17, when in fact Hunt turned 18 last August and the incidents at issue occurred between November and January. ...

"Prosecutors in the case are apparently determined to resist the politically correct demands of the ACLU, MSNBC and other liberals who don't care about the precedent that might be set by nullifying Florida's age of consent laws. What is remarkable – and alarming to many parents – is that liberals appear to be unashamed to argue for legalizing sex with 14-year-olds."[39]

And in another piece he writes, "Perhaps the most devastating blow to the 'Free Kate' campaign's narrative of victimhood, however, was a local TV station's interview Thursday with the younger girl's parents, a mixed-race couple who scarcely appeared to be 'vindictive bigots.' Jim and Laurie Smith (he's white, she's black) told WPEC-TV reporter Jana Eschbach that they had twice asked Hunt to leave their daughter alone, and only went to police after a January incident in which their daughter ran away and spent the night at Hunt's house."[40]

Another commentator also discusses these parents: "No matter what they feel they're protecting their daughter *from*, they have both the legal right and moral responsibility to protect their daughter, and that's exactly what they did. That they've become the biggest target of contempt because of the Hunt family's efforts is horrific. It's not just. It's unforgivable. That the basic truths of the case were wildly misrepresented by the Hunt family to do it make it that much more outrageous.

"That manipulation was used to take advantage of a community full of generous people with good hearts who are ready to fight for equality is just as offensive. The dishonesty of the architects of the Free Kate campaign does damage to the credibility of the effort of legitimately persecuted people fighting against real abuse...

"Not to mention the lives of the parents who fought to protect their daughter, and a 14 year old girl whose life will never be the same after becoming an unwitting participant in an international media firestorm that didn't need to happen. All of this... so an 18 year old doesn't have to accept the consequences of her own actions."[41]

And the lefties and homosexual activists insist that paedophilia has nothing to do with their agenda. Yeah right.

Incest

The push for incest "rights" is also sadly now upon us in a big way. Once again a number of voices are calling for this, and it is not just low-life types, but respectable leaders and educators. And once again, to even dare to suggest that the push for homosexual marriage rights will logically lead to incest rights results in plenty of abuse and derision.

One person knows this full well. Actor Jeremy Irons has asked whether we must now tolerate even incest, if we allow homosexual marriage to go ahead: "Academy Award winning actor Jeremy Irons said Wednesday that while he doesn't have much of a strong opinion either way on same-sex marriage, he believes it poses interesting questions, including whether allowing same-sex marriage would open the door for interfamilial relationships. 'Could a father not marry his son?' Irons asked *HuffPost Live* host Josh Zepps.

"Irons argued that 'it's not incest between men' because 'incest is there to protect us from inbreeding, but men don't breed,' and wondered whether same-sex marriage might allow fathers to pass on their estates to their sons without being taxed. 'It seems to me that now they're fighting for the name,' Irons said of advocates for same-sex marriage as opposed to civil unions. 'I worry that it means somehow we debase, or we change, what marriage is. I just worry about that'."[42]

He is clearly asking the right questions, but he took plenty of flak for daring to do so. But as I said, already many people are calling for the complete acceptance of incest, all in the name of tolerance and diversity. Consider the amazing claims of one American academic. Check out this headline: "Columbia Political Science Professor Equates His Incestuous Relationship With Daughter to Homosexual Sex".[43] He would not be the first to do this. One report says this:

> The political science professor at Columbia University, 46, allegedly slept with her between 2006 and 2009. Epstein, who specialises in American politics and voting rights, is also said to have exchanged twisted text messages with the woman during their relationship. Matthew Galluzzo, defending Epstein, has said that even though his daughter had emerged as a victim in the case, she could 'best be described as an accomplice'. He told ABCNews.com: "Academically, we are obviously all morally opposed to incest and rightfully so. At the same time, there is an argument to be made in the Swiss case to let go what goes on privately in bedrooms. It's ok for homosexuals to do whatever they want in their own home. How is this so different? We have to figure out why some behaviour is tolerated and some is not."[44]

His point is quite valid of course. If we tolerate, condone, and even celebrate sexual relations between two men, then why can we not do the same with relations between parent and child? Once you open the door to something as bizarre as homosexual marriage then it of course becomes much easier to make the case for incest and incestuous marriage.

And there were many voices happy to support the professor. As but one example, one group which describes itself as "a global voice for gender justice" was happy to see this being made public:

> One of the most taboo human activities has entered the privileged class, race, gender, and sexuality mainstream. This spells trouble. I'm guessing this guy will get skewered, ick-factored out of existence, practically, and everything else will be under rug swept. Shame, because I think – as unpleasant as it may be to discuss – there is an inherent value in bringing such a deeply troubling moral issue to the forefront. It could also be an entry point into frank conversations about class in this country, and how privilege so often keeps us removed from the nittiest, grittiest realities of human nature.
>
> Not least because it is an entry point into some very real, deep, and tough conversations about social and sexual norms. I'm of the opinion that discrimination against those who fall outside the hetero-norm in any way shape or form, queer, etc., is fuelled by our society's prissiness and aversion to addressing tough issues head on. I think the feminist community can play the role of prodding this conversation, and urging self-awareness of aimless moral judgments. Let's be efficient in our rhetoric. Less hot air and more constructive discussions about sexuality and morality.[45]

And others are not just asking about this connection – they are making the connection. If homosexual marriage is fine, why not incest? Consider film maker Nick Cassavetes who last year released the film *Yellow* with incest as the main theme. He saw no problem with this at all, and was happy to thank homosexual "progress" for all this. He said,

> We started thinking about [incest]. We had heard a few stories where brothers and sisters were completely, absolutely in love with one another. You know what? This whole movie is about judgment, and lack of it, and doing what you want. Who gives a shit if people judge you? I'm not saying this is an absolute but in

DANGEROUS RELATIONS: The Threat of Homosexuality

> a way, if you're not having kids – who gives a damn? Love who you want. Isn't that what we say? Gay marriage – love who you want? If it's your brother or sister it's super-weird, but if you look at it, you're not hurting anybody except every single person who freaks out because you're in love with one another.[46]

There we have it: homosexual marriage, incest – they are all on a par and why should anyone make a stink about any of it? And around the world even governments and parliaments are looking into this issue. Consider the case of Switzerland.

> The upper house of the Swiss parliament has drafted a law decriminalising sex between consenting family members which must now be considered by the government. There have been only three cases of incest since 1984. Switzerland, which recently held a referendum passing a draconian law that will boot out foreigners convicted of committing the smallest of crimes, insists that children within families will continue to be protected by laws governing abuse and paedophilia. Daniel Vischer, a Green party MP, said he saw nothing wrong with two consenting adults having sex, even if they were related. "Incest is a difficult moral question, but not one that is answered by penal law," he said.
>
> Barbara Schmid Federer of The Christian People's Party of Switzerland said the proposal from the upper house was "completely repugnant. I for one could not countenance painting out such a law from the statute books." The Protestant People's Party is also opposed to decriminalising the offence which at present carries a maximum three year jail term. A spokesman for the party said: "Murder is also quite rare in Switzerland but no one suggests that we remove that as an offence from the statutes."[47]

Then there is the creepy case of twin brothers who are gay porn stars – not just with others but with themselves. An article in *Salon* offers us some of the gory details:

Over the past few months, they have become two of the most controversial performers to hit the gay porn world in a very long time. That's because they're willing to break a taboo that, even in an industry that thrives on extremes, is too extreme for many: twin incest (or, more succinctly, twincest). While the concept of twin performers is not new to the gay porn world, the Peters twins are notable both because of the extent of their popularity and the things they are willing to do with each other on camera. They French kiss; they perform oral sex on each other; they have anal sex; and most shockingly of all, they do it in a tender and romantic way. "My brother is my boyfriend, and I am his boyfriend," says one of the twins during a phone call from Prague (Elijah and Milo sound so much alike on the phone it is impossible to tell which one is speaking). "He is my lifeblood, and he is my only love."

The twins' astonishing lack of shame – and their willingness to do anything with each other on camera – has helped turn them into a gay porn phenomenon. Since they first began appearing on Czech porn studio Bel Ami's website (NSFW, like all links in this story) in 2009, the company's traffic has doubled to 1.5 million users per month, and Milo and Elijah have become the subject of breathless coverage on adult blogging sites like *Fleshbot* and *The Sword*. They've even been flown from Prague to the United States for a whirlwind tour of Florida gay nightspots.[48]

And of course we must be open to the possibility that this is all just genetic. "After all, I was born that way – I can't help it." Yep, let's just add this to the list of "sexual orientations" which must be acknowledged, affirmed and legalised. And we already have groups seeking to give a pseudo-scientific backing to all this. Consider the site, Genetic Sexual Attraction. Yes I am afraid they mean just what it sounds like they mean: "GSA is a natural response to a broken situation. Humans have been designed to bond with their kin starting at the onset of the relationship and for whatever reasons (divorce, abandonment, adoption) it did not happen. This need to bond, which has been dormant for years, finally has the opportunity at the reunion to form a fierce and profound connection."[49]

Enough said. The push for the removal of all sexual boundaries seems to be proceeding apace. Once a society declares that homosexual acts and homosexual marriage are important social goods which must be given the full force of legal and social approbation, then the door of necessity just gets pushed open that much further.

Bestiality

Sadly there are also many calling for the legalisation of bestiality, or zoophilia. Yes, there is even a "scientific" name now assigned to those who want to enjoy "equal love" with animals. And these are not just a few cranks and misfits. Sadly we have academics, educational institutions, and plenty of other respectable type groups calling for this. Indeed, simply Google the euphemistic term "zoophilia". When I last did this some 1.2 million hits came up. There are all sorts of zoophilia sites, organisations, groups, societies and advocates out there seriously promoting all this.

In fact, there is far too much material here for me to do proper justice to it, so let me just select a few representative examples. Let's begin with this headline: "Those Who Practice Bestiality Say They're Part of the Next Sexual Rights Movement."[50] The headline alone says it all: If the homosexual lobby can get their way with full recognition and legalisation, then why can't we?

The article speaks of a Cody Beck who is quite serious in seeing his "rights" recognised: "Being a 'zoophile' in modern American society, Beck says, is 'like being gay in the 1950s. You feel like you have to hide, that if you say it out loud, people will look at you like a freak.' Now Beck believes he and other members of this minority sexual orientation, who often call themselves 'zoos,' can follow the same path as the gay rights movement. Most researchers believe 2 to

8 percent of the population harbours forbidden desires toward animals, and Beck hopes this minority group can begin appealing to the open-minded for acceptance."[51]

I mentioned that universities and academics are even happy to run with this. Here is another headline to get your head around: "Yale hosts workshop teaching sensitivity to bestiality".[52] Yes, that would be Yale University. The entire article is so incredible that I am tempted to quote the whole piece. But let me offer this much:

> On Saturday afternoon, Yale hosted a "sensitivity training" in which students were asked to consider topics such as bestiality, incest, and accepting money for sex. During the workshop, entitled, "Sex: Am I Normal," students anonymously asked and answered questions about sex using their cell phones, and viewed the responses in real time in the form of bar charts. The session was hosted by "sexologist" Dr Jill McDevitt, who owns a sex store called Feminique in West Chester, Pa. Survey responses revealed that nine percent of attendees had been paid for sex, 3 percent had engaged in bestiality, and 52 percent had participated in "consensual pain" during sex, according to an article published in the *Yale Daily News* on Monday.

> Event director Giuliana Berry told *Campus Reform* in an interview on Monday that the workshop was brought to campus to teach students not to automatically judge people who may have engaged in these sorts of activities, but rather to respond with "understanding" and "compassion." "People do engage in some of these activities that we believe only for example perverts engage in," she said. "What the goal is is to increase compassion for people who may engage in activities that are not what you would personally consider normal." McDevitt referred to the range of activities discussed in the workshop as "sexual diversity." "It tries to get people to be more sensitive ... to sexual diversity," McDevitt told *Campus Reform* in an interview on Monday. "We're not all heterosexual, able-bodied folks who have standard missionary sex."[53]

There you go: we need to offer "understanding" and "compassion" to those who are into zoophilia, or incest, or whatever. And the last thing we should do is cast any moral judgment on any of this: "'It's sensitivity training,' McDevitt told *Campus Reform*. 'Don't judge other people, because we all have something we are embarrassed about'."[54]

One well respected academic has been quite cavalier about bestiality for years now. I refer to Princeton University's Ira W. DeCamp Professor of Bioethics, Peter Singer. He is rather infamous for a piece he penned back in 2001 called "Heavy Petting".[55] The online magazine *Nerve*, the site where it first appeared, seems to have pulled it, but one can still find the entire article elsewhere. He said this, in part:

> The existence of sexual contact between humans and animals, and the potency of the taboo against it, displays the ambivalence of our relationship with animals. On the one hand, especially in the Judeo-Christian tradition – less so in the East – we have always seen ourselves as distinct from animals, and imagined that a wide, unbridgeable gulf separates us from them. Humans alone are made in the image of God. Only human beings have an immortal soul. In Genesis, God gives humans dominion over the animals. In the Renaissance idea of the Great Chain of Being, humans are halfway between the beasts and the angels. We are spiritual beings as well as physical beings. For Kant, humans have an inherent dignity that makes them ends in themselves, whereas animals are mere means to our ends. Today the language of human rights – rights that we attribute to all human beings but deny to all nonhuman animals – maintains this separation.
>
> On the other hand there are many ways in which we cannot help behaving just as animals do – or mammals, anyway – and sex is one of the most obvious ones. We copulate, as they do. They have penises and vaginas, as we do, and the fact that the vagina of a calf can be sexually satisfying to a man shows how similar these organs are. The taboo on sex with animals may, as I have

already suggested, have originated as part of a broader rejection of non-reproductive sex. But the vehemence with which this prohibition continues to be held, its persistence while other non-reproductive sexual acts have become acceptable, suggests that there is another powerful force at work: our desire to differentiate ourselves, erotically and in every other way, from animals. ...

But sex with animals does not always involve cruelty. Who has not been at a social occasion disrupted by the household dog gripping the legs of a visitor and vigorously rubbing its penis against them? The host usually discourages such activities, but in private not everyone objects to being used by her or his dog in this way, and occasionally mutually satisfying activities may develop. Soyka would presumably have thought this within the range of human sexual variety.

At a conference on great apes a few years ago, I spoke to a woman who had visited Camp Leakey, a rehabilitation centre for captured orangutans in Borneo run by Birute Galdikas, sometimes referred to as "the Jane Goodall of orangutans" and the world's foremost authority on these great apes. At Camp Leakey, the orangutans are gradually acclimatised to the jungle, and as they get closer to complete independence, they are able to come and go as they please. While walking through the camp with Galdikas, my informant was suddenly seized by a large male orangutan, his intentions made obvious by his erect penis. Fighting off so powerful an animal was not an option, but Galdikas called to her companion not to be concerned, because the orangutan would not harm her, and adding, as further reassurance, that "they have a very small penis." As it happened, the orangutan lost interest before penetration took place, but the aspect of the story that struck me most forcefully was that in the eyes of someone who has lived much of her life with orangutans, to be seen by one of them as an object of sexual interest is not a cause for shock or horror. The potential violence of the orangutan's come-on may have been disturbing, but the fact that it was an orangutan making the advances was not. That may be because Galdikas understands very well that we are animals, indeed more specifically, we are great apes. This does not make sex across the species barrier normal, or natural, whatever those much-misused words may mean, but it does imply that it ceases to be an offence to our status and dignity as human beings.[56]

Such a matter-of-fact discussion of bestiality from a professor of ethics. But perhaps we should put it down to a one-off case of over-exuberance. Alas, we cannot, for as recently as June 15, 2010 we had him saying much the same on the ABC program *Q&A*. In a four-minute session, he was asked about his 2001 article. Singer again said that if it is consensual, he sees no problem with it. He said it was "harmless" and asked, "Is it wrong?" He said, "I don't see why we have a huge taboo over it". Incredibly the host Tony Jones and much of the panel and audience were laughing throughout this exchange.[57]

But I fail to see the humour in this. Indeed, the amazing thing was that he was not booed off the show. This is quite mind-boggling. A reputable prime-time debate program which allows some "intellectual" to tell us there is nothing wrong with bestiality. And most of the other panellists did not seem concerned at all.

I still cannot believe he actually says such things. He can with a straight face insist that as long as the animal is not hurt or exploited, what is wrong with it having sex with them? Is that it? As long as the animal is happy, let's go for it? And this guy is a world-renowned ethicist and philosopher. As a strident vegetarian, all that he is really doing here is telling us that it is OK to have sex with animals, as long as we don't eat them afterwards. Amazing.

But this sole concern about the welfare of the animals often comes up here. Indeed, the most bizarre part about all this is that most of the people taking a stand against bestiality seem to be doing it not because they consider it to be morally wrong, but because the animal might get hurt, or may not be consenting! Europe, where we seem to have so many cases of bestiality occurring, provides a number of such cases where concerns about animal consent and wellbeing is the main worry.

Scandinavia for example is evidently fairly comfortable about having what are known as "animal brothels". I kid you not. Consider how one report opens on this matter:

> Laws in both Denmark and Norway are fairly open when it comes to a person's legal right to engage in sexual activity with an animal. The law states that doing so is perfectly legal, so long as the animal involved does not suffer. According to the Danish newspaper 24timer, this interesting gap in the law has led to a flourishing business in which people pay in order to have sex with animals. On the internet, several Danish animal owners openly advertise their services. The newspaper contacted several such individuals and was told that many of the animals have been engaged in this kind of activity for several years and that the animals crave the sexual stimulation. The newspaper found that the cost charged by the animal owners varied from DKK 500 to 1,000 (USD$85 to $170). Since Danish laws are so similar to Norwegian laws, the animal bordello phenomenon has led many to question if such a practice could be legal in Norway as well. Torunn Knaevelsrud is the section chief for animal welfare for the Norwegian Food Safety Authority. "It is difficult to say yes or no," he replied to a question about the legality of animal bordellos in Norway.[58]

Consider also the nation of Germany. The Germans also seem to be happy with their "bestiality brothels". Let me simply present to you an entire article on this:

> Animal sex abuse is on the rise in Germany, with bestiality brothels being set up across the country, according to a state animal protection officer demanding stronger laws to protect mankind's furry and feathered friends. Madeleine Martin, the animal protection official for Hessian state government, said the law needed to be changed to make sex abuse of animals – known

as zoophilia – a crime. "It is punishable to distribute animal pornography, but the act itself is not," she told the Frankfurter Rundschau daily paper on Friday. "There are even animal brothels in Germany," she said. Sex with animals was being increasingly seen as a lifestyle choice, and thus more acceptable. "The abuse seems to be increasing rapidly, and the internet offers an additional distribution platform," she said.

She said the justice authorities had found it exceptionally difficult to convict a man from Hesse, who had offered pictures and instructions for animal sex abuse over the internet. "Zoophilia must be completely banned in the reformed animal protection law," said Martin, referring to the government's plan to rework that section of the law. Sex with animals was banned until 1969, when the animal protection law was introduced, but failed to include a specific ban on zoophilia, the *Frankfurter Rundschau* said. Martin said the current legal situation makes it too difficult for authorities to intervene – an animal has to be shown to have massive injuries before the animal protection laws prescribe action.[59]

Another news item on this begins as follows:

Bestiality brothels are spreading through Germany faster than ever thanks to a law that makes animal porn illegal but sex with animals legal, a livestock protection officer has warned. Madeleine Martin told the *Frankfurter Rundschau* that current laws were not protecting animals from predatory zoophiles who are increasingly able to turn to bestiality as a 'lifestyle choice'. She highlighted one case where a farmer in the Gross-Gerau region of southwest Germany, noticed his once friendly flock of sheep were beginning to shy away from human contact. So he rigged a CCTV camera in the rafters of his barn to discover multiple men sneaking in during the night to sexually abuse his beloved livestock. 'There are now animal brothels in Germany,' Martin told the paper, adding that people were playing down the issue by describing it as a 'lifestyle choice'. Armed with a host of similar case studies, Ms Martin is now calling for the government to categorically ban bestiality across the country.[60]

The story does not end there however. In early 2013 a report appeared about protests – not over bestiality, but the attempt to restrict it! "As Germany tightened its laws against having sex with animals, zoophile advocates gathered in central Berlin on Friday to fight for their right to choose who, or what, they love."[61] The article begins this way:

> Michael Kiok and his partner Cissy have been in a caring relationship for the past seven years, which would be unremarkable if not for the fact that Cissy is a dog. Angry that Germany wants to criminalize his unusual love affair, Kiok joined other zoophiles at Berlin's Potsdamer Platz on Friday to protest against new legislation banning bestiality. "I found her advertised in a newspaper after my old dog passed away," Kiok told *The Local*, saying the new law was unfair. "We feel like criminals. This is all because of fanatical animal rights demonstrators who think we hurt the animals." Late last year, Germany's lower house of parliament made having sex with animals a criminal offence carrying a fine of up to €25,000. The upper house, the Bundesrat, signed off on the measures on Friday, as part of a package of measures aimed at bolstering animal protection. "We are going to appeal to the highest court," said Kiok, whose hat was covered in Cissy's hair.[62]

Kiok is part of the group ZETA, or Zoophiles Engaging for Tolerance and Enlightenment, a German group "lobbying for more acceptance of human-animal relations. The leaflet the organization put together for the protest says that 'animals, which have been domesticated by humans for years, see people as pack members – the step from that to sexual partner is not large.' Kiok said he could not see how he was committing a crime, if an animal is big enough to protect itself from human sexual advances yet still submits willingly. For him it's love, but in a different package."[63]

Staying in Europe, consider also this news item: "Swedish man accused of sex with sheep". Here is how the story goes:

> A Swedish man in his fifties who was allegedly caught having sex with a sheep near Alingsås in western Sweden denies being guilty of animal cruelty. In the beginning of June last year a sheep farmer and his wife heard a curious bleating sound from one of the farm's pastures. When they went to investigate they were shocked to find a man engaged in sexual conduct with one of the ewes. "This is an unusual case. Earlier it would have been classified as bestiality but nowadays it is seen as cruelty to animals," Tomas Tell of the police told daily *Göteborgsposten* (GP).
> The witness reports are in themselves not enough to convict the man of cruelty to animals. Therefore a specialist veterinary surgeon has been called in from the Swedish Board of Agriculture (Jordbruksverket) as an expert witness. "Because there were no visible injuries the prosecutor must be able to prove that the ewe has suffered from the unpleasant event," Tell told GP.[64]

Once upon a time bestiality was seen as the utter epitome of moral depravity and sexual suicide. Now the only thing the Swedish authorities are worrying about is whether the sheep was injured or not. As long as both parties are unharmed – especially the animal – then everything is just fine. This is where contemporary Sweden has gotten to. Put these various ingredients together – super secularism, sexual anarchy, and a war against the family – and you have some very fertile ground for this sort of behaviour. Indeed, the article goes on to say this: "Sex crimes against animals have been reported to be on the rise in Sweden earlier this year with an increase in reported cases of sexual mutilation of horses and other livestock."

And have a look at this case from Spain. It seems a homosexual pride march in there was quite happy to have some bestiality advocates along for the ride. As one report states, "'I like dogs, I like apples, in my bed I sleep with whomever I want,' was one of the principal chants in the Gay Pride Parade last week in Madrid, where hundreds of thousands marched through the streets to advocate 'gay rights' and homosexualist ideology, according to local media reports."[65]

Europe is not alone in this of course. It is happening throughout the so-called civilised West. There are plenty of other recent cases of 'human-animal love' that can be mentioned here. Australia is not immune from all this. Indeed, our elites seem to find the topic well within bounds, as this headline confirms: "Donkey sex gets thumbs-up from censors". As the press at the time reported, "Gay sex is more likely to offend standards of morality and decency than men having sex with donkeys, as far as Australia's censors are concerned. A film depicting sex acts between men and donkeys was screened at a Sydney film festival last week after an exemption from classification was granted to the festival by the Classification Board. The federal government agency responsible for classifying films, the Classification Board, did not ask to view *Donkey Love* before granting permission for it to screen at the Melbourne Underground Film Festival and Sydney Underground Film Festival."[66]

And perhaps our elites take heart from real life. A few months earlier we had a case of this taking place. The incredible story goes as follows:

> Tina Marion Reichelt, 52, Garry Paul Reichelt, 51, both of Clare, and Kathleen Modystack, 58, of Ovingham, appeared in the District Court today. They have previously pleaded guilty to one count each of bestiality. The court has heard the Reichelts considered the action "taboo, not illegal". Today, Judge Geoffrey Muecke said Modystack did not have any sexual contact with the animals but was in contact with Tina Reichelt, via the internet, to arrange the activity. Lawyers for the trio claim the two dogs involved were not harmed and said investigations by the RSPCA had not led to their removal. However, Judge Muecke said there was no way to know for certain if it was a "victimless crime". "I don't quite know how one trains a dog to (perform sexual acts)

with a woman but there is other evidence before me that indicates one (of the dogs) at least seemed to know what to do," Judge Muecke said.[67]

Let's continue. Consider this recent case from Florida. It seems legal loopholes are allowing folks to share the love with their animal friends. As one news item says,

> Eric Antunes, 29, was arrested in May on charges of child pornography and bestiality. Prosecution has now dropped the bestiality charges due to a "loophole" in Florida law. One man's unique case may have uncovered a loophole in Florida law that allows for certain forms of oral sex between humans and animals. Eric Antunes, 29, was arrested in May on charges of child pornography and bestiality. After allegedly finding images of child pornography on his home computer, investigators say they searched his cell phone and discovered photos of Antunes engaged in sexual acts with his girlfriend's three-legged dog. Florida outlawed bestiality in October 2011. When Antunes was first arrested, many believed he would be among the first few people to be prosecuted under the new law.[68]

Probably the most bizarre story has to do with a guy who claims to have had a sexual relationship with a dolphin. As one recent report states:

> Malcolm Brenner, 60, wrote *Wet Goddess*, a new book about a man's nine-month sexual relationship with a dolphin – an affair that bears "a striking degree of resemblance" to his own interspecies romance. The author claims he started his relationship with a dolphin named Dolly back in 1970, when he was in his early 20s. Brenner was a sophomore at New College of Florida in Sarasota. A writer hired Brenner to take photographs for a children's book about the dolphin show at an amusement park in nearby Nokomis. He was given free access to the park and introduced to the staff. If Brenner is to be believed, the dolphin courted him. Initially, "she became more and more

aggressive," said Brenner, who lives in Punta Gorda, Fla. "She would thrust herself against me." But over time, Dolly became more gentle, he claimed. "I found that extraordinarily erotic," Brenner said. ...

Brenner insists his relationship did not harm the dolphin. "Some people find it hard to imagine that I wasn't abusing the animal," Brenner said. "They didn't see me interacting with the dolphin. They weren't there. These creatures basically have free will." Brenner points out that some researchers have argued dolphins should be considered "non-human persons," because of their intelligence. "What is repulsive about a relationship where both partners feel and express love for each other?" Brenner asked. "I know what I'm talking about here because after we made love, the dolphin put her snout on my shoulder, embraced me with her flippers and we stared into each others' eyes for about a minute. This was not some dog trying to hump my leg, okay. This was a 400-lb. wild-born female dolphin. She was an awesome creature.

"As self-aware mammals, dolphins are capable of making profound emotional attachments to other dolphins and, apparently, to selected humans as well," Brenner said. "A dolphin can die of loneliness, of a broken heart, of separation anxiety." As evidence of his claims, Brenner points to the story of former trainer turned animal rights activist Richard O'Barry, who said he watched a dolphin living in captivity commit suicide in his arms. He's not married, but Brenner said he has two ex-wives who knew about his fling with Dolly. "Neither one objected," Brenner said. His daughter from his first marriage even designed the book cover.[69]

And these demands for recognition of their lifestyle also include demands for "marriage rights" as well. These folks not only want public support and recognition of what they are doing, they want to be able to marry the objects of their "love" as well. Consider this headline: "Indiana Woman Wants to Marry Her Pet Dog – Tries to Rally Support From Gay Rights' Activists". The story begins:

"Cassandra White of Northern Indiana has petitioned her local government to allow her to marry her dog Brutus. White has sent several letters to gay rights activists to help her lead the march to stop discrimination against her and those like her who should get to 'marry whomever they want'. Ms White has made several unsuccessful attempts to get a marriage license after listing only 'Brutus' in the section asking for FULL NAME OF PARTY B on marriage certificate form."

It concludes: "Ms. White applauded President Obama for announcing that he is in support for gay marriage and quoted the president saying, 'I was so happy to hear President Obama yesterday comment on gay marriage.' Ms White is asking the state of Indiana to recognize what the president said and change their perspective on allowing her to marry Brutus. White has also received support from 'Freedom To Marry Our Pets Society' who plan to organize a protest in Washington to change definition of marriage to include pets."[70]

Or take a look at this incredible but true headline: "'Gay Rights' Icon Frank Kameny Says Bestiality OK 'as Long as the Animal Doesn't Mind'". Said Kameny, "Bestiality is not my thing ... But it seems to be a harmless foible or idiosyncrasy of some people. So, as long as the animal doesn't mind (and the animal rarely does), I don't mind, and I don't see why anyone else should. If bestiality with consenting animals provides happiness to some people, let them pursue their happiness."[71]

And of course just as the homosexual activists have claimed they are born this way and can do no other, so too the zoophilia crowd is claiming the same thing. They insist this is an innate predisposition and orientation which they have no choice over, and the loving and compassionate thing to do would be to not only officially endorse and promote their lifestyle, but allow them the right to marry as well.

In the article I cite above we find this revealing paragraph: "Among the seven zoophiles I consulted for this article, all say that theirs is an orientation and that to meet the definition, one must not harm an animal. For this reason, a man who has sex with chickens, for instance, is not a zoophile because the act is sure to hurt if not kill the chicken. Zoophiles I spoke with say they are as opposed to forcing sex upon animals as the rest of society is opposed to the rape of humans."

There you have it: if you have a kinky thing for animals, it is simply an "orientation" which obviously you have no control over whatsoever. And given that laws are being changed all over the Western world to make it illegal to "discriminate" against someone on the basis of their "sexual orientation" then nothing is to stop these folks from doing their thing, and from demanding their marriage rights as well.

"Zoophiles" are now certainly coming out of the closet. What I offer above are just a few of many examples which I could present here. The implications of all this are quite clear: once we allow marriage to be destroyed by the sexual militants, then it seems anything goes. And all the various sexual activist groups know it.

But despite all this evidence, people are still being attacked for daring to suggest that homosexual marriage will nicely pave the way for things like bestiality. Indeed, an Australian Liberal Party Senator actually lost his position as shadow parliamentary secretary for bravely making such a claim. Senator Cory Bernardi went through all sorts of grief when he took a stand back in September 2012. He even had to pull out of a conservative summit in the UK because of all the commotion.[72]

As mentioned, there are organisations out there dedicated to all this. Consider just one, and what it says on its homepage:

> We may be a small minority, scorned by the majority who may consider our movement to be immoral or perhaps even twisted. But who is truly twisted and immoral, those who yearn to live with animals as partners and love them as equal creatures, or

those who violently abuse nature, raise themselves [sic] above the rest of creation and, for their perverse comfort, destroy everything and everyone around them. We cannot heal the entire world but we can try to remedy the small portion which directly affects us. E.F.A., Equality for All, is an organization which is trying to rehabilitate the Animal Spirit.[73]

Consider this very proud headline from their website: "WORLD'S FIRST ZOOPHILE-RIGHTS / BESTIALITY-RIGHTS DEMONSTRATION / MARCH / PROTEST GOES PEACEFULLY IN BERLIN, FEBRUARY 1, 2013!!!" The article begins: "On February 1, 2013 zoophiles and non-zoophile supporters of zoophile-rights, came out of the shadows and bravely demonstrated right in the heart of Berlin, Germany! The demonstration was organized by Germany's zoophile-rights group, Zeta, and was attended by members of E.F.A. some of whom took part in a performance piece conceived by Sir Tijn Po especially for this occasion."

Thus all this is not just theory or speculation. The zoophiles are acting on their beliefs. We have already had a number of cases of people "marrying" their beloved animals. In addition to some examples I refer to above, let's consider just a few more. As but one Australian example of this, consider this odd story: "A young Toowoomba man yesterday tied the knot with his best friend – a five-year-old labrador. In perhaps a first for the Garden City, Laurel Bank Park hosted the wedding of Joseph Guiso and Honey, a labrador he adopted five years ago. Thirty of the couple's closest friends and family were in attendance for the emotional ceremony, held at dusk."

The news item continues: "Mr Guiso said as a 'religious guy', he could no longer take the guilt of living with Honey out of wedlock. 'It's not sexual,' he assured the onlookers. 'It's just pure love.' The couple is planning a short honeymoon to one of Toowoomba's parks."[74] There is no clear indication that this is meant to be some sort of joke, or April Fool's Day stunt. But even if it were, we have other examples to choose from.

To give cat lovers equal space here, consider this story of a German man who married his own cat:

> A German man has unofficially married his cat after the animal fell ill and vets told him it might not live much longer, *Bild* newspaper reports. It says Uwe Mitzscherlich, 39, paid an actress 300 euros (£260, $395) to officiate at the ceremony, as marrying an animal is illegal in Germany. Mr Mitzscherlich said he had wanted to tie the knot before his asthmatic cat Cecilia died. The cat and groom have lived together for 10 years. "Cecilia is such a trusting creature. We cuddle all the time and she has always slept in my bed," Mr Mitzscherlich, a postman from the eastern town of Possendorf, told Bild. Actress Christin-Maria Lohri, who officiated the ceremony, was quoted as saying: "At first I thought it was a joke. But for Mr Mitzscherlich it's a dream come true".[75]

And what about a woman in Ghana who has married her dog? The bride, Emily Mabou, 29 said this: "For so long I've been praying for a life with a partner who has all the qualities of my dad. My dad was kind, faithful and loyal to my mum, and he never let her down." She claims that her relationships have all been with "skirt-chasers and cheaters." The priest who performed the ceremony told people not to mock the wedding, but instead "rejoice with her, as she has found happiness at last."[76]

Bestiality, zoophilia, and marriage rights with animals then is clearly the next step in the sexual revolution. Albert Camus once said, "A man without ethics is a wild beast loosed upon the world." In this case it might be more accurate to say, "A man without ethics is a man loosed upon wild beasts."

Objectamory

I might have coined a term here, but there is nonetheless some reality behind the term. I refer to those who love inanimate objects, and even "marry" them. This small but growing movement may easily just be dismissed as so much foolishness, but of course the same could have been said about homosexuals "marrying" a few short decades ago. Back then such a concept was laughable. But today of course the laughable has become the actual, and there is most certainly a slippery slope now going on here. I have documented many, many cases of the slippery slope in action, since the push for homosexual marriage has become reality.

All sorts of radical sexual lifestyle groups are demanding their rights to marry as well. And in my book *Strained Relations* I spoke about those even marrying objects. Let me offer a few paragraphs from my book:

> Consider a recent article in the *Futurist*, produced by the World Futurist Society based in America. A cultural historian wrote an article entitled "The Transformation of Marriage". Stephen Bertman, professor emeritus of languages, literatures, and cultures at Canada's University of Windsor, argued that marriage may be "a semantic artefact of a lost world". He argued that it is not just the transience of marriage that is at issue now. "It is the very definition of the term that futurists must now address. A radical redefinition of marriage is now under way that promises to transform its meaning for all future time"...

> And finally, presumably still with the utmost seriousness, he speaks of the "theoretical possibility" of "the marriage of human beings to inanimate objects". He speaks of how many men love their cars, or how many people have formed an intimate relationship with their computer. "Why should not this bond of tactile intimacy be validated by more than an owner's manual?" he asks, seemingly in complete sincerity.[77]

Well, there have been plenty of objects that people have "married". I have documented some of them elsewhere. And consider this article which features "13 People Who Married Inanimate Objects".[78]

While many of them may well be a joke, it is no joke that some folks are taking all this quite seriously. Let me offer another example, which also may be regarded as a joke, and then look at a rather serious exploration of all this. The recent case comes from Europe:

"An Australian woman has taken her desire for the 'strong and silent'-type to a new extreme when she married a bridge. Jodi Rose married Le Pont du Diable Bridge in Céret, southern France after falling head over heels for the 'sensual' 14th century stone structure....

"The wedding between Jodi and Le Pont du Diable, which translates to The Devil's Bridge, took place in front of 14 guests and was blessed by the mayor of neighbouring town Saint-Jean-de-Fos. The pair made their vows at the groom's entrance. Rose wore a custom bridal gown and veil, and commissioned rings for both her and the bridge. 'He understands that I love other bridges – and men – ours is a love that embraces the vagaries of life, as materialised in the swirling currents of the river that flows beneath his magnificent body,' Rose wrote on her website. ...

"Their union is not legally recognised in France, but Rose claims their marriage is as strong as any other. 'This is not a decision I undertake lightly, just as our curves complement, we truly bring joy to each other, and the strength of his pylons will always carry me home.' Ms Rose, who says she is completely devoted to her new husband, have [sic] yet to explain how she determined the sex of the bridge."[79]

But leaving aside this case without further comment, consider a very lengthy interview done in a rather serious magazine, *The Atlantic*. It has to do with a guy in love with, and married to, a doll. Yep. While the whole interview is quite revealing, let me offer a few excerpts from it:

> Davecat met his future wife, Sidore Kuroneko at a goth club in 2000, so the story goes. The less romantic but perhaps more true version is that he saved up for a year and a half to buy her online. She cost about $6,000. Sidore is a RealDoll, manufactured by Abyss Creations in the shape of a human woman. She is covered in artificial skin made of silicone, so she's soft. These high-end, anatomically correct – even equipped with fake tongues – love dolls (or capital-D Dolls) are ostensibly made for sex. But 40-year-old Davecat (a nickname acquired from videogames that he now prefers to go by) and others who call themselves iDollators see their dolls as life partners, not sex toys. Davecat and Sidore (or, as he sometimes calls her, Shi-chan) obviously aren't legally married, but they do have matching wedding bands that say "Synthetik [sic] love lasts forever," and he says they're considering some sort of ceremony for their 15th anniversary. Davecat considers himself an activist for synthetic love. ...
>
> **Have you always been interested in dolls, and if so, was it always in a sexual way?**
>
> I've always been fascinated by the idea of artificial people, specifically artificial women. Before I knew Dolls existed, I'd long identified as being a technosexual, even before I knew there was a word for it. A technosexual is someone who is attracted to robots. Like any subculture, there's many shades within the term. Some technosexuals prefer their organic partners to dress as robots; others are attracted to robots who don't necessarily have a humanoid appearance, such as R2-D2. My preference is for humanoid robots that are covered in artificial flesh, so they look organic upon first glance; both Geminoid-F and the Actroid series of Gynoids by Hiroshi Ishiguro are excellent examples. Obviously, I'm sexually attracted to synthetic humans, such as Gynoids and Dolls, but the much larger part of their appeal is that they're humans, but they don't possess any of the unpleasant

qualities that organic, flesh and blood humans have. A synthetic will never lie to you, cheat on you, criticize you, or be otherwise disagreeable. It's rare enough to find organics who don't have something going on with them, and being able to make a partner of one is rarer still. ...

In your episode of *My Strange Addiction*, you talk about how you're perfectly aware she's a doll, and you're not trying to pretend she's a person. Yet you consider yourself married to Sidore, a marriage/relationship being something that is inherently two-sided. How do you reconcile those two things in your head at once?

Both Sidore and Elena have two backstories. One in which Sidore is the daughter of a Japanese father and an English mother, and was born in Japan and raised in Manchester, England. Elena's is similar; she grew up in Vladivostok, Russia. The other backstory they have is that they're Dolls. Self-aware Dolls, but Dolls nonetheless. In one backstory they have favourite foods; in the other, they don't eat, because they don't have digestive tracts... because they're Dolls. You get the idea. ...

Also, I have to ask – do you really feel fulfilled? Does it ever get lonely, is there anything that Sidore and Elena can't offer that you wish you had?

At this stage in the game, I'd have to say that I'm about 99 percent fulfilled. Every time I return home, there are two gorgeous synthetic women waiting for me, who both act as creative muses, photo models, and romantic partners. They make my flat less empty, and I never have to worry about them becoming disagreeable. Because of my status as an iDollator, I've met people across several countries and forged solid friendships. I've seen things I would never have seen were I not an iDollator. I've been interviewed for various television programs and websites, and asked to speak in front of a room full of psychology students about the benefits of synthetic partners. I've collaborated with performance artists and sociology teachers. To this day, I still get people contacting me online, saying that they saw how happy I am with Sidore, and they're saving up for a Doll of their own, to pull them out of their own loneliness. It's true that Sidore and Elena wouldn't exist without me, but without them, I'd be a much more reduced individual, so I owe them quite a lot. However, that 1 percent of unfulfillment? That's only there because neither Sidore nor Elena are Gynoids. Once that technology becomes affordable, I'll have one made in my wife's likeness, and that'll be the final piece of the puzzle. She'd be able to hug me back whenever I embrace her, we'd be able to attend films and concerts together, and do all manner of things besides. There would be genuine interaction. The foundation for the technology is already there, so I'm convinced it'll happen; it's just a matter of waiting.[80]

On and on it goes. The fact that this mainstream periodical chose to even run with the story shows that something is underfoot. Whether or not this guy is a bit of a nutter is immaterial here. Increasingly the serious, respectable parts of the mainstream media are devoting a lot of attention to all this.

And that simply helps to make my point: there is a real slippery slope going on here, and once we countenance an oxymoron like homosexual marriage then we might as well push the door wide open and allow any "love" to be formally recognised, and even become the stuff of marriage.

Conclusion

What we have here is a real clear case of the slippery slope in action. A few decades ago pro-family forces were mocked, ridiculed and treated with contempt when they said that allowing de facto unions full marriage rights would open the door to the demand for homosexual marriage rights. They were derided and scorned as hysterical, fear-mongering extremists holding repugnant views.

But everything they warned about has exactly come to pass. And of course now the very same thing is happening all over again: those who warn about a slippery slope or an open door because of homosexual marriage are mercilessly attacked and ridiculed. But as I document here, the can is fully open, the door is already ajar, and the slope is as slippery as you can get.

The simple truth is this: once you destroy the fundamental nature of marriage, then anything goes. And the four fundamental and non-negotiable components of marriage have always been:
-one from each gender;
-only two people;
-of the proper age;
-not a close blood relative.

Meet those basic conditions of marriage, and anyone can marry. But start to mess around with these fundamental components, then we no longer have marriage, but sexual anarchy. And now that the homosexual militants have kicked out the first leg of opposite gender, then the polyamorists are fully justified in kicking out the second leg of two in number.

And of course then the paedophiles can kick out the third leg of proper age, and the incest crowd can kick out the final leg of close family ties. And while we are at it, then the bestiality fans can get rid of a fifth criterion: only between human beings. Hey, why be so intolerant and discriminating? We demand our right to marry Fido.

So thanks, homosexual militants. You have done exactly what we said would happen: you have opened the Pandora's Box, and once it is opened, it is very difficult indeed to shut again. Thanks for destroying marriage, for destroying family, and for destroying society. You ought to be real proud of yourselves.

When a society starts to hit rock bottom, you can be sure that sexual anarchy is a big part of the chain of events leading up to it. When immorality skyrockets, then societies plummet. When people start going over the top with all things sexual, then it is not long before their nations start going over the cliff.

We must remind ourselves that all this has not just sprung out of nowhere. This is simply the logical and inevitable outworking of the radical sexual revolution which began in the late 60s. The push for complete and utter sexual freedom is now simply resulting in the inevitable directions we read about above. And why not, is the only thing we can really ask. If all sexual constraints have been seen as binding and restrictive, and complete sexual expression is seen as the only way to go, then why are we surprised at all this?

Sexual insanity abounds wherever we look. Each day new headlines alert us to yet more sexual perversion and sexual suicide. Yet all this is being defended and promoted by our intelligentsia and so many activist groups. How much further can we go before we as a society are likely beyond redemption? Mark Steyn nicely summarises the bitter fruit of this decades-old act of sexual suicide:

"The wreckage is impressive. The Sexual Revolution was well-named: it was a revolt not just against sexual norms but against the institutions and values they supported; it was part of an assault against any alternatives to government, civic or moral. Utopianism, writes the philosopher Roger Scruton, is 'not in the business of perfecting the world' but only of demolishing it: 'The ideal is constructed in order to destroy the actual.' Who needs families, or marriage, or morality? Who needs nations, especially nations with borders? We'll take a jackhammer to the foundations of functioning society and proclaim paradise in the ruins."[81]

Quite so. We are now witnessing before our very eyes what may be the final destruction of the West. Whether there is any turning back from this point remains to be seen. But the sexual revolutionaries have not given us the utopia they promised. They have given us instead death and destruction. They ought to be real proud of themselves.

CHAPTER 4

Deconstructing the Family

A major assault weapon of the homosexual activists is the claim heard so tediously often that the family is just a fluke of history, a recent invention, a social construct, and so on. The same with marriage: it is an ever-changing thing with no permanent or universal features. Therefore we must accept and embrace the notion that families mean whatever you want them to mean, and marriage is entirely flexible, to meet the mood of the times.

The activists think that by throwing these claims around ad infinitum, ad nauseam, enough people will fall for this and simply capitulate. Sure, that is how propaganda and indoctrination works, but it is not how history, truth and facts work. These last three items all mitigate against the claims of the militants. Thus it is worth retelling the story, this time from the vantage point of evidence, reason and the weight of history.

The family is one of the most basic and universal of human institutions. And from a biblical point of view, it is one of the most crucial. Indeed, it is the first and most important institution created by God. It precedes the state and all other divinely ordained institutions. But it is not just religion that praises marriage and family. The Spanish philosopher George Santayana once remarked that the family is "one of nature's masterpieces". Indeed, it has been enjoyed by millions of people around the world for many centuries. The family unit is a major force of social cohesion and stability, the ideal means to raise and nurture children, and the best means of dispensing social services, such as education, health and welfare. No social invention comes close to comparing with the institution of the family, and its close companion, the institution of marriage.

Because of its central importance in the divine scheme, and to much of "bourgeoisie" history, it is perhaps to be expected that it should be subject to continued attack. Indeed, the family today is undergoing a radical assault from a number of quarters. This battering is almost unprecedented in recent history. It seems that the institutions of marriage and family have come under exceptionally heavy fire, with hostile salvos coming from all sides.

Many social commentators have noted this all-out attack on the family. Consider the many books which have appeared lately – from secular and religious publishing houses alike – with titles such as, *The War Against the Family*,[1] *The Family Under Siege*,[2] *In Defence of the Family*,[3] *Farewell to the Family?*,[4] *War Over the Family*,[5] *Utopia against the Family*,[6] *Haven in a Heartless World: The Family Besieged*,[7] *The Family on Trial*,[8] *The Broken Hearth*,[9] *The War Against Parents*,[10] *The Traditional Family in Peril*,[11] *The War Over the Family*,[12] and *Taken Into Custody: The War Against Fathers, Marriage, and the Family*.[13]

This war on the family of course also involves a war on marriage, a war on parenthood, and a war on children. More representative titles include: *The Abolition of Marriage*,[14] *The Retreat from Marriage*,[15] *The Marriage Problem*,[16] *Nation of Bastards: Essays on the End of Marriage*,[17] *The Assault on Parenthood*,[18] *Can Motherhood Survive?*,[19] *Fatherless America*,[20] *Life Without Father*,[21] *Home-Alone America*,[22] and *The War Against Boys*.[23]

A few representative quotes can help to set the stage. Family expert Allan Carlson puts it this way: "The natural family – *part of the created order, imprinted on our natures, the source of bountiful joy, the fountain of new life, the bulwark of ordered liberty* – stands reviled and threatened in the early twenty-first century. Foes have mounted attacks on all aspects of the natural family, from the bond of marriage to the birth of children to the true democracy of free homes."[24]

The battle over the family can especially be found in the intellectual and political arenas. As Philip Abbott has stated, "The attack on the family in modern political thought has been sweeping and unremitting. Although the critiques vary in their intensity, dissatisfaction with the family is nearly universal in modern political thought".[25]

James Q. Wilson echoes these thoughts: "Since the Enlightenment, the dominant tendency in legal and philosophical thought has been to emancipate the individual from all forms of tutelage – the state, revealed religion, ancient custom – including the tutelage of kin. This emancipation has proceeded episodically and unevenly, but relentlessly. Liberal political theory has celebrated the individual and constrained the state, but it has been silent about the family."[26]

Professor John Witte also speaks to this transformation, one that he calls "From Sacrament to Contract". Looking specifically at marriage in relation to religion and law, he says this: "The same Enlightenment ideals of individualism, freedom, equality, and privacy, which had earlier driven reforms of traditional marriage law, are now being increasingly used to reject traditional marriage laws altogether. The early Enlightenment ideal of marriage as a permanent contractual union designed for the sake of mutual love, procreation, and protection is slowly giving way to a new reality of marriage as a terminal sexual contract designed for the gratification of the individual parties."[27]

He continues, "We seem to be living out the grim prophecy that Friedrich Nietzsche offered a century ago: that in the course of the twentieth century, 'the family will be slowly ground into a random collection of individuals,' haphazardly bound together 'in the common pursuit of selfish ends' – and in the common rejection of the structures and strictures of family, church, state, and civil society"[28]

Yet as sociologist Robert Nisbet has remarked: "It should be obvious that family, not the individual, is the real molecule of society, the key link in the social chain of being. It is inconceivable to me that either intellectual growth or social order or the roots of liberty can possibly be maintained among a people unless the kinship tie is strong and has both functional significance and symbolic authority. On no single institution has the modern political state rested with more destructive weight than on the family. From Plato's obliteration of the family in his *Republic*, through Hobbes, Rousseau, Bentham, and Marx, hostility to family has been an abiding element in the West's political clerisy."[29]

And as Nisbet remarks elsewhere, governments are often the source of greatest danger to the family: "From Burke on it has been a conservative precept and a sociological principle since Auguste Comte that the surest way of weakening the family, or any other vital group, is for the government to assume, and then monopolize, the family's historic functions."[30]

The fact that the family is under attack seems pretty clear. The reasons why this is the case are less certain and more complex however. There are many variables in the equation.[31] One can argue that the secularisation process in the Western world is a leading factor.[32] Changing economic conditions, resulting in the mass employment of women in the workforce is another factor.[33] Changing social and cultural values also have their role to play. The counter culture of the 1960s and 1970s is a case in point,[34] with the rise of feminism,[35] homosexual liberation,[36] the sexual revolution,[37] and other radical social upheavals. Changes in the legal world, especially with introduction of no-fault divorce, have also contributed.[38] The rise in mother-headed households, and the disappearance of fatherhood could also be explored.[39] And the general devaluation of marriage is also an important consideration.[40]

While other factors could be mentioned, and each could merit its own discussion, I want to focus on just one part of the equation. This has to do with the tendency amongst many of our intelligentsia (educators, social commentators, media personalities, politicians and the like) to try to attack the family from a social/historical angle. That is, by seeking to alter the facts of history, they hope to convince many that the family is simply an historical aberration. They want us to believe not only that the natural family[41] is a recent invention, but that very few people in fact live in the setting of the natural family. Thus there is a concerted effort to undermine the family both in terms of its historicity and its universality.

The historicity and universality of the natural family

The remainder of this chapter will argue that the natural family has been a constant of human history. Most cultures throughout most of human history have organised their lives around the family unit – both nuclear and extended. To make this argument is not to deny the many permutations and variations of the family unit which can be found amongst the world's cultures, both past and present. Yes families have come in different shapes and sizes. And such differentiation is to be expected. However, the "fact that family has varied from time to time and place to place does not prove that family is a recent historical invention, or that it has not existed in all societies."[42] Indeed, this chapter will demonstrate that as a general rule, with many obvious exceptions, the natural family has been the norm of human history, and that the institution of marriage has played a major role in this family structure.

Critics of the family claim that marriage and family are repressive, patriarchal, selfish, inward-looking and enslaving. Some critics go even further, alleging that the traditional family is basically dead, that few people live in traditional families any more, and that the traditional family was just some invention of the 1950s. Indeed, how often do we hear today from anti-family spokesmen that those of us who seek to promote family values are just trying to turn the clock back to the fifties? It is as if the family was born in America some time in the fifties, and died a few decades later.

This claim that the traditional family is only a recent "invention", something which is no longer relevant, has been made by many detractors of the family. Various feminists, homosexual activists and civil libertarians have repeated this claim, and repeated it so often, that now it has almost become the accepted wisdom.

Take for example a speech given during the International Year of the Family in 1994 by a professor of anthropology from Charles Sturt University, Albury campus, in New South Wales. The professor said that today's nuclear family is an "aberration" left over from the 40s and 50s. "It's not functional now, and it never has been. That is why this type of family is surrounded by so much legislation and moral discourse. It needs propping up because it's not a natural unit."[43]

She continues, "It has not arisen from biology or an imperative from human nature, but was structurally created to promote gender, sexual and racial order." Even in its prime form in the 50s, it was only a minority, she claims. "No other society that I am aware of has ever tried it ... it was basically a white middle-class Anglo-Celtic family that was part of the new postwar economic and gender order."[44]

Other examples could be produced. For example, lesbian commentator Susan Mitchell wrote an opinion piece tearing into the notion of the natural family, saying the "narrow legal definition of family as illustrated by that fragile unit known as the nuclear family has been the most destructive influence on all our human relationships. Such a notion of family is all about who is excluded, not who is included. ... [A]ny notion of family being defined by direct biological links is a nonsense. The reduction of a family to a mother, a father and two children was a result of economics and the demands of a shifting workforce".[45]

Or consider these remarks by Dr Warwick Hartin, former director of Marriage Guidance Australia: "The '50s were the golden era of the nuclear family. It wasn't the way it was before or the way it has been since. It's an historical blip, an aberration".[46]

We get more of the same from a Melbourne University academic who argues for lesbian access to assisted reproductive technologies. She speaks of "the continuation of outdated 1950s family values that are deeply homophobic and fearful of women raising children without men".[47]

Just one more. Feminist writer Fiona Stewart took me to task in a column entitled, "Beware the back-to-the-kitchen brigade." She complained about "conservative groups such as the Australian Family Association" who imagined "doomsday thoughts" concerning the changing fortunes of the family. She claimed they exist to "rail against social change, particularly where women are concerned." She clinched her argument with the now-standard throwaway line: Their concerns are "born out of nostalgia for the 1950s version of the nuclear family with the stay-at-home mother."[48]

Perhaps these critics need to become more widely read: the historical, anthropological and sociological record gives a much different picture. The traditional family unit, cemented by marriage, is not just a 1950s social construct. It has in fact been the predominant form of family life in most cultures throughout history. The evidence is all too plain for anyone without ideological blinders to see.

The family in history

Just a few examples will suffice to show that the family is clearly not a recent 'invention,' nor is it a localised institution. Late Harvard sociologist Carle Zimmerman's historical overview of the family shows that the nuclear family is the heart of society. He demonstrates that when families break down, so do societies.[49]

Boston University sociologist Peter Berger has said, "Recent research into the history of the family, both in Western Europe and in northern America, shows that the nuclear family, far from being a product of modernization processes (such as urbanization and industrialization), *antedates* these processes *by centuries*".[50]

Indeed, the family antedates the state as well. Writing two and a half millennia ago, Aristotle put it this way: "Man is by nature more inclined to live as a couple than to associate politically, since the family is something that precedes and is more necessary than the State."[51]

The family not only spans the centuries, but it extends across cultures as well. Bronislaw Malinowski was the first great anthropologist to live among primitive peoples. After years of research and painstaking observations of the daily habits of these people, he came to see that the family was a universal institution:

"Indeed, at first sight, the typical savage family, as it is found among the vast majority of native tribes ... seems hardly to differ at all from its civilized counterpart. Mother, father, and children share the camp, the home, the food, and the life.... Attached to each other, sharing life and most of its interests, exchanging counsel and help, company and cheer, and reciprocating in economic cooperation ... the individual, undivided family stands out conspicuous, a definitive social unit marked off from the rest of society by a clear line of division."[52]

Another important anthropologist, Robert Lowie, notes that communal arrangements in sexuality and child-rearing are the exception, whereas families are the universal norm: "Sexual communism as a condition taking the place of the individual family exists nowhere at the present time; and the arguments for its former existence must be rejected as unsatisfactory ... we are justified in concluding that regardless of all other social arrangements the individual family is an omnipresent social unit.... [T]he one fact stands out beyond all others that everywhere the husband, wife and immature children constitute a unit apart from the remainder of the community."[53]

Anthropologist George Murdock's exhaustive investigation into 250 human societies revealed this elementary conclusion: "The nuclear family is a universal human social grouping. Either as the sole prevailing form of the family or as the basic unit from which more complex familial forms are compounded, it exists as a distinct and strongly functional group in every known society. No exception, at least, has come to light in the 250 representative cultures surveyed for the present study. ... In no case have we found a reliable ethnographer denying either the existence or the importance of this elemental social group. ... The nuclear family is always recognizable and always has its distinctive and vital functions."[54]

More recent research by Peter Laslett of Cambridge University has confirmed Murdock's claims, that the nuclear family is universal.[55] Says Laslett, "In England and elsewhere in Northern and Western Europe the standard situation was one where each domestic group consisted of a simple family living in its own house, so that the conjugal family unit was identical with the household ... in spite of the important differences which comparison reveals ... this standard situation seems to have obtained to a remarkable extent everywhere else."[56]

Elsewhere Laslett says that "the distinguishing feature of the family in the Western tradition, in so far as it is discernible to the sociological historian over the last two or three centuries at least" has been the presence of several characteristics, the first of which is the "shape and membership of the familial group. In the West this has been confined for the most part to the parents and children themselves, what is called the nuclear family form or simple family household."[57]

Sociologist Amitai Etzioni has put it this way: "There never was a society throughout all of history ... without a family as the central unit for launching the education of children, for character formation, and as the moral agent of society."[58]

Harvard University's James Q. Wilson concurs: "In every community and for as far back in time as we can probe, the family exists and children are expected, without exception, to be raised in one. By a family I mean a lasting, socially enforced obligation between a man and a woman that authorizes sexual congress and the supervision of children. Its style and habits will vary greatly, of course, but nowhere do we find a place where children are regularly raised by a mother who has no claims on the father."[59]

And again, "The family is not only a universal practice, it is the fundamental social unit of any society."[60]

And this seems to be the constant pattern of history. As the *Times Literary Supplement* Editor, Ferdinand Mount has commented, "The family is not an historical freak. If the evidence we have put together is correctly interpreted, the family as we know it today – small, two-generation, nuclear, based on choice and affection...is neither a novelty nor the product of unique historical forces. The way most people live today is the way most people have preferred to live when they had the chance."[61]

Michael Levin, professor of philosophy at the City College of New York, puts the case even more forcefully:

> Human beings have always been reared within "traditional" families. It is true that in many cultures children are raised after

infancy by communal groups, but these groups are generally composed of mothers who know each other. Not only has there never been an open, democratic society not based on the family, there has never been any society of any sort not based on the family. In every society a child's upbringing has been the responsibility of close blood relations, with his daily care a female task and his protection a male task. Some societies have favoured polygamy, a very few polyandry; in some societies a number of married couples live together under a communal roof, while in others each of the basic units live separately. But no society has tolerated reproductive units with more than one member of both sexes, a temporary bond, or sex outside the reproductive unit.[62]

Given all these claims, one has to ask, why should there be any doubt that the traditional family is the norm? As suggested earlier, there are those who simply are pushing an agenda, and will not let the facts stand in their way. Many social scientists are hostile to marriage and family and are quite happy to ignore or skew the historical record and the social data. But not all of them are.

One anthropologist from Boston University is worth quoting at length in this regard:

> Anthropology – hometown to cultural relativists and all-night diner for disaffected intellectuals – may not be where you would most expect to find good reason to defend traditional American family values. But anthropology, in fact, guards a treasure house of examples of what happens when a society institutionalizes *other* arrangements...

> The Leftist political convictions of many of my fellow anthropologists tend to keep them silent about some of the scientific findings that have accumulated over 150 years or so of systematic ethnographic study. But these findings strongly suggest that the family is a bedrock institution and that the kinds of modifications to the family advocated by gays, feminists, and

others who speak in favour of relaxing traditional restrictions on sexual self-expression will have huge consequences.[63]

Thus in spite of the ideological musings of some intellectuals, the family unit is the preferred way of living for most people. It is also the best. No other social relationship comes close to the family unit. It is in the family that all other social relationships are learned and developed. Without the family, social cohesion would be much more difficult to achieve. As late Harvard sociologist Pitirim Sorokin has said, the family is the "first fundamental form of social relationships."[64]

Marriage the norm

Marriage is also an historical given. Commentators old and new have noted this fact. Back in 1725 Italian philosopher and social theorist Giambattista Vico wrote his monumental treatise, *The New Science*. In this wide-ranging work, Vico argued that marriage was an essential characteristic of civilisation. Having made an exhaustive study of ancient history, he declared marriage to be the "seed-plot" of society.

In an important article written by J D Unwin of Cambridge University, marriage is seen as the crucial element in the development and maintenance of healthy societies: "Marriage as a life-long association has been an attendant circumstance of all human achievement, and its adoption has preceded all manifestations of social energy. ... Indissoluble monogamy must be regarded as the mainspring of all social activity, a necessary condition of human development."[65]

Writing in 1938, Stanford University psychologist Lewis Terman opened his book on marital happiness with these words: "Marriage is one of the most nearly universal of human institutions. No other touches so intimately the life of practically every member of the earth's population".[66] And more recent studies arrive at similar findings. Dr Helen Fisher, anthropologist at the American Museum of Natural History, puts it this way: "Marriage is a cultural universal; it predominates in every society in the world."[67]

American sociologist Kingsley Davis concurs: "Although the details of getting married – who chooses mates, what are the ceremonies and exchanges, how old are the parties – vary from group to group, the principle of marriage is everywhere embodied in practice. ... No matter how bizarre or peculiar the marriage customs of a given society, they are still recognizable as *marriage* customs. In any particular society there may be individuals, couples, or even groups who reject marriage as a norm, but these, being in the minority, do not determine the norms of the whole society. Other people may fail to marry because of conditions beyond their control, but the institution of marriage is present in the society."[68]

He goes on to note that "the unique trait of what is commonly called marriage is social recognition and approval ... approval of a couple's engaging in sexual intercourse and bearing and rearing offspring."[69] And these aspects of marriage are both universal and historical. They are not unique to just a few cultures, nor are they found sporadically in history: "compared to most other aspects of human society, marriage has changed surprisingly little. As an institution, contemporary wedlock bears an indubitable likeness to marriage three centuries or three millennia ago. It still has the same essential character that it had then."[70]

Indeed, monogamy, not communal or group relationships, has been the long-standing norm. As Mount says, "Anthropologists have firmly denied that group marriage was the rule in primitive society.... Westermarck in his *History of Marriage* (1891) asserts that, on the contrary, monogamy is the rule almost everywhere; even where polygamy or any other variant of sexual, parental and social relations is found, monogamy continues to be the normal rule of life."[71]

American social commentator Karl Zinsmeister goes so far as to put it this way: "The preference for monogamy thus seems to be a kind of Iron Rule of human culture. Even in today's hyper-liberated America, the instinct retains a powerful grip on us: The data ... show that the proportion of married people having sexual relations beyond the marital boundary is only a few percent a year."[72]

A major purpose of marriage of course is the regulation of human sexuality. Cultures that do not tame this most basic and uncontrollable instinct ask for, and get, trouble. As Brandeis University anthropologist David Murray put it: "Cultures differ in many ways, but all societies that survive are built on marriage. Marriage is a society's cultural infrastructure, its bridges of social connectedness. The history of human society shows that when people stop marrying, their continuity as a culture is in jeopardy."[73]

James Q. Wilson also emphasises this point: "In virtually every society, the family is defined by marriage; that is, by a publicly announced contract that makes legitimate the sexual union of a man and a woman. Even in societies where men and women have relatively unrestricted sexual access to one another beginning at an early age, marriage is still the basis for family formation. It is desired by the partners and expected by society. Marriage, in short, is not simply a way of legitimizing sex, and so it cannot be dispensed with just because sexual activity need not be made legitimate. Marriage exists because people must take responsibilities for child care and assume economic obligations. Marriage, and thus the family that it defines, is a commitment."[74]

Writing a decade later, Wilson finds the evidence just as strong: "Marriage, broadly defined, is a universal feature of all societies and apparently has been since records first were kept."[75] Blankenhorn concurs: "Marriage as a man-woman bond is fundamentally a natural and social institution – what Claude Levi-Strauss calls 'a social institution with a biological foundation' – that exists in all or nearly all human societies."[76]

Sociologist Patricia Morgan says that "there has been no known human society built upon the mother/child unit. Indeed, for an anthropologist, a widespread failure to marry is a sign of impending disaster. All societies that have survived have been built on marriage, and children have always been raised within 'traditional' families."[77]

Finally, a further word from Zinsmeister. He argues that the historical record is quite clear on the existence and importance of the institution of marriage: "History suggests marriage is the oldest and probably most indispensable of all human institutions. It varies in name, and sometimes in detail, but as anthropologist David Gilmore says, 'all societies have marriage – there are *none* that do not.' And the reason is simple: marriage regulates sex. And sex, as everyone knows, is humanity's original impulse."[78]

Marriage is natural

Some radical feminists and other critics however want to argue that marriage is just an artificial social construction, as is the nuclear family. They seek to downplay marriage by claiming that it is socially constructed by male rulers to dominate women and keep them in their place.

However, the evidence points in the opposite direction. As family law expert Lynne Marie Kohn has stated, "Marriage was not invented, codified, or planned by human government. Rather, human government gave the stamp of approval to a design already manifested, honoured, maintained, and flourishing."[79]

Indeed, the claim that marriage is simply a flexible and changing institution, and has originated as the result of government decrees and transient laws is not borne out by the historical evidence. American professor of law William Duncan puts it this way: "marriage preexisted the state and is recognized (not created) by the state because of its intrinsic value. This is not a theological point.

Whether one understands that marriage preexisted state recognition as a matter of religious belief or whether one believes that marriage has developed from the machinations of a 'selfish gene,' one thing is clear – marriage did not come into being by statute. ... It is not, therefore, wholly malleable."[80]

Charles Reid, another American law professor, concurs: "Historically, marriage has been considered the creation of natural law. It was understood as existing prior to the state. Indeed, state and society alike were seen as the products of marriage. And marriage conferred rights and privileges, as well as obligations, on the parties, which the parties were not free to discard."[81]

Or as family researcher Jennifer Roback Morse puts it, "Marriage is an organic, pre-political institution that emerges spontaneously from society. ... Government does not create marriage any more than government creates jobs. Just as people have a natural 'propensity to truck, barter and exchange one thing for another,' in Adam Smith's famous words from the second chapter of *The Wealth of Nations*, we likewise have a natural propensity to couple, procreate, and rear children. People instinctively create marriage, both as couples and as a culture, without any support from the government whatsoever."[82]

Emory University (Atlanta) Professor of Law and Ethics, John Witte, admits that an appeal to the historical record is not in itself sufficient: "History alone, of course, is not reason enough to maintain traditional marriage laws. But history must be an essential part of any serious arguments for the maintenance of traditional marriage."[83]

Thus in his essay on the "tradition of traditional marriage" he notes how marriage and its importance can be traced back to writers in antiquity, long antedating the Christian church. He concludes with these words: "For all of its theological and philosophical diversity, therefore, the West has had a long and thick overlapping consensus that marriage is good, does good, and has goods both for the couple and for the children."[84]

Mind you, the marriage spoken of here is not same sex-marriage, as some are now pushing, but the traditional male-female form. Even the evolutionary biologists, like C. Owen Lovejoy have acknowledged that the paleo-anthropological evidence makes clear that male-female bonding in lasting pairs was the critical step in human evolution.[85] And other evolutionists acknowledge that this long-term male-female bonding is not some social construct, but is built into us by nature itself: "There is one big difference between human beings and chimpanzees and that is the institution we call marriage. In virtually all human cultures, including hunter-gatherer societies, males monopolise their mates, and vice versa. Even if he ends up with more than one wife ... each man enters a long-term relationship with each woman who bears his children. ... Long-term pair bonds are not a cultural construct of our particular society; they are a habit universal to our species."[86]

Boston University anthropologist Peter Wood argues that the ethnographic and anthropological data on this are quite clear: "The anthropological evidence is overwhelmingly on the side of those who argue that large social consequences follow from a society's decisions about which sexual practices are legitimate. The rules that govern marriage and sexuality are, directly and indirectly, the basis of family life and have enormous influence over the formation of good (or bad) character in children. Marriage channels the primary relations between the sexes and the generations, and it is the template for most other relations in society. This is true not just in the United States. It is true everywhere."[87]

Indeed, the arguments for same-sex marriage and adoption rights ignore the historic, sociological and anthropological evidence. Families always have been defined by the male/female relationship, and children have almost always been raised within that unit. Few exceptions can be found. As Bronislaw Malinowski put it, "I know of no single instance in anthropological literature of a community where illegitimate children, that is children of unmarried girls, would enjoy the same social treatment and have the same social status as legitimate ones. The universal postulate of legitimacy has a great sociological significance ... It means that in all human societies moral tradition and the law decree that the group consisting of a woman and her offspring is not a socially complete unit. The ruling of culture runs here ... it declares that the human family must consist of a male as well as a female."[88]

David Popenoe, professor of sociology at Rutgers University, and a leading expert on families, explains the significance of such pair-bonding. He speaks of this as "the fundamental biological and psychological makeup of humankind". He continues, "If the evolutionary biologists are correct, human beings are a pair-bonding species. Unlike most other species, we have an innate predisposition to mate with one member of the opposite sex (homosexuals notwithstanding) and form a pair-bond for the purpose of raising children.

"Pair-bonds are considered to be an evolutionary development of enormous importance to the human species, a major reason for our extraordinary success in the world of nature. Our predisposition to pair-bond appears to be a legacy of the fact that, in our ancestral environment of evolutionary adaptation, the mother- child bond alone was inadequate for favourable child outcomes. The most successful childrearing occurred when fathers were involved in the endeavour, bonding with the child's mother at least to the extent of providing the resources necessary for survival."[89]

The raising of children has in most cultures taken place within that male/female relationship. This was one of the discoveries made by Margaret Mead: "When we survey all known societies, we find everywhere some form of the family, some set of permanent arrangements by which males assist females in caring for children while they are young."[90] Not any old relationship will do here. As Wilson puts it, "A family is not an association of independent people; it is a human commitment designed to make possible the rearing of moral and responsible children. Governments care – or ought to care – about families for this reason, and scarcely for any other."[91]

And the raising of children involves more than just maternal involvement. Fathers play an equally important role. To quote further from David Popenoe: "Across time and cultures, fathers have always been considered by societies to be essential – and not just for their sperm. Indeed, until today, no known society ever thought of fathers as potentially unnecessary. Biological fathers are everywhere identified, if possible, and play some role in their children's upbringing. Marriage and the nuclear family – mother, father, and children – are the most universal social institutions in existence. In no society has nonmarital childbirth been the norm. To the contrary, a concern for the 'legitimacy' of children is another cultural near universal: The mother of an illegitimate child virtually everywhere has been regarded as a social deviant, if not a social outcast, and her child has been stigmatized."[92]

Malinowski puts it this way: "Through all societies there runs the rule that the father is indispensable for the full sociological status of the child [and] that the group consisting of a woman and her offspring is sociologically incomplete and illegitimate.... The most important moral and legal rule [in primitive societies] is that no child should be brought into the world without a man – and one man at that – assuming the role of sociological father, that is guardian and protector, the male link between the child and the rest of the community. ... This is by no means only a European or Christian prejudice; it is the attitude found amongst most barbarous and savage people as well. ... I think that this generalization amounts to a universal sociological law."[93]

Not only is marriage and family defined by the male/female relationship, but by a life-long commitment as well. Says Mead: "No matter how free divorce, how frequently marriages break up, in most societies there is the assumption of permanent mating, of the idea that the marriage should last as long as both live. ... No known society has ever invented a form of marriage strong enough to stick that did not contain the 'till death us do part' assumption."[94]

Marriage is important for a variety of reasons, but one main reason historically has been the need to bind fathers to the mother-child relationship. Marriage, simply put, helps to civilise young men and refocus their energies into productive and committed relationships. This is a common understanding in the findings of anthropology. As Margaret Mead once said, "The central problem of every society is to define appropriate roles for the men."[95] Or as George Gilder more crudely puts it, marriage is all about "taming the barbarians."[96]

Gilder makes the case in startling terms: "Biology, anthropology, and history all tell the same story. Every society, each generation, faces an invasion by barbarians. ... These barbarians are young men and boys, in their teens and early twenties. If the truth be known, all too many of them are entirely unsuited for civilized life. Every society must figure out ways to bring them into the disciplines and duties of citizenship."[97]

Gilder is right in this regard: men simply need extra incentives to get married and stay married. As Popenoe explains, "biology was never enough to hold a father to the mother-child bond. That's why every society has set up the institution of marriage – virtually every society – and they did it for this purpose of holding the father to the mother-child bond. They realized that the outcome for the children would be better."[98]

David Popenoe also speaks to this truth: "In recognition of the fatherhood problem, human cultures have used sanctions to bind men to their children, and of course the institution of marriage has been culture's chief vehicle. Marriage is society's way of signalling that the community approves and encourages sexual intercourse and the birth of children, and that the long-term relationship of the parents is socially important. Margaret Mead once said, with the fatherhood problem very much in mind, that there is no society in the world where men will stay married for very long unless culturally required to do so."[99]

The overwhelming importance of marriage for the wellbeing of children has to be argued for elsewhere, which I have done.[100] Suffice it to say that the wellbeing of children has always been a central component of the institution of marriage, and that has been the case throughout history and across cultures.

As David Blankenhorn puts it, "In the study of kinship, a central finding of anthropology is that in the crucial area of filiation – defined as who the child affiliates with, emotionally, morally, practically, and legally – the overwhelming majority of human societies are bilateral. Almost *all* human societies strongly seek for the child to affiliate with *both* its mother and its father."[101]

At this point some might argue that polygamy in its various forms has been a notable feature of many cultures throughout history. The short answer to this objection is both yes and no. Polygamy has certainly existed, but it appears to be the exception, not the rule. Philosopher Stephen Post puts it this way: "Historically, men have a reasonably strong record of monogamy. When polygamy has existed, it has been almost entirely the result of the sheer power of despots over men and women."[102] Or as Matt Ridley notes in his book on sex and the evolution of human nature, "even in openly polygamous societies, most men have had only one wife and virtually all women have only one husband."[103]

Levin unites these various truths in this way: "Some societies have favoured polygamy, a few polyandry; in some societies a number of married couples live together under a communal roof, while in others each of the basic units live separately. But no society has tolerated reproductive units with more than one member of both sexes, a temporary bond, or sex outside the reproductive unit."[104]

Matt Ridley likewise offers this summarising perspective: "The harems of ancient despots ... cannot have been typical of the human condition for most of its history. ... In many ways modern people probably live in social systems that are much closer to those of their hunter-gatherer ancestors. ... No hunter-gatherer society supports more than occasional polygamy; and the institution of marriage is virtually universal. People live in larger bands than they used to, but within those bands the kernel of human life is the nuclear family: a man, his wife and children. Marriage is a child-rearing institution: wherever it occurs the father takes at least some part in rearing the child even if only by provision of food. In most societies, men strive to be polygamists; but few succeed. Even in the polygamous societies of pastoralists, the great majority of marriages are monogamous ones. It is our usual monogamy, not our occasional polygamy, that sets us apart from other animals, including apes."[105]

Marriage and the nuclear or extended family, therefore, appear to be the norm throughout human history. And children are almost always raised by their biological parents. However, at this point someone may raise the issue of the kibbutz in Israel. Therefore, let me deal with it here. Very briefly, the experiment has been tried and found wanting. Many references could be cited here. Let me offer the words of sociologist Amitai Etzioni of George Washington University: "Israeli kibbutzim are rapidly dismantling their collective child care centres and returning children to live with their families – because both the families and the community established that even a limited disassociation of children from their parents at a tender age is unacceptable."[106]

Zinsmeister, in his article assessing the downside to the kibbutzim, summarises: "Today, nearly all kibbutzim have overthrown the communal childrearing practices that were once at the very heart of their efforts. Infant care has shifted back to parents. Children's houses are disappearing. Single family dwellings have sprung up, and the private family dinner has returned. Parent-child intimacy and closeness are enjoying a great revival."[107]

Moreover, not only has the kibbutz movement stopped collectivised child rearing, but recent allegations of widespread rape and child sexual abuse in the kibbutzim have sparked outrage in Israel.[108]

Conclusion

Modern legal and political documents have always – at least until recently – acknowledged the importance of marriage and family. Consider but four statements:

"Marriage is defined as the civil status, condition or relation of one man and one woman united in law for life, for the discharge to each other and the community of the duties legally incumbent upon those whose association is founded on the distinction of sex."[109]

The family has been acknowledged by the United Nations in its Covenant on Civil and Political Rights as "the natural and fundamental group unit of society entitled to protection by society and State."[110] Also, "Men and women of full age, without limitation due to race, nationality or religion, have the right to marry and found a family."[111] Marriage is defined by the Marriage Act (1961) and the Family Law Act (1975) as "the union of a man and a woman to the exclusion of all others voluntarily entered into for life".

The faulty use of historical fact by the Charles Sturt University professor I mention above is not all, however. Indeed, one is left wondering which is greater, her capacity to mislead and misinform, or her intense dislike of "traditional" families. She says: "While some privileged people can look back to a happy childhood or a fulfilling career in motherhood during the 1950s, for many others that same family structure produced and hid violence, isolation, depression, despair and the truncation of opportunity for the women so central to them."[112]

The fact is, however, for the overwhelming majority of Australians, the nuclear family is the norm, a source of great joy and warmth, not the dysfunctional mess that the professor makes it out to be. One can only speculate as to why she seems to hate the family so, but we have a clue when she goes on to discuss "alternatives to the idealised nuclear family," including "same-sex partner families". Perhaps it is this agenda – this attempt to redefine the family to include various "alternative lifestyles" – that explains her apparent disregard for historical and social fact, and her loathing of traditional family life.

But of course she is not alone in this attempt to redefine the family. It has been tried by many others. But as the brief remarks above indicate, the traditional family is not so easily disposed of. It remains an historical and social reality, which will not easily succumb to its enemies. The truth is, of course, it is not the family which is an aberration. The real aberration is the various groups who seek to denigrate and/or overthrow the family.

Yet as we noted in the introduction, the family has been under sustained attack. But as James Q. Wilson comments, "What is remarkable is how well the family has survived this process. Were the family the mere social convention that some scholars imagine, it would long since have gone the way of cottage industries, and the owner-occupied farm, the inevitable victim of the individualizing and rationalizing tendencies of modern life. But, of course, the family is not a human contrivance invented to accomplish some goal and capable of being reinvented or reformulated to achieve different goals. Family – and kinship generally – are the fundamental organizing facts of all human societies, primitive or advanced, and have been such for tens of thousands of years."[113]

The words of Simon Leys offer a fitting summary: "The family has stood as the most enduring and successful experiment in the entire cultural history of mankind. ... In the history of the civilised world, no substitute has ever been found for the family. Any society that allows it to disintegrate, or endeavours actively to destroy it (as we are now doing here) does it at its own horrific risks and costs. ... That such a matter of common sense could become now a subject for challenge and debate is a telling sign of the times. Chesterton said it well: when common sense ceases to be common, a society is in terminal decay."[114]

And to conclude, I defer to the wise words of the UK's Chief Rabbi, Jonathan Sacks: "The fact that we have deconstructed the family – morally, psychologically, economically, politically – is the single most fateful cultural development of our times."[115]

CHAPTER 5

The Importance of Both Fathers and Mothers

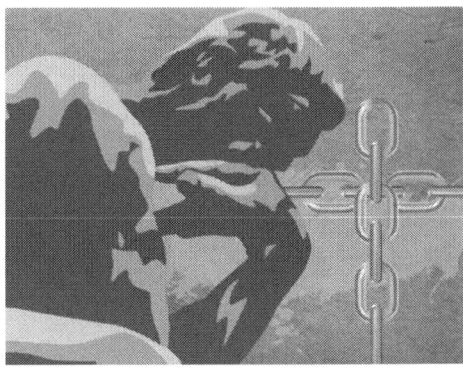

As the push for homosexual marriage continues apace, with various countries succumbing to the pressure of the homosexual activists, the issue of homosexual parenting is also gaining prominence and importance. In my book *Strained Relations* I had several chapters documenting this issue, showing how children do best when raised in a two-parent married household, and do less well when raised in any other household.

I examined some of the studies purporting to show that children do fine when raised in homosexual households, offering plenty of data as to the flawed nature of such studies, and demonstrating that the traditional heterosexual family is always in the best interests of the child.

The simple truth is, men and women are different, and both a father and a mother are necessary to ensure the best environment for raising children. One helpful recent booklet on this is well worth consulting here. The 2007 publication *21 Reasons Why Gender Matters* is a fact-filled document put together by a team of family experts, medical practitioners, and social science researchers. In just 24 pages it presents a tremendous amount of information and statistics as to why gender matters. Buttressed with 178 endnotes, the document makes it very clear that attempts at same-sex parenting are fundamentally unhelpful to children.[1]

As it says in its introduction: "This document lays out the case for the importance of male and female genders, and argues against the new androgyny and the social engineering taking place in the arena of gender. It examines some of the evidence that shows men and women are different, including the fact that our brains are different, our biochemistry is different, our hormones are different, our strength levels are different, our physical designs and sizes are different, and therefore our needs for protection and security are different. Such hardwired differences explain why men and women are so different in areas of behaviour, perceptions, the way they process information, and so on."[2]

Given these fundamental differences between men and women, the case against homosexual parenting becomes that much stronger. Two men cannot take the place of a mother and a father, and neither can two women. Children deserve both, and they have a basic right to be raised, whenever possible, by their own two biological parents – a mother and a father.

This chapter will look at some of this evidence. It will first look at how father-absence harms children. Next it will discuss the importance of mothers. Finally, it will briefly examine in a bit more detail why mothers and father are different, and why children need both.

The facts on fatherlessness

In 1861 Queen Victoria said this: "The poor fatherless baby of eight months is now the utterly broken-hearted and crushed widow of forty-two! My life as a happy one is ended! The world is gone for me! If I must live on (and I will do nothing to make me worse than I am), it is henceforth for our poor fatherless children – for my unhappy country, which has lost all in losing him – and in only doing what I know and feel he would wish."

Fatherlessness is a growing problem all over the Western world. Whether caused by divorce and broken families, or by deliberate single parenting, more and more children grow up without fathers. Indeed, 85 per cent of single parent families are fatherless families.

Writing about the situation in the United States in 1996, sociologist David Popenoe said this: "The decline of fatherhood is one of the most basic, unexpected, and extraordinary social trends of our time. Its dimensions can be captured in a single statistic: In just three decades, between 1960 and 1990, the percentage of U.S. children living apart from their biological fathers more than doubled, from 17 percent to 36 percent. By the turn of the century, nearly 50 percent of American children may be going to sleep each evening without being able to say good night to their dads."[3]

And these trends are not without negative consequences. Father absence has been shown to be a major disadvantage to the well-being of children. The following is a summary of the evidence for the importance of fathers and the need for two-parent families.

The US-based National Fatherhood Initiative starkly puts it this way: "Children who live absent their biological fathers are, on average, at least two to three times more likely to be poor, to use drugs, to experience educational, health, emotional and behavioural problems, to be victims of child abuse, and to engage in criminal behaviour than those who live with their married, biological (or adoptive) parents."[4]

One expert from Harvard medical school who has studied over 40 years of research on the question of parental absence and children's well-being said this: "What has been shown over and over again to contribute most to the emotional development of the child is a close, warm, sustained and continuous relationship with both parents."[5] Or as David Blankenhorn has stated in *Fatherless America*: "Fatherlessness is the most harmful demographic trend of this generation."[6]

Another expert puts it this way: "There exists today no greater single threat to the long-term well-being of children, our communities, or our nation, than the increasing number of children being raised without a committed, responsible, and loving father."[7]

Bryan Rodgers of the Australian National University has recently re-examined the Australian research. Says Rodgers: "Australian studies with adequate samples have shown parental divorce to be a risk factor for a wide range of social and psychological problems in adolescence and adulthood, including poor academic achievement, low self-esteem, psychological distress, delinquency and recidivism, substance use and abuse, sexual precocity, adult criminal offending, depression, and suicidal behaviour." He concludes: "There is no scientific justification for disregarding the public health significance of marital dissolution in Australia, especially with respect to mental health."[8]

A New Zealand summary of the data based on national and international research conducted over the past two decades also found major positive outcomes for children when fathers are present, and negative outcomes when fathers are absent. The report states:

"The weight of the evidence is that fathers can make unique, direct contributions to their children's well-being. These findings held true after controlling for a range of factors, including mothers' involvement, children's characteristics, children's early behavioural problems, family income, socio-economic status over time, stepfather involvement and family structure." It goes on to list the many specific ways in which fathers positively contribute to the well-being of children.[9]

And the importance of fathers is neither a recent nor a merely Western truth. The need and importance of fathers is an historical and universal given. As anthropologist Bronislaw Malinowski put it, "The most important moral and legal rule concerning the physiological side of kinship is that no child should be brought into the world without a man – and one man at that. ... I think that this generalization amounts to a universal sociological law." There may be cultural variations, yet "through all the variations there runs the rule that the father is indispensable for the full sociological status of the child as well of its mother, that the group consisting of a woman and her offspring is sociologically incomplete and illegitimate." [10]

Because there is now just so much social science data on the problems of fatherlessness, this topic can easily blow out in size. Thus to keep things brief, I have resorted to bullet points here. They are only a small part of the overall data, but provide clear witness to the importance of fathers and how children suffer when they are not raised by fathers. Here then is a sampling of the evidence:

Economic difficulties

- In America, among families with dependent children, only 8.3 per cent of married couples were living below the poverty line, compared to 47.1 percent of female-headed households.[11]
- Also in the US, a nationally representative sample found this: "In 2005, the median income for married couples was $66,067, which was $35,000 more than the median income for single mothers, $19,000 more than that of single fathers, $43,000 more than that of single women, and $24,000 more than that of single men. Married couples made up 79 percent of the highest quintile income and 17.9 percent of the lowest income quintile."[12]
- In Australia, a recent study of 500 divorcees with children five to eight years after the separation found that four in five divorced mothers were dependent on social security after their marriages dissolved.[13]

- Figures from Monash University's Centre for Population and Urban Research show that family break-up, rather than unemployment, is the main cause of the rise in poverty levels in Australia.[14]
- A joint report from AMP Life and Canberra University's National Centre for Social and Economic Modelling says that divorce leaves both partners worse off economically, but women tend to experience the biggest fall in disposable income.[15]
- A recent US study "found that by far the 'biggest factor' associated with child poverty in a county is the proportion of households headed by unwed mothers with children under 18 years of age." The researchers established that every 1 percentage-point increase in these households correlates with a 1.2 percentage-point increase in the county's child-poverty rate.[16]

Educational performance

- American children from intact families have a 21 per cent chance of dropping out of high school whereas children from broken families have a 46 per cent chance.[17]
- American school children who became father-absent early in life generally scored significantly lower on measures of IQ and achievement tests.[18]
- A recent Concordia University found clear positive effects of a father's influence on the behavioural and cognitive development of children. For example, "for both boys and girls, fathers' positive parental control predicted higher Performance IQ and fewer internalizing problems over six years later."[19]
- A study of Australian primary school children from three family types (married heterosexual couples, cohabiting heterosexual couples and homosexual couples) found that in every area of educational endeavour (language; mathematics; social studies; sport; class work, sociability and popularity; and attitudes to learning), children from married heterosexual couples performed better than the other two groups. The study concludes with these

words: "Married couples seem to offer the best environment for a child's social and educational development".[20]
- A Melbourne University study of 212 children found that fathers, even more than mothers, had a major beneficial influence on children in their first year of school. The study found that kids with regular father involvement were more cooperative and self-reliant in school than kids who did not have father involvement. The more regular involvement the father has with the child, the study's author said, the better the child does in his or her first year of school.[21]

Criminal involvement

- A British study found a direct statistical link between single parenthood and virtually every major type of crime, including mugging, violence against strangers, car theft and burglary.[22]
- Also in the UK, studies have shown that "children from broken homes are nine times more likely to commit crimes than those from stable families" and "seven out of 10 offenders come from broken homes".[23]
- One American study even arrived at this startling conclusion: the proportion of single-parent households in a community predicts its rates of violent crime and burglary, but the community's poverty level does not. Neither poverty nor race seem to account very much for the crime rate, compared to the proportion of single parent families.[24]
- In Australia, a recent book noted the connection between broken families and crime. In a discussion of rising crime rates in Western Australia, the book reported that "family breakdown in the form of divorce and separation is the main cause of the crime wave".[25]
- Maryland researchers found that bullying and aggressive behaviour are associated with family breakdown. This is especially the cause of girls' aggressiveness: "the percentage of single men and mother-alone families rival neighbourhood

violence as providing the most explanatory power" for aggressiveness among girls.[26]

Involvement with drugs and alcohol

- A UCLA study pointed out that inadequate family structure makes children more susceptible to drug use "as a coping mechanism to relieve depression and anxiety."[27]
- Another US study found that among the homes with strict fathers, only 18 per cent had children who used alcohol or drugs at all. In contrast, among mother-dominated homes, 35 per cent had children who used drugs frequently.[28]
- A National Institutes of Health study showed a clear connection between non-intact families and child drug abuse: "Our analyses indicated that children from intact families used significantly less inhalants, marijuana, and amphetamines than children from single-parent families."[29]
- A New Zealand study of nearly 1000 children observed over a period of 15 years found that children who have watched their parents separate are more likely to use illegal drugs than those whose parents stay together.[30]
- A South African study found that teens from single parent homes were more likely to consume alcohol and do so from an earlier age. Of those who ever drank, 81 per cent of the teens aged 16-18 lived with parents who were divorced compared to 51 per cent of students whose parents were married and living together.[31]

Sexual problems

- Studies from many different cultures have found that girls raised without fathers are more likely to be sexually active, and to start early sexual activity. Father-deprived girls "show precocious sexual interest, derogation of masculinity and males, and poor ability to maintain sexual and emotional adjustment with one male".[32]

- A US study found that girls who grow up without fathers were "53 percent more likely to marry as teenagers, 111 percent more likely to have children as teenagers, 164 percent more likely to have a premarital birth, and 92 percent more likely to dissolve their own marriages."[33]
- Another US study made this conclusion: "youth who spend part of their childhood/youth living in a household that does not include their biological father are more likely to smoke regularly, become sexually active, and be convicted of a crime."[34]
- New Zealand research has found that the absence of a father is a major factor in the early onset of puberty and teenage pregnancy. Dr Bruce Ellis, Psychologist in Sexual Development at the University of Canterbury in Christchurch found that one of the most important factors in determining early menarche is the father: "There seems to be something special about the role of fathers in regulating daughters' sexual development".[35]
- A British study found that girls brought up by lone parents were twice as likely to leave home by the age of 18 as the daughters of intact homes; were three times as likely to be cohabiting by the age of 20; and almost three times as likely to have a birth out of wedlock.[36]

Mental, emotional and physical well-being

- From nations as diverse as Finland and South Africa, a number of studies have reported that anywhere from 50 to 80 per cent of psychiatric patients come from broken homes.[37]
- A Canadian study of teenagers discharged from psychiatric hospitals found that only 16 per cent were living with both parents when they were admitted.[38]
- A study of nearly 14,000 Dutch adolescents between the ages of 12 to 19 found that, "In general, children from one parent and stepparent families reported lower self-esteem, more symptoms of anxiety and loneliness, more depressed mood and more suicidal thoughts than children from intact families."[39]

- A massive longitudinal study undertaken in Sweden involving over one million children found that children from single parents showed increased risks of psychiatric disease, suicide or suicide attempt, injury and addiction. The authors, writing in *The Lancet*, concluded that growing up in "a single-parent family has disadvantages to the health of the child". Bear in mind that Sweden is one of the most highly advanced welfare states on earth. Thus even with a comprehensive welfare net, children still suffer when not in two-parent families.[40]
- A US study of 2,733 adolescents found this: "The greater the fathers' involvement was, the lower the level of adolescents' behavioural problems, both in terms of aggression and antisocial behaviour and negative feelings such as anxiety, depression, and low self-esteem."[41]
- Researchers at the Children's Hospital of Los Angeles have shown that fatherlessness is directly related to childhood obesity. Statistical analysis of the data established that "family structure was significantly associated with the obesity rate." In each grade, children from single-mother families had higher rates of obesity than children from two-parent families.[42]
- A researcher from the University of South Australia's School of Health Sciences found that children from single families do less well than those from married families because they are less active and do not have as much opportunity for physical activity.[43]
- A more recent Australian study showed that obesity among girls in single-parent households continues to be a major problem. Deakin University health researchers studied nearly 9000 children aged between four and nine and found higher rates of overweight and obesity in girls from single-parent families than those in two-parent families.[44]
- A recent study from Rhode Island found that while "the incidence of mental-health problems ran particularly high (33 percent) among children living with parents reporting high levels of parental stress... the complete story involves not just parental stress. It involves family structure as well: the rate for mental-

health problems came in significantly higher among children living with a single mother (25.7 percent) or in a stepfamily (26.6 percent) than it did among children living with two biological or adoptive parents (13.3 percent; p<.001)."[45]

Social costs

- In the UK the costs of family breakdown is astronomical: "The 2012 total cost of family breakdown to the UK was £44 billion (£43.94 billion), up from £42 billion last year. The annual cost per taxpayer is now £1,470."[46]
- An even newer UK study said this: "Family breakdown is costing taxpayers almost £50 billion a year and the bill is rising fast, a new analysis said yesterday. The costs generated by family breakdown – including subsidised housing, crime, health and social care and disrupted education – have gone up by nearly a quarter in just four years."[47]
- Dr Bruce Robinson, University of Western Australia, and author of *Fathering from the Fast Lane*, has estimated the cost of fatherlessness in Australia to be over 13 billion dollars per year.[48]
- In Australia it has been estimated that marriage breakdown costs $2.5 billion annually. Each separation is estimated to cost society some $12,000.[49]
- Also, Australian industry is reported to lose production of more than $1 billion a year due to problems of family breakdown.[50]
- Homelessness is also closely linked with family breakdown. A recent Australian study conducted at two Melbourne universities has found that children whose biological parents stay together are about three times less likely to become homeless than those from other family types.[51]

Child abuse

- A 1994 study of 52,000 children found that those who are most at risk of being abused are those who are not living with both parents.[52]
- A recent American review of the studies found that "fathers, especially married fathers who live with their children, play an important role in protecting their children from abuse and neglect". It found that 15.5 children out of 1000 children were mistreated in married-parent families, whereas 27.3 children per 1000 were mistreated in single-parent families.[53]
- A Finnish study of nearly 4,000 ninth-grade girls found that "stepfather-daughter incest was about 15 times as common as father-daughter incest".[54]
- A study examining 126 profiles of perpetrators of fatal assault in United States found that non-biological parents were 17 times more likely to commit a fatal assault toward a child than biological parents.[55]
- In Australia, former Human Rights Commissioner Mr Brian Burdekin has reported a 500 to 600 per cent increase in sexual abuse of girls in families where the adult male was not the natural father.[56]
- A recent study by the Australian Institute of Health and Welfare found that "a relatively high proportion of substantiations [of child abuse] involved children living in female-headed one-parent families and in two-parent step or blended families."[57]
- And more recent Australian research continues to bear this out: "The data shows that almost half of all proven cases of child abuse and neglect involved 'broken' families in 2010-11, even though (according to the ABS Family Characteristics Survey) only 26 per cent of all Australian children lived in sole-parent and step or blended families."[58]

Conclusion

The evidence of the harmful effects of father absence could fill many pages. The above is just a small sampling of a very large body of research findings on the issue. The social science research on the need for children to be raised by both a biological mother and father, preferably cemented by marriage, is vast and growing.

Indeed, the evidence is so overwhelming that the reader is advised to look at recent summaries of the data.[59] However, several recent academic studies can be mentioned here, which demonstrate the importance of children growing up with their married biological mother and father.

One American study of 19,000 young people conducted by the Bowling Green State University (Ohio) found that teens fare best when living with two married biological parents: "Adolescents in married, two-biological-parent families generally fare better than children in any of the family types examined here, including single-mother, cohabiting stepfather, and married stepfather families. The advantage of marriage appears to exist primarily when the child is the biological offspring of both parents. Our findings are consistent with previous work, which demonstrates children in cohabiting stepparent families fare worse than children living with two married, biological parents."[60]

Another large-scale American study found that there are "overall disadvantages" in not living with both biological parents.[61] The author concludes, "My analyses have clearly demonstrated some overall disadvantages of living with neither parent. Among adolescents from all six family types, those in non-biological-parent appear to rank the lowest in academic performance, educational aspiration, and locus of control. Further, they appear to fare less well in the remaining outcome areas (self-esteem, behaviour problems, and cigarette smoking)."[62]

Cornell University Professor Urie Bronfenbrenner, a leading expert in developmental psychology, summarises the evidence in this fashion:

> Controlling for associated factors such as low income, children growing up in [single-parent] households are at greater risk for experiencing a variety of behavioural and educational problems, including extremes of hyperactivity or withdrawal; lack of attentiveness in the classroom; difficulty in deferring gratification; impaired academic achievement; school misbehaviour; absenteeism; dropping out; involvement in socially alienated peer groups; and, especially, the so-called 'teenage syndrome' of behaviours that tend to hang together – smoking, drinking, early and frequent sexual experience, a cynical attitude to work, adolescent pregnancy, and in the more extreme cases, drugs, suicide, vandalism, violence, and criminal acts.[63]

Similar comments can be made about the situation in Britain. After amassing a wealth of data on the negative effects of fatherlessness in the UK, Rebecca O'Neil makes this concluding remark:

> The weight of evidence indicates that the traditional family based upon a married father and mother is still the best environment for raising children, and it forms the soundest basis for the wider society. For many mothers, fathers and children, the 'fatherless family' has meant poverty, emotional heartache, ill health, lost opportunities, and a lack of stability. The social fabric – once considered flexible enough to incorporate all types of lifestyles – has been stretched and strained. Although a good society should tolerate people's rights to live as they wish, it must also hold adults responsible for the consequences of their actions. To do this, society must not shrink from evaluation of the results of these actions. As J.S. Mill argued, a good society must share the lessons learnt from its experience and hold up ideals to which all can aspire.[64]

The Importance of Both Fathers and Mothers

An American family expert offers these summarising words as he introduces his 370-page book on the war against fathers, marriage and family:

> No successful human society has ever been based on the mother-child dyad or on any other structure than the married, two-parent family. So much has been written in recent years about the destructive effects on both children and society of fatherlessness that it hardly needs to be laboured. Virtually every major social pathology of our time: violent crime, drug and alcohol abuse, truancy and scholastic failure, unwed pregnancy, suicide, and other psychological disorders – all these correlate more strongly to fatherlessness than to any other single factor.[65]

Wade Horn, the head of the National Fatherhood Initiative in the USA offers this concluding word: "The news is not good when large numbers of children are growing up disconnected from their fathers. It's not that every child who grows up in a fatherless household is going to have these kinds of difficulties. But it is true that there's an increased risk of these negative outcomes when kids grow up without fathers."[66]

With the rise of fatherlessness Australia and the Western world has also experienced a marked rise in social problems. And the brunt of these problems has been borne by children. We owe it to our children to do better. We urgently need to address the twin problems of fatherlessness and family breakdown. Public policy must begin to address these crucial areas. Until we tackle these problems, our children and our societies will continue to suffer. And all this will be further exacerbated by the increase in homosexual parenting.

The importance of mothers

Not only are fathers extremely important in the wellbeing and development of children, but so too are mothers. They are absolutely crucial in the development of a child's life, and without them children suffer in many ways. And the research we have on this is just as substantial and just as clear as the social science data on the importance of fathers. Indeed, even before the homosexual parenting debate arose, a huge amount of data was collected concerning the need of maternal care, especially as found in the debate over extended periods of child care. So let me approach this topic from that angle. The implications for homosexual parenting should be obvious.

The most important question in the child care debate (and the one that is least asked) is this: "How does it affect the child?" Most discussions about child care revolve around issues like employment or a woman's right to choose. Seldom is the child given any consideration. As family psychologist Steve Biddulph has said, "Childcare was not invented for children's sakes, but for adult needs".[67] Or as Anne Manne put it, "In this issue, those affected most deeply, children, are wordless, hence cannot be participants in that conversation".[68] What then are the effects long term day care can have on young children?

Numerous international studies have shown that maternal deprivation at an early age can affect the mother-child bonding process, and can impair a child's emotional, social and psychological development. For example, a major 1990 American report found that a higher proportion of children under age one in day care "show anxious-avoidance attachment to their mothers than do home-reared infants".[69] More recent research has found that maternal separation can profoundly affect the brain's biochemistry, with lifelong consequences for growth and mental ability.[70] Commenting on the new research, Mary Carlson of the Harvard Medical School said, "Our findings support clinical research showing that infants cared for in institutions grow slowly and have behavioural retardation".[71]

The work of people like John Bowlby,[72][73] Selma Fraiberg,[74] Robert Karen[75], Jay Belsky,[76][77] Ronald Haskins[78] and Mary Ainsworth[79], to name but a few, has shown a clear connection between extended periods of maternal absence, and lengthy stays in day care (as little as 10 hours a week) for infants, and later developmental problems.

Not only is the important role of instilling values, purpose and responsibility best met by a child's biological parents at an early age, but so too is the cultivation of a sense of security and well-being. Indeed, as one expert put it, the attachment relationship that a young child forges with his mother "forms the foundation stone of personality."[80] Regular and prolonged detachment from the mother can demonstrably impair a child's intellectual and emotional development, and affect a child throughout his or her life.

Studies in bonding and attachment theory have shown that a child's emotional and mental well-being are inexorably tied up with continuous, sustained, stable physical and emotional contact between mother and child. Taking the child away from its mother during this critical period can result in a number of harmful results: "Children deprived of parental care in early childhood are likely to be withdrawn, disruptive, insecure, or even intellectually stunted. New research [even suggests] that the depression resulting from separation anxiety in early childhood can cause a permanent impairment of the immune system making these children prone to physical illness through their lives."[81]

Or as family expert Steve Biddulph writes, "It now appears that mother-baby interaction, in the first year especially, is the very foundation of human emotions and intelligence. In the most essential terms, love grows the brain. The capacities for what make us most human – empathy, co-operation, intimacy, the fine timing and sensitivity that makes a human being charismatic, loving, and self-assured – are passed from mother to baby, especially if that mother is herself possessed of these qualities, and supported and cared for, so that she can bring herself to enjoy and focus on the task."[82]

A parent's absence or inaccessibility, either physical or emotional, can have a profound effect on a child's emotional health. Harvard psychiatrist Armand Nicholi has observed that individuals who suffer from severe nonorganic emotional illness have one thing in common: they all have experienced the "absence of a parent through death, divorce, a time demanding job or other reasons".[83]

One study from Norway, for example, found that children experiencing less maternal care than others had higher levels of behaviour problems.[84] Learning can also be impaired. Ernest Foyer, former U.S. commissioner of education, and president of the Carnegie Foundation for the Advancement of Teaching, has said that children in day care suffer in terms of language skills development.[85] A recent American study of 4000 children found that mothers who return to work soon after giving birth may harm their child's school performance. The study showed that children of mums who work full-time struggled academically compared with those whose mums stayed at home.[86] Other studies have even found that children who spend a lot of time in child care are more likely to join gangs as surrogate families.[87]

A recent 10-year study involving 1,300 American children found that the more hours that toddlers spend in child care, the more likely they are to turn out aggressive, disobedient and defiant. The researchers said the correlation held true regardless of whether the children came from rich or poor homes.[88]

More recent American studies bear this out. The largest long term study, which began in 1991, conducted by the National Institute of Child Health and Human Development found that the longer the hours a child stays in day care, the more aggressive, disobedient and difficult to get along with they become. And the Institute of Child Development of the University of Minnesota found similar problems of aggression and anxiety among young children who spend long hours in day care.[89]

An American study published in 2003 found that babies in childcare are more likely to show behavioural problems and low self-control later in life. The study of 17,000 children found that those who had the most problems were those who were in care for more than 30 hours a week and who were in day care before the age of one.[90]

A more recent long-term study conducted by the National Institute of Child Health and Human Development in the US found that "spending a year or more in a long-daycare centre increases the likelihood that a child will be disruptive at school". The effect can last until the child is 11 or 12. The study said that the child's gender, family's income level and quality of daycare made no difference to its conclusions.[91]

Educational psychologist Burton White, director of the Harvard Preschool Project, has written extensively on the subject of nonparental care. This is how he summarises his experience: "After more than 20 years research on how children develop well, I would not think of putting a child of my own into any substitute care program on a full-time basis, especially a centre-based program."[92]

Babies need a mother's love and attention. Child development experts indicate that children do not engage in peer play until they are about two years old.[93] The late psychoanalyst Selma Fraiberg said that babies need mother most of the time until age three, and afterwards, can tolerate a half day's absence.[94] As Connie Marshner sums up, "The quality of love and care that a child receives in the first three to five years of life is the main factor in whether that child will be able to think, to learn, to love, to care, to cooperate with other people – in short, whether that child will merely exist or will thrive and flourish and add to human society".[95]

Children need their mothers. This is especially true in the early years of life. It goes without saying that a child raised in a homosexual household will not have a mother. And having two "mothers" as in a lesbian household is not much better. As the evidence presented here thus far has made clear, children need both a mother and a father. They primarily need their own biological mother and father. This is something homosexual and lesbian couples simply cannot provide.

Children need both parents

As the above evidence demonstrates, mothers and fathers are both absolutely indispensible for children and their wellbeing. Children simply need both. Both mothers and fathers bring unique gifts and abilities into the world of parenting which are essential to the best possible outcomes for children. A father simply cannot take the place of a mother, and a mother cannot take the place of a father. Both are different from the other, and the two complement each other and make for the optimum environment in which to raise children.
By way of a summary of what has already been written, let me offer the work of another family researcher here. He has done a very nice job of compactly making the case for the two-parent family, so let me just offer his own words at this point. His words will complete this chapter, and serve as a fitting conclusion:

"Why Children Need a Male and Female Parent" by Glenn T. Stanton[96]

- The cooperative input and influence of a male parent and a female parent is essential for proper child development.
- As fathering expert Dr Kyle Pruett of the Yale Medical School explains in *Fatherneed: Why Father Care is as Essential as Mother Care for Your Child,* "fathers do not mother."[97] *Psychology Today* explains, "fatherhood turns out to be a complex and unique phenomenon with huge consequences for the emotional and intellectual growth of children."[98] A father, as a male parent, brings unique contributions to the parenting project.
- Likewise, a mother, as a female, uniquely impacts the life and development of her child, as Dr Brenda Hunter explains in her book, *The Power of Mother Love: Transforming Both Mother and Child.* Erik Erikson, a pioneer in the world of child psychology, explained that father love and mother love are qualitatively different kinds of love.[99]

Mothers and fathers parent differently
- Dr Pruett: By 8 weeks of age, infants can tell the difference between a male or female interacting with them. This diversity, in itself, provides children with a broader, richer experience of contrasting relational interactions – more so than for children who are raised by only one gender. Whether they realize it or not, children are learning at earliest age, by sheer experience, that men and women are different and have different ways of dealing with life, other adults and children.

Mothers and fathers play differently
- Fathers tend to play *with*, and mothers tend to care *for*, children....Fathers encourage competition; mothers encourage equity. One style encourages independence while the other encourages security....Both provide security and confidence in their own ways by communicating love and physical intimacy.

Fathers push limits; mothers encourage security
- Either of these parenting styles by themselves can be unhealthy. One can tend toward encouraging risk without consideration of consequences. The other tends to avoid risk, which can fail to build independence, confidence and progress. Joined together, they keep each other in balance and help children remain safe while expanding their experiences and confidence.

Mothers and fathers communicate differently
- Father's talk tends to be more brief, directive and to the point. It also makes greater use of subtle body language. Mothers tend to be more descriptive, personal and verbally encouraging.

Fathers and mothers prepare children for life differently
- Dads tend to see their child in relation to the rest of the world. Mothers tend to see the rest of the world in relation to their child.

Fathers provide a look at the world of men; mothers, the world of women
- Girls and boys who grow up with a father are more familiar and secure with the curious world of men. Girls with involved, married fathers are more likely to have healthier relationships with boys in adolescence and men in adulthood because they learn from their fathers how proper men act toward women. They also learn from mom how to live in a woman's world. This knowledge builds emotional security and safety from the exploitation of predatory males.
- Mothers help boys understand the female world and develop a sensitivity toward women. They also help boys know how to relate and communicate with women.

Fathers and mothers teach respect for the opposite sex
- FACT: A married father is substantially less likely to abuse his wife or children than men in any other category. This means that boys and girls with married fathers in the home learn, by observation, how men should treat women.
- The *American Journal of Sociology* finds that, "Societies with father-present patterns of child socialization produce men who are less inclined to exclude women from public activities than their counterparts in father-absent societies."[100]
- Girls and boys with married mothers learn from their mothers what a healthy, respectful female relationship with men looks like.

Conclusion

When we disregard the gender distinctions of parental influence as unimportant or unnecessary, we seriously diminish the proper development of children. Kids need the active participation of a mother and a father, and both parents need to be true to their gender designs. Both bring different and equally important things to the parenting project. We impoverish children and society when we deny our kids the influence of a mother and father, because we limit their development into full, healthy adults.

Barbara Dafoe Whitehead: "All this evidence gives rise to an obvious conclusion: growing up in an intact two-parent family is an important source of advantage for American children. Though far from perfect as a social institution, the intact family offers children greater security and better outcomes than its fastest growing alternatives: single-parent families and stepparent families."[101]

APPENDIX 1

Homosexuality: A Select Bibliography

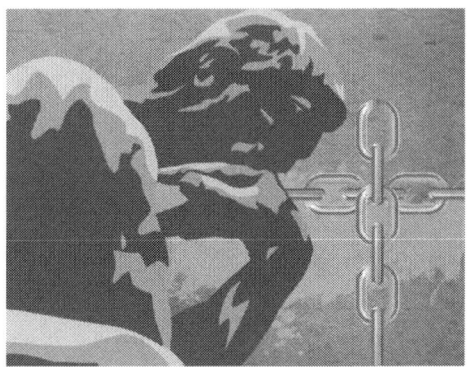

There are of course many thousands of books out on the subject of homosexuality. Those which promote and celebrate the homosexual lifestyle, homosexual marriage and the like far outnumber those which don't. The following books reflect the position as found in this book. This is not an exhaustive listing of such volumes, but nearly all of the helpful and important works in English are found here. It goes without saying that not everything contained in each of these volumes is something I necessarily fully agree with. I break up my listing into four parts: general works on homosexuality; volumes offering more of a pastoral or counselling angle; pro and con books which offer both sides of the argument; and volumes discussing HIV and AIDS.

General

Allberry, Sam, *Is God Anti-Gay?* The Good Book Company, 2013.

Anderson, Kerby, *A Biblical Point of View on Homosexuality*. Harvest House, 2008.

Ankerberg, John and John Weldon, *The Facts on Homosexuality*. Harvest House, 1994.

Bahnsen, Greg, *Homosexuality: A Biblical View*. Baker, 1978.

Brown, Michael, *Can You Be Gay and Christian? Responding With Love and Truth to Questions About Homosexuality*. Frontline, 2014.

Brown, Michael, *A Queer Thing Happened to America*. EqualTime Books, 2011.

Cameron, Paul, *The Gay Nineties: What the Empirical Evidence Reveals About Homosexuality*. Adroit Press, 1993.

Christopher, Mark, *Same-Sex Marriage: Is it Really the Same?* DayOne, 2009.

Dailey, Timothy, *Dark Obsession: The Tragedy and Threat of the Homosexual Lifestyle*. Broadman and Holman, 2003.

Davies, Bob and Lela Gilbert, *Portraits of Freedom*. InterVarsity Press, 2001.

De Young, James, *Homosexuality*. Kregal, 2000.

Dobson, James, *Marriage Under Fire: Why We Must Win this Battle*. Multnomah, 2004.

Gagnon, Robert, *The Bible and Homosexual Practice: Texts and Hermeneutics*. Abingdon, 2002.

Grant, George and Mark Horne, *Legislating Immorality: The Homosexual Movement Comes Out of the Closet*. Moody Press, 1993.

Grant, George and Mark Horne, *Unnatural Affections: The Impuritan Ethic of Homosexuality*. Legacy Communications, 1991.

Grenz, Stanley, *Welcoming But Not Affirming*. Westminster John Knox Press, 1997.

Harris, R. S., *Is There a Case for Same-Sex Marriage?* Anglican Mainstream, 2012.

Jones, Stanton and Mark Yarhouse, *Ex-Gay?: A Longitudinal Study of Religiously-Mediated Change in Sexual Orientation*. InterVarsity Press, 2007.

Jones, Stanton and Mark Yarhouse, *Homosexuality: The Use of Scientific Research in the Church's Moral Debate*. InterVarsity Press, 2000.

Keane, Christopher, ed., *What Some of You Were*. Matthias Media, 2001.

Kennedy, James and Jerry Newcombe, *What's Wrong with Same-Sex Marriage?* Crossway Books, 2004.

Keysor, Charles, ed., *What You Should Know About Homosexuality*. Zondervan, 1981.

Lansdown, Andrew, *Blatant and Proud: Homosexuals on the Offensive*. Perceptive Publications, 1984.

Lovelace, Richard, *Homosexuality: What Should Christians Do About It?* Revell, 1978, 1984.

Lutzer, Erwin, *The Truth about Same-Sex Marriage*. Moody, 2004.

McIlhenny, Chuck and Donna McIlhenny, *When the Wicked Seize a City*. Huntington House, 1993

Magnuson, Roger, *Are Gay Rights Right?* Multnomah Press, 1990.

Magnuson, Roger, *Informed Answers to Gay Rights*. Multnomah Press, 1994.

Muehlenberg, Bill, *Strained Relations: The Challenge of Homosexuality*. Melbourne: Freedom Publishing, 2011.

Nolland, Lisa, Chris Sugden and Sarah Finch, eds., *God, Gays and the Church*. Latimer Trust, 2008.

O'Leary, Dale, *One Man, One Woman: A Catholic's Guide to Defending Marriage*. Sophia Institute Press, 2007.

Paulk, John and Anne, *Love Won Out*. Tyndale House, 1999.

Reilly, Robert, *Making Gay Okay: How Rationalizing Homosexual Behaviour Is Changing Everything*. San Francisco: Ignatius Press, 2014.

Satinover, Jeffrey, *Homosexuality and the Politics of Truth*. Baker Books, 1996.

Schmidt, Thomas, *Straight & Narrow: Compassion & Clarity in the Homosexuality Debate*. InterVarsity Press, 1995.

Sears, Alan and Craig Osten, *The Homosexual Agenda*. Broadman and Holman, 2003.

Smith, F. LaGard, *Sodom's Second Coming*. Harvest House Publishers, 1993.

Sprigg, Peter, *Outrage: How Gay Activists and Liberal Judges are Trashing Democracy to Redefine Marriage*. Regnery Publishing, 2004.

Stanton, Glenn and Bill Maier, *Marriage on Trial: The Case Against Same-Sex Marriage and Parenting*. InterVarsity Press, 2004.

Staver, Mathew, *Same-Sex Marriage*. Broadman & Holman, 2004.

Stefanowicz, Dawn, *Out From Under: The Impact of Homosexual Parenting*. Annotation Press, 2007.

Stott, John, *Same-Sex Partnerships?: A Christian Perspective*. Revell, 1998.

Turek, Frank, Correct, *Not Politically Correct: How Same-Sex Marriage Hurts Everyone*. CrossExamined, 2008.

White, James and Jeffrey Niell, *The Same Sex Controversy*. Bethany House Publishers, 2002.

Whitehead, Neil and Briar, *My Genes Made Me Do It*. Huntington House Publishers, 1999.

Wold, Donald, *Out of Order*. Baker, 1998.

Wolfe, Christopher, ed., *Homosexuality and American Public Life*. Spence Publishing, 1999.

Wolfe, Christopher, ed., *Same-Sex Matters*. Spence Publishing, 2000.

Woods, Glenn and John Dietrich, *The AIDS Epidemic: Balancing Compassion and Justice*. Multnomah Press, 1990.

Yamamoto, J. Isamu, ed., *The Crisis of Homosexuality*. Victor Books, 1990.

Counselling, Testimonies

Baskett, Shirley, *The Woman Who Outran the Devil*. Monarch, 2005.

Bergner, Mario, *Setting Love in Order: Hope and Healing for the Homosexual*. Baker Books, 1995.

Boynes, Janet, *Called Out: A Former Lesbian's Discovery of Freedom*. Creation House, 2008.

Chambers, Alan, *Leaving Homosexuality: A Practical Guide for Men and Women Looking for a Way Out*. Harvest House, 2009.

Chambers, Alan, ed., *God's Grace and the Homosexual Next Door*. Harvest House, 2006.

Cohen, Richard, *Coming Out Straight : Understanding and Healing Homosexuality*. OakHill Press, 2001.

Comiskey, Andrew, *Pursuing Sexual Wholeness*. Creation House, 1989.

Comiskey, Andrew, *Strength in Weakness: Healing Sexual and Relational Brokenness*. InterVarsity Press, 2003.

Consiglio, William, *Homosexual No More*. Victor Books, 1991.

Dallas, Joe, *Desires in Conflict*. Harvest House Publishers, 1991.

Dallas, Joe, *A Strong Delusion: Confronting the 'Gay Christian' Movement*. Harvest House Publishers, 1996.

Dallas, Joe, *When Homosexuality Hits Home*. Harvest House, 2004.

Dallas, Joe and Nancy Heche, eds., *The Complete Guide To Understanding Homosexuality*. Harvest House, 2010.

Davies, Bob and Lori Rentzel, *Coming Out of Homosexuality*. InterVarsity Press, 1993.

Davies, Bob and Anita Worthen, *Someone I Love is Gay*. InterVarsity Press, 1996.

Haley, Mike, *101 Frequently Asked Questions About Homosexuality*. Harvest House, 2004.

Hallman, Janelle, *The Heart of Female Same-Sex Attraction: A Comprehensive Counselling Resource*. InterVarsity Press, 2008.

Hamilton, Julie Harren and Philip Henry, eds, *Handbook of Therapy for Unwanted Homosexual Attractions*. Xulon Press, 2009.

Harvey, John, *The Homosexual Person*. Ignatius, 1987.

Hopko, Thomas, *Christian Faith and Same-Sex Attraction: Eastern Orthodox Reflections*. Conciliar Press, 2006.

Howard, Jeanette, *Into the Promised Land: Beyond the Lesbian Struggle*. Monarch, 2005.

Howard, Jeanette, *Out of Egypt*. Monarch, 1991.

Konrad, Jeff, *You Don't Have to be Gay*. Monarch, 1993.

Moberly, Elizabeth, *Homosexuality: A New Christian Ethic*. Attic Press, 1983.

Nicolosi, Joseph, *Healing Homosexuality: Case Stories of Reparative Therapy*. Jason Aronson, 1997.

Nicolosi, Joseph, *A Parent's Guide to Preventing Homosexuality*. InterVarsity Press, 2002.

Nicolosi, Joseph, *Reparative Therapy of Male Homosexuality*. Jason Aronson, 1991, 1997.

Nicolosi, Joseph, *Shame and Attachment Loss: The Practical Work of Reparative Therapy*. InterVarsity Press, 2009.

Paulk, Anne, *Restoring Sexual Identity: Hope for Women Who Struggle With Same-Sex Attraction*. Harvest House Publishers, 2003.

Payne, Leanne, *The Broken Image*. Crossway Books, 1981.

Phelan, James, *Practical Exercises for Men in Recovery of Same-Sex Attraction (SSA)*. Morris Publishing, 2006.

Saia, Michael, *Counselling the Homosexual*. Bethany House, 1988.

Schmierer, Don, *An Ounce of Prevention*. Word, 1998.

Thompson, Chad, *Loving Homosexuals As Jesus Would: A Fresh Christian Approach*. Brazos Press, 2004.

Van Den Aardweg, Gerard, *The Battle for Normality: Self-Therapy for Homosexual Persons*. Ignatius, 1997.

Van Den Aardweg, Gerard, *Homosexuality and Hope*. Servant Books, 1985.

Whitehead, Briar, *Craving for Love: Relationship, Addiction, Homosexuality and the God Who Heals*. Monarch Publications, 1993.

Yarhouse, Mark, *Homosexuality and the Christian: A Guide for Parents, Pastors, and Friends*. Bethany House, 2010.

Yuan, Christopher and Angela Yuan, *Out of a Far Country: A Gay Son's Journey to God. A Broken Mother's Search for Hope*. WaterBrook Press, 2011.

Pro and Con

Croome, Rodney and Bill Muehlenberg, *Why vs Why: Gay Marriage*. Pantera Press, 2010.

Gagnon, Robert and Dan Via, *Homosexuality and the Bible: Two Views*. Fortress Press, 2003.

Sullivan, Andrew, ed., *Same-Sex Marriage: Pro and Con*. Vintage Books, 1997.

Wardle, Lynn, et. al., eds., *Marriage and Same-Sex Unions: A Debate*. Praeger, 2003.

Wardle, Lynn, ed., *What is the Harm? Does Legalizing Same-Sex Marriage Really Harm Individuals, Families or Society?* University Press of America, 2008.

Homosexuality and HIV/AIDS

Antonio, Gene, *The AIDS Cover-up?* Ignatius Press, 1986, 1987.

Antonio, Gene, *AIDS: Rage & Reality*. Anchor Books, 1993.

Cameron, Paul, *Exposing the AIDS Scandal*. Huntington House, 1988.

Day, Lorraine, *AIDS: What the Government Isn't Telling You*. Rockford Press, 1991.

Fumento, Michael, *The Myth of Heterosexual AIDS*. Basic Books, 1990.

Gasper, Jo Ann, ed., *What You Need To Know About AIDS*. Servant Books, 1989.

Green, Edward, *Broken Promises: How the AIDS Establishment has Betrayed the Developing World*. Left Coast Press, 2011.

McNamee, Lawrence and Brian McNamee, *AIDS: The Nation's First Politically Protected Disease*. National Medical Legal Publishing House, 1988.

Montieth, Stanley, *AIDS: The Unnecessary Epidemic*. Covenant House Books, 1991.

Redfield, Robert and Wanda Kay Franz, *AIDS & Young People*. Regnery Gateway, 1987.

Woods, Glenn and John Dietrich, *The AIDS Epidemic*. Multnomah, 1990.

APPENDIX 2

One Man's Story
by Haydn Sennitt (Australia)

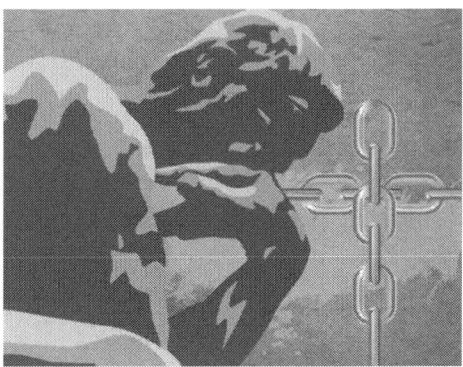

When I first became aware of having same-sex attraction I was 12-13 years old and I remember it as being a time of much uncertainty. I did not choose to have same-sex attraction; in fact, discovering it was like finding out that I had an unwanted disability. I did not know where to go or what to do with it. At that time I sought advice from a school counsellor, and I turned to him because I felt I had nowhere else to go, and I grew up on Sydney's wealthy North Shore, where problems like homosexuality are not meant to exist. That counsellor advised me to tell my parents; and against my better judgment, that's what I did. Although I was somewhat optimistic that he would be able to help me the reality was a complete dashing of that hope. For a week my parents were gripped with fear and anxiety and I was promptly told to just make the problem go away by whatever means because no son of theirs was meant to bring shame upon the family name by being gay. Worse still, I was meant to do this by telling not another soul. I was completely alone.

The reaction of my family was simply heartbreaking because what I wanted more than anything else were assurances that I was still loved even in spite of this confusing issue, that no thing I was going through would ever cost me my parents' love. I knew they were confused and hurting – I was too – but what I wanted was for my folks to at least admit their feelings and work with me to navigate through it all. Yet I felt like the family's Big Dirty Secret, an embarrassment that had to just disappear. I wrestled with the possibilities that perhaps I was 'born gay'- after all, I did not know where my homosexuality came from and at that stage I was not a Christian and had not the Holy Spirit to guide me through anything. At that stage in the 1990s, homosexuality was described as an 'alternative lifestyle' and none of the 'born gay' messages were very prevalent, but still I was undecided about what was at stake. To make matters worse some of the boys at high school started calling me names like fag and sissy, all which reinforced the idea that I was not cut out to be a man and that maybe I really was 'gay'.

Eventually I changed high schools to attend a traditional Anglican school, and against my father's advice I decided to explicitly tell everyone about my sexuality. I knew it was risky and would attract unwanted attention but I was just so desperate for someone – anyone – to know because who knew if it might net me a boyfriend or, even better, bring to me a wise man (like a father figure) who would guide me through all the confusion. It was like playing Russian roulette but it was better than suffering in silence, so I thought. So I was loud and proud and unashamed of it, and interestingly God used that very thing to introduce me to Himself. Some Christians at the school told me God could not love gay people and that the worst kind of hell was reserved for fags, yet others told me that although God did not approve of homosexuality He did love me and had a plan for me. Others said I could be gay and Christian. At this stage I was *more* confused! How could one group of Christians have three different views on God and sex? I started to believe that 'gay' was my identity, so hearing that God would love me but ask me to leave behind homosexuality made no sense. Nonetheless I read the New Testament for myself and found a God who loved the most sexually depraved people, including Jacob (Genesis 27), Kings David and Solomon, the woman at the well (John 4), the Corinthians (1 Corinthians 6:9-10), and the woman who was about to be stoned for adultery (John 8). Yet, just as Jesus said to the woman in John 8, He not only sought to love me but also to *call me out* of sin by the power of the Holy Spirit. I didn't understand it all but saw enough to believe that Jesus did love sexually broken people and had the power to heal their hearts, so I became a Christian just as I was finishing high school.

Once I became a Christian I had high hopes that God would just take away my same-sex attractions with a prayer like 2-4-6-8 Come on God! Make me straight to procreate! I prayed that a few times but God did not answer it by just removing the struggle. I then began to question his goodness. Soon after that I went to Mardi Gras to see what the gay lifestyle was like; it wasn't 'gay' at all but promiscuous and blasphemous. The homosexuality I saw was scary and I was determined to walk with Jesus, but I also wanted to see what homosexuality was like.

At that point I began to attend church and found a few that were good at teaching the Bible but and reactions to me were mixed. I told one pastor about my struggle, and he explicitly called me a 'freak'. Others just did not know what to do or did not care to know. Many lay people were sympathetic but could not offer more than commiseration. I joined a support group with Liberty Christian Ministries, which was informative, but the difficulty of finding local church fellowships that understood my struggles grew. I always felt ostracised, marginalised, and jaded. I kept changing churches because I never felt at home, and when my mother eventually died from cancer I was overwhelmed with grief and ever-increasing sexual temptations. Sad to say, I eventually yielded to them and began, in 2001, a 4-year span of acting out on my same-sex attractions. I did so in anger at God, at my earthly and spiritual fathers, and the ineptitude of the church. I was irate that at church I was surrounded by people who had such good theology, but seemed so inept at being able to speak grace to my aching and over-burdened heart. I hoped that by acting out sexually with men Christian brothers would rebuke me in love (e.g. 1 Corinthians 5:5ff; Matthew 18:15-20). But it did not happen and time and again people gave me cheap grace: they told me my sin was terrible but that all I had to do was ask God for forgiveness. They did not reinforce God's holiness (Hebrews 12:14) or the spiritual danger I was in (Hebrews 12:15-17) but told me that my sin was just as bad as theirs and that they were not in a place to judge. It was quite disheartening.

In the 'gay world' I never found a faithful partner. It was just a world of casual sex and none of my gay friends had ever found a partner long-term, even though they were lying to themselves that it really was possible. I did so many shameful things I thought God could never forgive me, but in all of it He was faithful and showed me that I did not have to sin but could refuse it (Titus 2:11-14; Psalm 40). He showed me what the real root of the problem was (Jeremiah 2:13) and that He cared about me. Being reminded of God's holy law was not what helped me to stop sleeping around: it was being reminded that He loved me so much that He sent Jesus to die for me and that He has called me to live a holy life so that I may live a much better way. He showed me that all of the hopes I had in having sex with men were about trying to find a substitute for my earthly father, but that I did not need to look for that any more because He would be that Father (Psalm 68:5). One pastor rebuked me in a way that I had been expecting and when he did it caused in me some anxiety but more than ever a desire to walk in purity.

It took a long time to be convinced of God's goodness again but God was very patient with me in seeing this. In many ways I still struggle to believe in His goodness because He is just so ... good! Over time He provided me with safe and well-grounded people at church who shared their hearts and lives with me. He also answered a big prayer by providing me also with a wife and, eventually, two beautiful daughters. These were a pleasant surprise although I was foolish enough at the time to bring same-sex attraction into my marriage. This turned out to be one of my biggest regrets: that I did not work through my deep brokenness before getting married as I should have. Yet even in this God has been good as He has shown me what *He* is like as a father and husband as I try to fulfil both of those roles. In the last four years I have been seeing a counsellor who has helped me to get to the roots of not only sexual brokenness, but other forms of brokenness that have been manifesting themselves in my life such as bitterness, anger, lack of mercy, emotional coldness, and immaturity. By doing this God showed that same-sex attractions can die away (Colossians 3:5; 1 Peter 2:11; Matthew 15:19-20) and that sin really can be resisted (Titus 2:11-14; Isaiah 61:1-7). This was all the more pertinent given that the stakes are the highest when it comes to sexual sin (1 Corinthians 6:18). My same-sex attractions are becoming both less frequent and less intense as I have taken the Holy Spirit's healing to the roots of my brokenness, as I found in reading books like *Sexual Healing* by David Kyle Foster. I am now enjoying my relationship with God more than ever before and it just keeps getting better.

APPENDIX 3

One Woman's Story: A Life Redeemed
by Anne Paulk (USA)

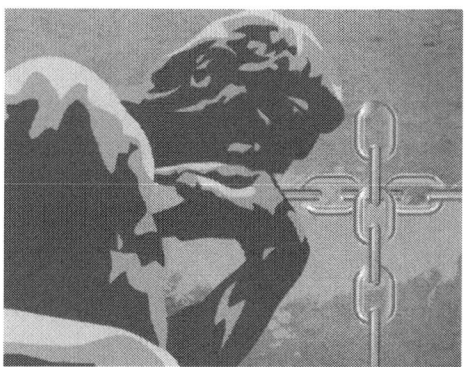

There are many reasons I think that God has a sense of humour – His sense of irony is one of them. For example, who would have guessed as I argued in my university English class in favour of abortion and the compatibility of Christianity and homosexuality, that I would become the woman I am today?

Back in those university days, I excelled at several things, one of which was logic, but that didn't necessarily mean my life bore the fruit of my logical mind. In fact, that first year at university, my life was full of confusion.

I had known for a long time that I had a strong romantic attraction for girls, though I tried to cover it up by dating men. But it was during that dramatic freshman year that I finally conceded I was definitely "gay." It was an exciting admission at the time to be able to identify myself by my long repressed struggles. The question now became: Would I be able to find that perfect woman for me?

It was at this time that I also discovered I was attracted to a particular third-year student. "Is she the one?" I wondered. As I began to imagine life with her, I also considered what would happen if we were separated by death or tragedy or betrayal. I've been known to look ahead, but this time I was looking quite far ahead. In my imagination, I saw my future self alone at some point; devastated and empty. Then one night as I looked up at the night sky and considered the permanence of the stars that have and will exist for numberless centuries, I asked myself, "Is there something more for me in life?"

That question was unexpectedly answered in my next year at university, though not by my college classes. I should preface this by saying that as a young woman embracing a "gay" identity and yearning for future relationships, I had come to see the idea of the Christian God as more of a difficulty than a help, so in my pursuit of my new "gay" identity, I had discarded my wobbly (and uninformed) concept of God as revealed in the Bible.

But then in my fall semester, as I was embracing my homosexuality I began having dreams troubled by the appearance of Jesus. I confided these dreams to my closest friends who happened to be Jewish, and they scratched their heads with me as to what the dreams could mean. Then, one day at a gay meeting on campus, the realization suddenly pierced through me – "You will not find what you are looking for here."

What?! Not find the love I was seeking in the gay community with a woman to spend the rest of my days with? But amazingly, this "other voice" was telling me the truth and in my heart I knew it. It was as if a light pierced through my soul from heaven. I left that meeting sobbing in grief at the truth that had found me.

But this new truth did not mean that I was ready to embrace Christianity. In fact, although I was ready to accept the truth, I didn't want it to be the Christian truth. I knew enough from reading the Bible that the Christian God did not approve of homosexual relationships and that if I became a Christian, my hope of a female life partner would be forever gone.

Something was going on, but I couldn't comprehend it. So my next question was, "If there really is a God, then who is the true god or gods?" In order to find the answer to this question, I put God – whoever He was – to the test. I asked that the true God would be shown to me by answering this request--to connect me with a woman who dealt with homosexuality in her own life, had short brown hair, was athletic and kind.

Within weeks I had forgotten this list, but my request was answered with the appearance of an upperclassman in my accounting class. She stood out to me as being very kind to a punk rock girl – and she had short brown hair and an athletic build. Very soon our paths inexplicably crossed again and again, and finally we ended up studying together, with me falling "head over heels" for her.

Meanwhile, she explained to me that while she understood my struggle personally, Jesus was her "husband." This made no sense to me. Oh no, Jesus again... I thought to myself.

Still, I decided to ask all my friends and dorm mates what they thought about Jesus. They all had flimsy answers so I asked at a campus Christian ministry and was soon enrolled in their "Evangelism Training" class. I pretended to fit in with these people, but God was not deceived.

One night as we prayed, God revealed Himself to me in an amazing way as a Person with great authority and tenderness, as this One moved about the room while students prayed. It also was very clear to me that where I was, there was a vacuum of space without this amazing Person.

Did God exist? Yes...but not in my life. He was revealing Himself to be the Christian God – and yet I was still faced with the tug-of-war between my own same-sex desires and this new reality.

After that experience I spoke with the campus pastor and told him about my experience, and then he shared with me how to receive Christ into my life and that, yes, it was true, homosexuality and Christianity were incompatible. As he shared with me from the Scriptures, I knew what he was saying was true. God *was* real, and He wanted a relationship with me and had provided the way through Jesus. I quickly knew I would trade everything – even the hope of having a female life partner – for this One to be in my life. For this reason, Matthew 13:44 has been such a joy to me: "The kingdom of heaven is like a treasure hidden in the field, which a man found and hid again; and from joy over it he goes and sells all he has and buys that field."

From that point on, my life became filled with rich adventure and healthy sister relationships with other women. Yes, some struggles too – daily battles with my own errant desires, but then victory as I surrendered my hurts, wounds, and wrong perceptions to God. It became a process of exchanging the lies I had believed for the truth of what God says. I also began to confront the demons of my past: molestation at the age of four and the resultant perception that men were generally dangerous and not trustworthy. I began to trust God to be my defence, which softened my heart and my mind as a woman.

Over the years, I had help from Christian ministries that walked alongside me and encouraged me. I learned that the homosexual struggle is often based on wounds of the past. In confronting and praying about these dark corners of my life, I began to experience greater freedom from the source of my heart's pain and as a result, the grip of homosexual struggle lessened. I found hope and freedom as I moved along this path, including the freedom to choose how to respond rightly to temptation. I found freedom to delight and enjoy being a woman. I found new possibilities that I had never thought would ever happen, romantic attraction to a particular man, then marriage and a family. I found that God is able to finish the work He began in me and that He's able and willing to align me with His great plans that are rich, right, and full of unadulterated beauty.

I have also found the intimate companion who will never leave or forsake me. I've faced many challenges along the way, including the betrayal of my husband and our subsequent divorce. Through it all, I've sensed God's nearness, care, and delight in me. Since embarking on this wonderful journey, I've been able to share the hope that is mine in Christ Jesus with many hurting people whom God loves.

Because of God's kindness, I'm able to thrive despite life's ups and downs and continue to share my hope with others. I can say that trading my ways for His ways was the best trade I have ever made in every sense. "I am my beloved's and my beloved is mine" (Song of Solomon 6:3).

Anne Paulk is the executive director and a board member of Restored Hope Network, mother of three boys, author, and popular speaker on homosexual issues. Anne has been interviewed on TV, radio and in magazines including Oprah Winfrey, Good Morning America, CBS Evening News, 700 Club, D. James Kennedy's Coral Ridge Ministry, Focus on the Family, and People magazine. She is the author of Restoring Sexual Identity: Hope for Women Who Struggle with Same-Sex Attraction.

REFERENCES

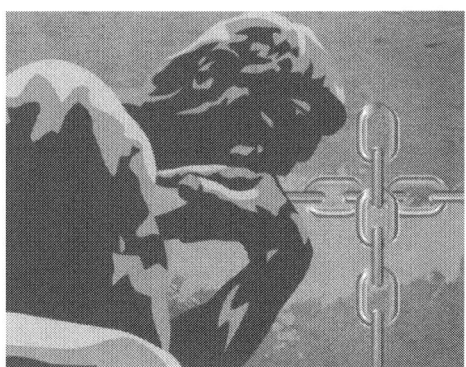

Chapter 1 The Homosexual War Against Freedom, Faith and Family

1. Mark Steyn, "Komen has its awareness raised", *The Orange County Register*, February 3, 2012.
   URL: www.ocregister.com/articles/komen-338772-planned-parenthood.html

2. *Ibid.*

3. My biggest problem here was knowing when to stop. With new cases occurring all the time, the temptation was to just keep listing them. But in that case of course this book would never have made it to the printer!

4. Thaddeus Baklinski, "Canadian court: marriage officials must marry homosexuals", *LifeSiteNews*, January 10, 2011.
   URL: www.lifesitenews.com/news/canadian-court-rejects-legislation-allowing-marriage-commissioners-to-opt-o/

5. Thaddeus Baklinski, "Quebec human rights tribunal fines man $12,000 for 'homophobic' remarks", *LifeSiteNews*, January 17, 2011.
   URL: www.lifesitenews.com/news/quebec-human-rights-tribunal-fines-man-12000-for-homophobic-remarks

6. Hilary White, "Death threats against UK columnist for opposing homosexualist agenda", *LifeSiteNews*, February 2, 2011.
   URL: www.lifesitenews.com/news/death-threats-against-uk-columnist-for-opposing-homosexualist-agenda

7. Kathleen Gilbert, "Gay couple files complaint against Christian B&B owners for refusing civil union ceremony", *LifeSiteNews*, March 7, 2011.
   URL: www.lifesitenews.com/news/gay-couple-files-complaint-against-christian-bb-owners-for-refusing-civil-u/

8. "Army: court-martial chaplains for 'religious, conscience' objection to homosexuality", *CatholicCitizens.org*, March 24, 2011.
   URL: catholiccitizens.org/press/pressview.asp?c=52791

9. Patrick B. Craine, "Mandated gay clubs in Catholic schools can't help students overcome homosexuality: Ontario gvmt", *LifeSiteNews*, April 8, 2011.

URL: www.lifesitenews.com/news/mandated-gay-clubs-in-catholic-schools-cant-help-students-overcome-homosexu

10. Rebecca Millette, "Pro-marriage U.S. Olympic official forced to resign after criticism from gay activists", *LifeSiteNews*, May 10, 2011.
URL: www.lifesitenews.com/news/pro-marriage-us-olympic-official-forced-to-resign-after-criticism-from-ga/

11. Kathleen Gilbert, "Gay columnist: let's face it, we want to indoctrinate children", *LifeSiteNews*, May 18, 2011.
URL: www.lifesitenews.com/news/gay-journalist-lets-face-it-we-want-to-indoctrinate-children

12. Patrick B. Craine, "Top sports anchor fired over beliefs on marriage", *LifesiteNews*, June 23, 2011.
URL: www.lifesitenews.com/news/top-sports-anchor-fired-over-beliefs-on-marriage-this-can-happen-to-you/

13. "Genderless preschool bans 'him' and 'her'", *Herald Sun* (Melbourne), June 27, 2011.
URL: www.heraldsun.com.au/news/the-other-side/pc-preschool-bans-words-him-and-her/story-e6frfhk6-1226082516997

14. John-Henry Westen, "Florida high school removes Christian teacher for criticizing gay 'marriage' on Facebook", *LifeSiteNews*, August 18, 2011.
URL: www.lifesitenews.com/news/florida-high-school-removes-teacher-for-criticizing-gay-marriage-on-faceboo/

15. Jessica Geen, "Tory MP calls for churches to be banned from holding marriages if they refuse gay couples", *PinkNews*, September 2, 2011.
URL: www.pinknews.co.uk/2011/09/02/tory-mp-calls-for-churches-to-be-banned-from-holding-marriages-if-they-refuse-gay-couples/

16. "Student's homosexuality comment leads to suspension", *CBS/DFW*, September 21, 2011.
URL: dfw.cbslocal.com/2011/09/21/students-homosexuality-comments-lead-to-suspension-first-amendment-discussion/

17. Christine Dhanagom, "New York clerk faces lawsuit for refusing to sign same-sex 'marriage' license", *LifeSiteNews*, September 30, 2011.
URL: www.lifesitenews.com/news/new-york-clerk-faces-lawsuit-for-refusing-to-sign-same-sex-marriage-license

18. Jeremy Kryn, "Teacher under investigation for criticizing homosexuality on Facebook page", *LifeSiteNews*, October 17, 2011.
URL: www.lifesitenews.com/news/teacher-under-investigation-for-criticizing-homosexuality-on-facebook-page

19. "MPs vote to stop civil servants refusing to carry out gay weddings" *DutchNews.nl*, November 15, 2011.
URL: www.dutchnews.nl/news/archives/2011/11/mps_vote_against_gay_marriage.php

20. Kathleen Gilbert, "Lesbian couple mulls action against Christian wedding cake baker", *LifeSiteNews*, November 16, 2011.
URL: www.lifesitenews.com/news/lesbian-couple-mulls-action-against-christian-wedding-cake-baker/

21. Christine Dhanagom, "Gay rights activist calls for boycott of Salvation Army Christmas fundraiser", *LifeSiteNews*, November 28, 2011.
URL: www.lifesitenews.com/news/gay-rights-activist-calls-for-boycott-of-salvation-army-christmas-fundraise

22. Ben Johnson, "Case of counseling student forced to undergo pro-homosexual 'sensitivity training' goes to court", *LifeSiteNews*, December 2, 2011.

URL: www.lifesitenews.com/news/case-of-counselling-student-forced-to-undergo-pro-homosexual-sensitivity-tr/

23. Peter Baklinski, "Macy's fires woman for refusing 'transgender' man access to women's fitting room", *LifeSiteNews*, December 8, 2011.
URL: www.lifesitenews.com/news/macys-fires-woman-for-refusing-transgender-man-access-to-womens-fitting-roo/

24. Patrick B. Craine, "All Ontario teachers will be forced to undergo 'diversity' training by 2013: minister", *LifeSiteNews*, December 22, 2011.
URL: www.lifesitenews.com/news/all-ontario-teachers-will-be-forced-to-undergo-diversity-training-by-2013-m/

25. Neil Harman, *"Australian Open braced for anti-Margaret Court protest"*, *The Australian*, January 11, 2012.
URL: www.theaustralian.com.au/sport/tennis/australian-open-braced-for-anti-margaret-court-protest/story-fnbe6xeb-1226241552090

26. Ben Johnson, "Judge rules Christian facility cannot ban same-sex civil union ceremony on its own premises", *LifeSiteNews*, January 13, 2012.
URL: www.lifesitenews.com/news/judge-rules-christian-facility-cannot-ban-same-sex-civil-union-ceremony-on/

27. Cnaan Liphshiz, "Amsterdam chief rabbi suspended for gay stance", *The Jerusalem Post*, January 18, 2012.
URL: www.jpost.com/JewishWorld/JewishNews/Article.aspx?id=254108

28. Todd Starnes, "Attorney says school threatened, punished boy who opposed gay adoption", *Fox News*, January 24, 2012.
URL: radio.foxnews.com/toddstarnes/top-stories/atty-says-school-threatened-punished-boy-who-opposed-gay-adoption.html

29. Amy Edwards, "Gay activists attack church over same-sex marriage message", *Newcastle Herald*, February 15, 2012.
URL: www.theherald.com.au/news/local/news/general/vandals-attack-church-over-samesex-marriage-message/2454817.aspx

30. "All schools must teach about homosexuality, cabinet decides", *DutchNews*, February 17, 2012.
URL: www.dutchnews.nl/news/archives/mobile/all_schools_must_teach_about_h.php

31. Hilary White, "Criticize homosexuality in Sweden and go to jail: No problem for European rights court", *LifesiteNews*, February 17, 2012.
URL: www.lifesitenews.com/news/eu-family-roundup-criticize-homosexuality-in-sweden-and-go-to-jail-no-probl/

32. Matt Wordsworth, et. al., "Qld Labor candidate expelled after homophobic rant", *ABC News*, February 21, 2012.
URL: www.abc.net.au/news/2012-02-20/queensland-labor-candidate-peter-watson-quits/3841192

33. Matthew Cullinan Hoffman, "Brazilian government demands apology from televangelist for 'homophobia'", *LifeSiteNews*, February 21, 2012.
URL: www.lifesitenews.com/news/brazilian-government-demands-apology-from-televangelist-for-homophobia/

34. Ben Johnson, "14-year-old homeschooled girl receives death threats for defending marriage", *LifeSiteNews*, February 22, 2012.
URL: www.lifesitenews.com/news/14-year-old-homeschooled-girl-receives-death-threats-for-defending-marriage/

35. Patrick B. Craine, "Alberta readies to impose 'diversity' education on homeschoolers", *LifeSiteNews*, February 22, 2012.
URL: www.lifesitenews.com/news/alberta-readies-to-impose-diversity-education-on-homeschoolers/

36. "Preacher's remarks spark USQ ban", *The Chronicle*, February 23, 2012.
   URL: www.thechronicle.com.au/story/2012/02/23/preachers-anti-gay-remarks-spark-usq-ban/
37. Hilary White, "Stop Catholic schools from distributing 'homophobic' literature: leader of UK's largest union" *LifeSiteNews*, February 27, 2012.
   URL: www.lifesitenews.com/news/stop-catholic-schools-from-distributing-homophobic-literature-leader-of-uks/
38. Bob Kellogg, "Christian vendor blocked from campus", *OneNewsNow*, March 5, 2012.
   URL: www.onenewsnow.com/education/2012/03/05/christian-vendor-blocked-from-campus#.UmZBAnbtMUM =1549400
39. Thaddeus Baklinski, "'Truth about homosexuality' pamphleteer arrested, threatened with committal to psychiatric ward", *LifeSiteNews*, March 8, 2012.
   URL: www.lifesitenews.com/news/truth-about-homosexuality-pamphleteer-arrested-threatened-with-committal-to/
40. Bob Unruh, "Christians who signed petitions investigated", *WND*, March 10, 2012.
   URL: www.wnd.com/2012/03/christians-who-signed-petitions-investigated/
41. Amy Remeikis, "ABC presenter stood down for voicing Katter ad", *Brisbane Times*, March 12, 2012.
   URL: www.brisbanetimes.com.au/queensland/abc-presenter-stood-down-for-voicing-katter-ad-20120313-1uxji.html
42. Julio Severo, "Christian minister accused of 'crime against humanity' for homosexuality stance", *LifeSiteNews*, March 15, 2012.
   URL: www.lifesitenews.com/blog/christian-minister-accused-of-crime-against-humanity-for-homosexuality-stan/
43. Patrick B. Craine, "Lesbian with kids in Catholic school demands removal of catechism quote on homosexuality", *LifeSiteNews*, March 16, 2012.
   URL: www.lifesitenews.com/news/lesbian-with-kids-in-catholic-school-demands-removal-of-catechism-quote-on/
44. Matthew Cullinan Hoffman, "Liberal outrage in Spain: Homosexual groups seek prosecution of bishop over sermon on homosexuality", *LifeSiteNews*, April 18, 2012.
   URL: www.lifesitenews.com/news/liberal-outrage-in-spain-homosexual-groups-seek-prosecution-of-bishop-over/
45. Ben Johnson, "Kansas law would force churches to host same-sex 'weddings,' receptions", *LifeSiteNews*, April 24, 2012.
   URL: www.lifesitenews.com/news/kansas-law-would-force-churches-to-host-same-sex-weddings-receptions/
46. Stephen Beaven, "'Angry Queers' damage Driscoll's Portland church", *Washington Post*, April 25, 2012.
   URL: www.washingtonpost.com/national/on-faith/angry-queers-damage-driscolls-portland-church/2012/04/25/gIQA0zESbT_story.html
47. "Proposed Kansas law would force churches to host drag queen parties", *Liberty Counsel*, May 1, 2012.
   URL: www.lc.org/index.cfm?PID=14100&PRID=1186
48. Thaddeus Baklinski, "Nebraska football coach: I'd rather be fired than retract homosexuality remarks", *LifeSiteNews*, May 3, 2012.
   URL: www.lifesitenews.com/news/nebraska-football-coach-id-rather-be-fired-than-retract-homosexuality-remar/
49. "UK Catholic schools warned of breaking law in opposing gay marriage", *Newsmax*, May 9, 2012.
   URL: www.newsmax.com/Newsfront/wales-catholic-school-gay/2012/05/09/id/438581

References

50 Pete Winn, "California considers legislation making it a crime to counsel children not to be homosexual", *CNS News*, May 9, 2012.
URL: cnsnews.com/news/article/california-considers-legislation-making-it-crime-counsel-children-not-be-homosexual

51 "Victorian psychiatrist questioned over his stance on gay marriage", *AAP*, May 13, 2012.
URL: www.news.com.au/breaking-news/national/victorian-psychiatrist-opposes-gay-marriage/story-e6frfku9-1226354167424#ixzz22Cno63cE

52 "Christian marriage conference in UK banned for opposition to gay marriage", *Christian Post*, May 14, 2012.
URL: www.christianpost.com/news/christian-marriage-conference-in-uk-banned-for-opposition-to-gay-marriage-74872/

53 "Doctor quits equal rights board after same-sex row", *ABC News* (Australia), May 15, 2012.
URL: www.abc.net.au/news/2012-05-15/doctor-quits-equal-rights-board-after-same-sex-row/4011928

54 "City in Kansas votes to outlaw discrimination against gays amid push to exempt churches", *Fox News*, May 15, 2012.
URL: www.foxnews.com/politics/2012/05/15/kansas-town-approves-amended-anti-discrimination-ordinance/#ixzz22BYCjxmn

55 Thaddeus Baklinski, "Boxing superstar Manny Pacquio banned from shopping mall over gay 'marriage' remarks", *LifeSiteNews*, May 17, 2012.
URL: www.lifesitenews.com/news/boxing-superstar-manny-pacquio-banned-from-shopping-mall-over-gay-marriage/

56 Jeanette Rundquist, "NJ teacher accused of anti-gay Facebook posts may retire to avoid charges", *NJ.com*, May 17, 2012.
URL: www.nj.com/news/index.ssf/2012/05/nj_teacher_charged_with_postin.html

57 Hilary White, "UK Christian blogger under investigation by gov't ad authority for running pro-marriage ad", *LifeSiteNews*, May 18, 2012.
URL: www.lifesitenews.com/news/uk-christian-blogger-under-investigation-by-govt-ad-authority-for-running-p/

58 Sophie Borland, "NHS removes word 'Dad' from pregnancy handbook in case it offends same sex couples", *Daily Mail* (UK), May 27, 2012.
URL: www.dailymail.co.uk/news/article-2150672/NHS-remove-word-Dad-pregnancy-handbook-case-offends-sex-couples.html

59 "'Dad' deleted from NHS baby guide – for sake of gay couples", *The Christian Institute* (UK), May 30, 2012.
URL: www.christian.org.uk/news/dad-deleted-from-nhs-baby-guide-for-sake-of-gay-couples/

60 Bob Unruh, "Court: Christians can be ordered to violate beliefs", *WND*, June 5, 2012.
URL: www.wnd.com/2012/06/refuse-to-photograph-lesbians-get-fined-7000/

61 Ben Johnson, "Denmark forces churches to perform same-sex 'marriages'", *LifeSiteNews*, June 7, 2012.
URL: www.lifesitenews.com/news/denmark-forces-churches-to-perform-same-sex-marriages

62 Jason Groves and Steve Doughty, "Cameron CANNOT protect Church against gay marriage laws (says his own Justice minister)", *Daily Mail* (UK), June 13, 2012.
URL: www.dailymail.co.uk/news/article-2158442/Cameron-CANNOT-protect-Church-gay-marriage-laws-says-Justice-minister.html#ixzz22BPTxCx0

63 Siobhan Duck, "Angry response to Salvation Army's gay stance", *Herald Sun* (Melbourne), June 18, 2012.
URL: www.heraldsun.com.au/news/victoria/angry-response-to-salvation-armys-gay-stance/story-fn7x8me2-1226398031984

64. Bruce Golding, "First gay-marriage suit hits Catholic institution", *New York Post*, June 20, 2012.
URL: www.nypost.com/2012/06/20/first-gay-marriage-suit-hits-catholic-institution

65. Dominic Sutton, "Church groups suspended from school over homophobic leaflet", *The Guardian* (UK), June 28, 2012.
URL: www.guardian-series.co.uk/news/rbnews/9788251.WANSTEAD__Church_groups_suspended_from_school_over_homophobic_leaflet/

66. "Schools could be forced to teach gay marriage", *The Christian Institute* (UK), July 2, 2012.
URL: www.christian.org.uk/news/schools-could-be-forced-to-teach-gay-marriage/

67. Katie Craine, "Toronto school board promotes curriculum encouraging students to cross-dress", *LifeSiteNews*, July 5, 2012.
URL: www.lifesitenews.com/news/toronto-school-board-encourages-students-to-cross-dress

68. Patrick B. Craine, "Christian B&B owners ordered to pay gay couple $4,500 in damages", *LifeSiteNews*, July 19, 2012.
URL: www.lifesitenews.com/news/christian-bb-owners-ordered-to-pay-gay-couple-4500-in-damages

69. Greg Turner, "Mayor Menino on Chick-fil-A: Stuff it: Vows to block eatery over anti-gay attitude", *Boston Herald*, July 20, 2012.
URL: www.bostonherald.com/business/business_markets/2012/07/mayor_menino_chick_fil_a_stuff_it

70. Angela O'Brien, "Swedish high school student fails bio class for saying homosexuality 'abnormal'", *LifeSiteNews*, July 27, 2012.
URL: www.lifesitenews.com/news/swedish-high-school-student-fails-bio-class-for-saying-homosexuality-abonor

71. Billy Hallowell, "Activists call for boycott on cake shop after owner refuses to bake gay wedding cake", *The Blaze*, July 30, 2012.
URL: www.theblaze.com/stories/activists-call-for-boycott-on-cake-shop-after-owner-refuses-to-bake-gay-wedding-cake/

72. Dave Jolly, "Pastor's sermon defending Chick-fil-A causes school to consider revoking lease", *Godfather Politics*, August 1, 2012.
URL: godfatherpolitics.com/6412/pastors-sermon-defending-chick-fil-a-causes-school-to-consider-revoking-lease/

73. Ben Johnson, "Democrat admits, 'Attack on parental rights' is 'the whole point' of banning sex orientation therapy", *LifeSiteNews*, August 2, 2012.
URL: www.lifesitenews.com/news/democrat-admits-attack-on-parental-rights-is-the-whole-point-of-banning-sex

74. Cameron Harris, "University suspends Chick-fil-A from campus", *Campus Reform*, August 9, 2012.
URL: www.campusreform.org/blog/?ID=3122

75. Greg Buckle, "St Kilda's Milne fined over gay slur", *Sydney Morning Herald*, August 9, 2012.
URL: news.smh.com.au/breaking-news-sport/st-kildas-milne-fined-over-gay-slur-20120809-23x9n.html

76. Charles McVety, "Canadian schools teaching 8-year-olds there are six genders without parental permission", *National Organisation for Marriage*, August 10, 2012.
URL: www.nomblog.com/26781/

77. Ben Johnson, "Vermont Catholic couple pays $30,000 in dispute over hosting lesbian 'wedding' reception", *LifeSiteNews*, August 24, 2012.

URL: www.lifesitenews.com/news/vermont-catholic-couple-pays-30000-for-not-hosting-lesbian-wedding-receptio

78 "Catholic college teacher suspended in gay marriage row", *TVNZ, OneNews*, August 29, 2012.
URL: www.tvnz.co.nz/national-news/catholic-college-teacher-suspended-in-gay-marriage-row-5052167

79 Graeme Paton, "Teachers 'face sack' for refusing to endorse gay marriage", *The Telegraph* (UK), September 10, 2012.
URL: www.telegraph.co.uk/news/9531803/Teachers-face-sack-for-refusing-to-endorse-gay-marriage.html

80 Patrick B. Craine, "Ontario dad sues school board over no opt out classes on sex", *LifeSiteNews*, September 10, 2012.
URL: www.lifesitenews.com/news/ontario-dad-sues-school-board-over-no-opt-out-classes-on-sex

81 Thaddeus Baklinski, "Ontario Christian minister forced to conduct same-sex 'marriages' or get sacked", *LifeSiteNews*, September 11, 2012.
URL: www.lifesitenews.com/news/ontario-christian-minister-forced-to-conduct-same-sex-marriages-or-get-sack

82 Johanna Dasteel, "Franciscan U of Steubenville under investigation for teaching homosexuality as deviant", *LifeSiteNews*, September 11, 2012.
URL: www.lifesitenews.com/news/breaking-franciscan-u-of-steubenville-faces-sanction-for-teaching-homosexua

83 Kathleen Gilbert, "Seminary professor fired for beliefs on homosexuality: complaint", *LifeSiteNews*, September 12, 2012.
URL: www.lifesitenews.com/news/black-seminary-professor-fired-for-beliefs-on-homosexuality-complaint

84 Jeanne Smits, "No allowances for conscience in French 'gay marriage' bill: French Justice Minister", *LifeSiteNews*, September 12, 2012.
URL: www.lifesitenews.com/news/no-allowances-for-conscience-in-french-gay-marriage-bill-french-justice-min/

85 Ben Johnson, "Pro-family views cost ex-Marine a superintendent job in Berkeley", *LifeSiteNews*, September 19, 2012.
URL: www.lifesitenews.com/news/pro-family-views-views-cost-ex-marine-a-superintendent-job-in-berkeley

86 Jane Fryer, "Christian couple reveal how they have suffered a two-year campaign of death threats and abuse for refusing to let two gay men share a room in their B&B", *Daily Mail* (UK), September 21, 2012.
URL: www.dailymail.co.uk/news/article-2206952/Christian-couple-reveal-suffered-year-campaign-death-threats-abuse-refusing-let-gay-men-share-room-B-B.html

87 Ian Sparks, "France is set to ban the words 'mother' and 'father' from all official documents under controversial plans to legalise gay marriage", *Daily Mail* (UK), September 24, 2012.
URL: www.dailymail.co.uk/news/article-2207860/France-set-ban-words-mother-father-official-documents-controversial-plans-legalise-gay-marriage.html

88 Anon., "Rupert Everett receives death threats over gay parenting comments", *Hollywood.com*, September 29, 2012.
URL: www.hollywood.com/news/Rupert_Everett_receives_death_threats_over_gay_parenting_comments/41210560

89 Todd Starnes, "University punishes staffer for signing marriage petition", *FoxNews*, October 15, 2012.
URL: radio.foxnews.com/toddstarnes/top-stories/university-punishes-staffer-for-signing-marriage-petition.html

[90] Miranda Devine, "Being straight no longer normal, students taught", *Daily Telegraph* (Sydney), October 17, 2012.
URL: www.dailytelegraph.com.au/news/sydney-news/being-straight-no-longer-normal-students-taught/story-e6freuzi-1226497360980

[91] Anon., "B&B fined for hurting gay couple's feelings", *CharismaNews*, October 18, 2012.
URL: www.charismanews.com/world/34336-bab-fined-for-hurting-gay-couples-feelings

[92] Billy Hallowell, "Lesbians launch discrimination complaint against NY farm owners for refusing to host their gay wedding", *The Blaze*, October 22, 2012.
URL: www.theblaze.com/stories/lesbians-launch-discrimination-complaint-against-ny-farm-owners-for-refusing-to-host-their-gay-wedding/

[93] Heather Clark, "Texas pastor jailed for preaching at pride event awaits court date", *Christian News*, October 31, 2012.
URL: christiannews.net/2012/10/31/texas-pastor-jailed-for-preaching-at-pride-event-awaits-court-date/

[94] Jim Hoft, "Washington college OK's exposure of young girls to transgender male in locker room", *Gateway Pundit*, November 1, 2012.
URL: www.thegatewaypundit.com/2012/11/washington-college-oks-exposure-of-young-girls-to-transgender-male-in-locker-room/

[95] Thaddeus Baklinski, "Last UK Catholic adoption agency loses final appeal over homosexual adoption", *LifeSiteNews*, November 2, 2012.
URL: www.lifesitenews.com/news/last-uk-catholic-adoption-agency-loses-final-appeal-over-homosexual-adoptio

[96] Peter Baklinski, "Judge: Parents have no right to know what homosexual activist taught their children in school", *LifeSiteNews*, November 10, 2012.
URL: www.lifesitenews.com/news/judge-parents-have-no-right-to-know-what-homosexual-activist-taught-their-c

[97] Christopher Agee, "Middle schoolers subjected to graphic gay indoctrination", *The Western Center for Journalism*, November 10, 2012.
URL: www.westernjournalism.com/middle-schoolers-subjected-to-graphic-gay-indoctrination/

[98] Tarringo Vaughan, "A school district being sued for removing a book about a lesbian couple", *Examiner*, November 13, 2012.
URL: www.examiner.com/article/a-school-district-being-sued-removing-a-book-about-a-lesbian-couple

[99] Ben Johnson, "Obama nominates black homosexual judge to 'ensure that the judiciary resembles the nation'", *LifeSiteNews*, November 15, 2012.
URL: www.lifesitenews.com/news/obama-nominates-gay-black-judge-to-ensure-the-judiciary-resembles-the-nat

[100] John Bingham, "Primary school teachers 'could face sack' for refusing to promote gay marriage", *The Telegraph*, November 18, 2012.
URL: www.telegraph.co.uk/news/politics/9686306/Primary-school-teachers-could-face-sack-for-refusing-to-promote-gay-marriage.html

[101] Ben Johnson, "San Francisco set to vote on ban on public nudity, except at 'gay pride' events", *LifeSiteNews*, November 19, 2012.
URL: www.lifesitenews.com/news/public-nudity-out-in-san-francisco-except-for-8216-gay-pride8217-events

[102] "A Newcastle blogger and taxi driver has been ordered to pay thousands of dollars in damages for vilifying homosexuals", *ABC News*, November 28, 2012.
URL: www.abc.net.au/news/2012-11-28/newcastle-cabbie-fined-for-vilifying-homosexuals/4397212

References

[103] Bethany Monk, "Commission opposes t-shirt company's refusal to print 'gay pride' message", *CitizenLink*, November 29, 2012.
URL: www.citizenlink.com/2012/11/29/commission-opposes-t-shirt-companys-refusal-to-print-gay-pride-message/

[104] Hilary White, "Ban children's books depicting traditional families: 'gender stereotyping' says EU report", *LifeSiteNews*, November 30, 2012.
URL: www.lifesitenews.com/news/ban-childrens-books-depicting-traditional-families-gender-stereotyping-says

[105] Jeff Schapiro, "DOE investigating school over Bible and homosexuality comments", *Christian Post*, December 1, 2012.
URL: www.christianpost.com/news/doe-investigating-school-over-bible-and-homosexuality-comments-85891/

[106] Simon Johnson, "Scottish parents 'cannot withdraw children from all gay marriage lessons'", *The Telegraph* (UK), December 13, 2012.
URL: www.telegraph.co.uk/news/uknews/scotland/9740898/Scottish-parents-cannot-withdraw-children-from-all-gay-marriage-lessons.html

[107] "BBC 'should be bold in gay coverage'", *BBC News*, December 14, 2012.
URL: www.bbc.co.uk/news/entertainment-arts-20725345

[108] "Wedding vendor opposed to same sex marriage shuts down", *Breitbart*, December 27, 2012.
URL: www.breitbart.com/Big-Government/2012/12/27/Company-shuts-doors-over-same-sex-marriage

[109] "Socialist politician says Spanish bishop should be 'muzzled'", *Catholic News Agency*, January 7, 2013.
URL: www.catholicnewsagency.com/news/socialist-politician-says-spanish-bishop-should-be-muzzled/

[110] Matthew Cullinan Hoffman, "French government warns Catholic schools to stay 'neutral' on homosexual 'marriage'", *LifeSiteNews*, January 7, 2013.
URL: www.lifesitenews.com/news/french-government-warns-catholic-schools-to-stay-neutral-on-homosexual-marr

[111] Joe Carter, "Pastor disinvited from giving inaugural prayer because of sermon on homosexuality", *The Gospel Coalition*, January 10, 2013.
URL: thegospelcoalition.org/blogs/tgc/2013/01/10/pastor-disinvited-from-giving-inaugural-prayer-because-of-sermon-on-homosexuality/

[112] Charlie Butts, "'Gay' issue threatens plans for Christian law school", *OneNewsNow*, January 22, 2013.
URL: onenewsnow.com/education/2013/01/22/%E2%80%98gay%E2%80%99-issue-threatens-plans-for-christian-law-school#.UmdBC3btMUM

[113] Simon Johnson, "Catholic adoption agency faces punishment for gay 'discrimination'", *The Telegraph* (UK), January 23, 2013.
URL: www.telegraph.co.uk/news/uknews/scotland/9822253/Catholic-adoption-agency-faces-punishment-for-gay-discrimination.html

[114] Mike Benner, "The Oregon Department of Justice is looking into a complaint that a Gresham bakery refused to make a wedding cake for a same sex marriage", *NBC News*, February 2, 2013.
URL: www.nbcnews.com/id/50679304/ns/us_news-life/?ocid=msnhp&pos=7#.UQ3cNvLPURp

[115] "Over 40,000 teachers 'face sack' over gay marriage", *The Christian Institute* (UK), February 4, 2013.
URL: www.christian.org.uk/news/over-40000-teachers-face-sack-over-gay-marriage/

[116] Patrick Craine, "Canadian gvmt halts overseas funding to Christian group over beliefs on homosexuality", *LifeSiteNews*, February 11, 2013.

URL: www.lifesitenews.com/news/canadian-gvmt-halts-overseas-funding-to-christian-group-over-beliefs-on-hom/

[117] John Bingham, "Gay marriage: no opt-out for Christian registrars", *The Telegraph* (UK), February 15, 2013.
URL: www.telegraph.co.uk/news/politics/9870468/Gay-marriage-no-opt-out-for-Christian-registrars.html

[118] Tim Graham, "AP caves into gay PC: 'His husband' and 'Her wife' are now accepted stylebook terms", *NewsBusters*, February 21, 2013.
URL: newsbusters.org/blogs/tim-graham/2013/02/21/ap-caves-gay-pc-his-husband-and-her-wife-are-now-accepted-stylebook-term

[119] Heather Clark, "Canadian Supreme Court rules biblical speech opposing homosexual behavior is a 'hate crime'", *ChristianNews*, February 28, 2013.
URL: christiannews.net/2013/02/28/canadian-supreme-court-rules-biblical-speech-opposing-homosexual-behavior-is-a-hate-crime/

[120] "Police chaplain dumped for opposing gay marriage", *The Christian Institute* (UK), March 1, 2013.
URL: www.christian.org.uk/news/police-chaplain-dumped-for-opposing-gay-marriage/

[121] William Bigelow, "Two 11-year-olds receive threats for testifying against same-sex marriage", *Breitbart*, March 31, 2013.
URL: www.breitbart.com/Big-Government/2013/03/31/Children-Viciously-Attacked-For-Testifying-Against-Same-Sex-marriage

[122] Tim Drake, "Homosexual students hope to oust Catholic chaplain from university campus", *Catholic Education Daily*, April 4, 2013.
URL: www.cardinalnewmansociety.org/CatholicEducationDaily/DetailsPage/tabid/102/ArticleID/2116/Homosexual-Students-Hope-to-Oust-Catholic-Chaplain-from-University-Campus.aspx

[123] AAP, "U.S. florist refused to serve gay couple", *9News*, April 10, 2013.
URL: news.ninemsn.com.au/world/2013/04/10/16/39/us-florist-refused-to-serve-gay-couple

[124] Hilary White, "Force 'gay marriage' on Northern Ireland through courts: Amnesty International", *LifeSiteNews*, April 10, 2013.
URL: www.lifesitenews.com/news/force-gay-marriage-on-northern-ireland-through-courts-amnesty-international/

[125] Kirsten Andersen, "Supporting marriage may be offensive: Public school students need permission slips to hear Santorum", *LifeSiteNews*, April 11, 2013.
URL: www.lifesitenews.com/news/supporting-marriage-may-be-offensive-public-school-students-need-permission/

[126] Kim Trobee, "Bill rescinds tax breaks for groups with Christian views on sexuality", *CitizenLink*, April 11, 2013.
URL: www.citizenlink.com/2013/04/11/bill-rescinds-tax-breaks-for-groups-with-christian-views-on-sexuality/

[127] Simon Collins, "Gender-neutral terms possible for marriage forms", *New Zealand Herald*, April 13, 2013.
URL: www.nzherald.co.nz/nz/news/article.cfm?c_id=1&objectid=10877294

[128] Hilary White, "Judge: Firing teacher who called homosexuality a sin reflects 'modern British values of tolerance'", *LifeSiteNews*, April 26, 2013.
URL: www.lifesitenews.com/news/judge-firing-teacher-who-called-homosexual-sin-reflects-modern-british-valu

References

129. Alex Murashko, "Gay activists push for gov't officials to drop Greg Laurie from national day of prayer events", *Christian Post*, April 29, 2013.
URL: www.christianpost.com/news/gay-activists-push-for-govt-official-to-drop-greg-laurie-from-national-day-of-prayer-events-94850/

130. Kirsten Andersen, "Columbus bishop risks jail defending Catholic school that fired teacher for coming out as lesbian", *LifeSiteNews*, May 3, 2013.
URL: www.lifesitenews.com/news/columbus-bishop-risks-jail-defending-catholic-school-that-fired-teacher-for

131. "Rohit Singh, Canadian transgender woman, allegedly denied service at bridal boutique", *Huffington Post*, May 3, 2013.
URL: www.huffingtonpost.com/2013/05/03/rohit-singh-transgender-wedding-dress-_n_3210219.html?utm_hp_ref=gay-voices

132. Vaimoana Tapaleao, "Homosexual rejected, heads to tribunal", *The New Zealand Herald*, May 6, 2013.
URL: www.nzherald.co.nz/nz/news/article.cfm?c_id=1&objectid=10881716

133. Heather McCracken, "Family First NZ faces deregistration", *The New Zealand Herald*, May 6, 2013.
URL: www.nzherald.co.nz/nz/news/article.cfm?c_id=1&objectid=10881782

134. Hilary White, "Young Christians will be locked out of public professions by 'gay marriage', ministers warn", *LifeSiteNews*, May 20, 2013.
URL: www.lifesitenews.com/news/young-christians-will-be-locked-out-of-public-professions-by-gay-marriage-m

135. "'You're not doing this in my home': lesbian bed ban sparks threats and abuse", *The Age* (Melbourne), May 21, 2013.
URL: www.theage.com.au/travel/travel-news/youre-not-doing-this-in-my-home-lesbian-bed-ban-sparks-threats-and-abuse-20130521-2jxem.html#ixzz2X5wqcbFt

136. Peter Baklinski, "Police investigate teacher who posted graphic gay sex brochures in 7-8 Toronto classroom", *LifeSiteNews*, May 31, 2013.
URL: www.lifesitenews.com/news/police-investigate-teacher-who-posted-graphic-gay-sex-brochures-in-7-8-toro

137. Ivan Moreno, "Colo. gay discrimination alleged over wedding cake", *Yahoo News*, June 6, 2013.
URL: news.yahoo.com/colo-gay-discrimination-alleged-over-wedding-cake-195825831.html

138. Kirsten Andersen, "Army soldier disciplined for serving Chick-Fil-A at promotion party", *LifeSiteNews*, June 6, 2013.
URL: www.lifesitenews.com/news/army-soldier-disciplined-for-serving-chick-fil-a-at-promotion-party

139. Matt C. Abbott, "Court awards lesbian $170,000 after being fired from Catholic school for using IVF", *LifeSiteNews*, June 7, 2013.
URL: www.lifesitenews.com/news/court-awards-lesbian-170000-after-being-fired-from-catholic-school-for-usin

140. "Boy, 3, taught about gay marriage in nursery", *The Christian Institute* (UK), June 11, 2013.
URL: www.christian.org.uk/news/boy-3-taught-about-gay-marriage-in-nursery/

141. Matthew Cullinan Hoffman, "French mayor refuses to 'marry' homosexual couple: risks years in jail", *LifeSiteNews*, June 12, 2013.
URL: www.lifesitenews.com/news/french-refuses-to-marry-homosexual-couple-risks-years-in-jail

142. Hilary White, "Scottish Catholic adoption agency threatened with closure over gay adoption", *LifeSiteNews*, June 12, 2013.
URL: www.lifesitenews.com/news/scottish-catholic-adoption-agency-threatened-with-closure-over-gay-adoption/

143. Ben Johnson, "Boston cops must defer to transgender crooks", *LifeSiteNews*, June 13, 2013.
    URL: www.lifesitenews.com/news/boston-cops-must-defer-to-transgender-crooks
144. Todd Starnes, "Professor orders students to support gay rights", *FoxNews*, June 18, 2013.
    URL: radio.foxnews.com/toddstarnes/top-stories/professor-orders-students-to-support-gay-rights.html
145. "Teachers told 'watch what you say' on gay marriage", *The Christian Institute* (UK), June 25, 2013.
    URL: www.christian.org.uk/news/teachers-told-watch-what-you-say-on-gay-marriage/
146. David Hacker, "University fires employee for op-ed standing against gay rights as civil rights", *Charisma News*, July 2, 2013.
    URL: www.charismanews.com/us/40089-university-fires-employee-for-op-ed-standing-against-gay-rights-as-civil-rights
147. John Bingham, "Christian arrested for calling homosexuality a 'sin' warns of 'real-life thought police'", *The Telegraph* (UK), July 4, 2013.
    URL: www.telegraph.co.uk/news/religion/10159420/Christian-arrested-for-calling-homosexuality-a-sin.html
148. Ben Johnson, "Judge orders Ohio to recognize out-of-state gay 'marriage' despite state's marriage amendment", *LifeSiteNews*, July 23, 2013.
    URL: www.lifesitenews.com/news/judge-orders-ohio-recognize-out-of-state-gay-marriage-amendment-will-only-i
149. "Gay couple to sue church over gay marriage opt-out", *The Christian Institute*, August 1, 2013.
    URL: www.christian.org.uk/news/gay-couple-to-sue-church-over-gay-marriage-opt-out/
150. Thaddeus Baklinski, "Scottish man fined $62,000 for 'homophobic' Twitter message", *LifeSiteNews*, August 9, 2013.
    URL: www.lifesitenews.com/news/scottish-man-fined-62000-for-homophobic-twitter-message
151. Gina Meeks, "Chaplain assistant facing punishment for calling homosexuality a sin on Facebook", *CharismaNews*, August 9, 2013.
    URL: www.charismanews.com/us/40568-chaplain-assistant-facing-punishment-for-calling-homosexuality-a-sin-on-facebook
152. Ben Johnson, "Business owners threatened, face legal action for refusing to rent facility for gay 'wedding'", *LifeSiteNews*, August 12, 2013.
    URL: www.lifesitenews.com/news/f-k-you-f-k-your-god-f-k-your-religion-business-owners-threatened-for-refus
153. "War on Christianity? Airman allegedly relieved of duty for opposing gay marriage", *Examiner*, August 16, 2013.
    URL: www.examiner.com/article/war-on-christianity-airman-allegedly-relieved-of-duty-for-opposing-gay-marriage
154. Wendy Wright, "Judge allows lawsuit against pastor for opposing homosexuality", *LifeSiteNews*, August 23, 2013.
    URL: www.lifesitenews.com/news/judge-allows-lawsuit-against-pastor-for-opposing-homosexuality
155. Cheryl K. Chumley, "Christian bakers who refused cake order for gay wedding forced to close shop", *Washington Times*, September 2, 2013.
    URL: www.washingtontimes.com/news/2013/sep/2/christian-bakers-who-refused-cake-order-gay-weddin/
156. Thaddeus Baklinski, "One complaint, Facebook campaign force restaurant owners to take down 'anti-gay' newspaper clipping", *LifeSiteNews,* September 3, 2013.

URL: www.lifesitenews.com/news/one-complaint-facebook-campaign-force-restaurant-owners-to-take-down-anti-g

[157] Kirsten Andersen, "Fox Sports football announcer fired over 2011 remarks on homosexuality", *LifeSiteNews*, September 9, 2013.
URL: www.lifesitenews.com/news/fox-sports-football-announcer-fired-over-2011-remarks-on-homosexuality

[158] Kirsten Andersen, "Air force sergeant claims he was fired for refusing to endorse gay 'marriage': faces court martial", *LifeSiteNews*, September 10, 2013.
URL: www.lifesitenews.com/news/air-force-sergeant-claims-he-was-fired-for-refusing-to-endorse-gay-marriage

[159] Thaddeus Baklinski, "Transgender man wins complaint against bridal shop for not letting him try on wedding dress", *LifeSiteNews*, September 19, 2013.
URL: www.lifesitenews.com/news/transgender-man-wins-complaint-against-bridal-shop-for-not-letting-him-try

[160] Hilary White, "Gay activists launch complaint against teacher who included homosexuality on list of possible sins", *LifeSiteNews*, September 23, 2013.
URL: www.lifesitenews.com/news/gay-activists-launch-complaint-against-teacher-who-included-homosexuality-o

[161] Kirsten Andersen, "Washington state judge faces formal reprimand for refusing to officiate same-sex 'weddings'", *LifeSiteNews*, October 8, 2013.
URL: www.lifesitenews.com/news/washington-state-judge-faces-formal-reprimand-for-refusing-to-officiate-sam

[162] Todd Starnes, "US Army defines Christian ministry as 'domestic hate group'", *Fox News*, October 14, 2013.
URL: www.foxnews.com/opinion/2013/10/14/us-army-defines-christian-ministry-as-domestic-hate-group/

[163] "Katter Party candidate Tess Corbett ordered to apologise over election comments", *ABC News*, October 16, 2013.
URL: www.abc.net.au/news/2013-10-16/katter-party-candidate-tess-corbett-ordered-to-apologise-over-e/5026084

[164] Jeanne Smits, "Mayors cannot refuse to 'marry' homosexual couples: French Constitutional Court", *LifeSiteNews*, October 22, 2013.
URL: www.lifesitenews.com/news/mayors-cannot-refuse-to-marry-homosexual-couples-french-constitutional-cour

[165] Brian Camenker, "What same-sex 'marriage' has done to Massachusetts", *MassResistance*, October 20, 2008.
URL: www.massresistance.org/docs/marriage/effects_of_ssm.html

[166] *Ibid.*

[167] *Ibid.*

[168] Michael Coren, "Canadian crackdown", *National Review Online*, June 11, 2012.
URL: www.nationalreview.com/articles/301641/canadian-crackdown-michael-coren

[169] *Ibid.*

[170] Bradley Miller, "Same-sex marriage ten years on: Lessons from Canada", *Public Discourse*, November 5, 2012.
URL: www.thepublicdiscourse.com/2012/11/6758/

[171] Robert George, "Marriage, religious liberty, and the 'grand bargain'", *Public Discourse*, July 19, 2012.
URL: www.thepublicdiscourse.com/2012/07/5884

[172] Matthew J. Franck, "Same-sex marriage and religious freedom, fundamentally at odds", *Public Discourse*, June 18, 2013.
URL: www.thepublicdiscourse.com/2013/06/10393/

[173] *Ibid.*

[174] *Ibid.*

[175] Michael Brown, *A Queer Thing Happened To America*. Concord, NC: EqualTime Books, 2011, p. 501.

[176] Cited in Andrew Johnson, "CNN distorts Arizona's right-to-refuse bill", *National Review*, February 25, 2014.
URL: www.nationalreview.com/article/371934/cnn-distorts-arizonas-right-refuse-bill-andrew-johnson

[177] Albert Mohler, "Caesar, coercion, and the Christian conscience: A dangerous confusion", *albertmohler.com*, February 24, 2014.
URL: www.albertmohler.com/2014/02/24/caesar-coercion-and-the-christian-conscience-a-dangerous-confusion/

[178] Matt Walsh, "Yes, of course a business owner should have the right to refuse service to gay people", *The Matt Walsh Blog*, February 25, 2014.
URL: http://themattwalshblog.com/2014/02/25/yes-of-course-a-business-owner-should-have-the-right-to-refuse-service-to-gay-people/

[179] Gary DeMar, "Should a pro-abortion printer be forced to print 'Abortion is murder' signs and shirts?", *Godfather Politics*, February 25, 2014.
URL: http://godfatherpolitics.com/14503/pro-abortion-printer-forced-print-abortion-murder-signs-shirts/

[180] Ryan T. Anderson, "On religious liberty, Arizona gets it right and NY Times gets it wrong again", *The Foundry*, February 25, 2014.
URL: http://blog.heritage.org/2014/02/25/religious-liberty-arizona-gets-right-ny-times-gets-wrong/

Chapter 2. How Families, Parenthood and Identity Suffer

[1] Ian Sparks, "France is set to ban the words 'mother' and 'father' from all official documents under controversial plans to legalise gay marriage", *Daily Mail* (UK), September 24, 2012.
URL: www.dailymail.co.uk/news/article-2207860/France-set-ban-words-mother-father-official-documents-controversial-plans-legalise-gay-marriage.html

[2] Jessica Geen, "UK passport forms to accommodate gay parents", *PinkNews*, October 3, 2011.
URL: www.pinknews.co.uk/2011/10/03/uk-passport-forms-to-accommodate-gay-parents/

[3] "Definition of confusion: UK govt to re-term 'husband' and 'wife'", *Russia Today* (Moscow), June 28, 2013.
URL: http://rt.com/news/uk-husband-wife-overrule-379/

[4] "Obama's State Dept. removes mother, father from passports", *NewsMax*, January 9, 2011.
URL: www.newsmax.com/InsideCover/passport-mother-father-abolished/2011/01/09/id/382319

[5] U.S. Department of Education, "Education Department announces changes to FAFSA form to more accurately and fairly assess students' need for aid", USDE media release, April 29, 2013.
URL: www.ed.gov/news/press-releases/education-department-announces-changes-fafsa-form-more-accurately-and-fairly-ass

[6] "U.S: Words 'husband' and 'wife' axed from marriage certificates", *The Christian Institute* (UK), November 28, 2012.
URL: www.christian.org.uk/news/us-words-husband-and-wife-axed-from-marriage-certificates/

References

7. Thaddeus Baklinski, "Florida judge OKs 3-parent family: two lesbians and a homosexual man", LifeSiteNews, February 8, 2013.
URL: www.lifesitenews.com/news/florida-judge-oks-3-parent-family-two-lesbians-and-a-homosexual

8. *Ibid.*

9. "'Man and woman', 'wife', 'husband', 'widow', 'widower' banished from all Ontario law", *LifeSiteNews*, February 25, 2005.
URL: www.lifesitenews.com/news/archive//ldn/2005/feb/05022511

10. "Genderless preschool bans 'him' and 'her'", *Herald Sun* (Melbourne), June 27, 2011.
URL: www.heraldsun.com.au/news/the-other-side/pc-preschool-bans-words-him-and-her/story-e6frfhk6-1226082516997

11. Bill Muehlenberg, "Can Sweden get any worse?", *CultureWatch*, June 27, 2011.
URL: www.billmuehlenberg.com/2011/06/27/can-sweden-get-any-worse/

12. "First gay 'marriage' legalized, now Spain bans terms 'mother' and 'father'", *LifeSiteNews*, March 10, 2006.
URL: www.lifesitenews.com/news/first-gay-marriage-legalized-now-spain-bans-terms-mother-and-father

13. "'Mother' and 'father' to be scrapped from Scottish law", *The Christian Institute* (UK), February 11, 2013.
URL: www.christian.org.uk/news/mother-and-father-to-be-scrapped-from-scottish-law/

14. *Ibid.*

15. Hilary White, "City of Venice to ban 'mother' and 'father' terms on official forms", *LifeSiteNews*, Septembner 4, 2013.
URL: www.lifesitenews.com/news/city-of-venice-to-ban-mother-and-father-terms-on-official-forms

16. Terry Vanderheyden, "P.E.I. amending marriage laws to replace 'husband', 'wife', 'bride', 'groom' with gender-neutral 'spouse'", *LifeSiteNews*, November 18, 2005.
URL: www.lifesite.net/ldn/2005/nov/05111810.html

17. Bill Muehlenberg, "Mums and dads to be banned", *CultureWatch*, June 5, 2006.
URL: www.billmuehlenberg.com/2006/06/05/mums-and-dads-to-be-banned/

18. Heath Gilmore, "Fathers to go from birth certificates", *Sydney Morning Herald*, May 17, 2008.
URL: www.smh.com.au/news/national/father-to-go-from-birth-certificates/2008/05/17/1210765258007.html

19. Katherine Weber, "Germany introduces 'third gender' on birth certificates; New 'gender blank' option implemented", *Christian Post Europe*, August 19, 2013.
URL: http://global.christianpost.com/news/germany-introduces-third-gender-on-birth-certificates-new-gender-blank-option-implemented-102569/#sgJaPMLRTMcZ01tW.99

20. Eric Owens, "Taxpayer-funded college offers SEVEN gender choices on application", *Daily Caller*, November 28, 2013.
URL: http://dailycaller.com/2013/11/28/taxpayer-funded-college-offers-seven-gender-choices-on-application/#ixzz2mUx0gRSW

21. Ben Johnson, "Colorado college lists five genders, including 'queer,' on applications", *LifeSiteNews*, November 8, 2013.
URL: www.lifesitenews.com/news/colorado-college-lists-five-genders-including-queer-on-applications

22. Brendan O'Neill, "How the gay-marriage campaign has unleashed a bureaucratic assault on people's identities", *The Telegraph* (UK), March 24, 2012.
URL: http://blogs.telegraph.co.uk/news/brendanoneill2/100146397/how-the-gay-marriage-camapign-has-unleashed-a-bureaucratic-assault-on-peoples-identities/

23   *Ibid.*

Chapter 3. What Slippery Slope?

1. Bill Muehlenberg, *Strained Relations: The Challenge of Homosexuality*. Melbourne: Freedom Publishing, 2011, pp. 109-116.
2. Kirsty McMurray, "Legalise multi-partner marriage-group", *Stuff.co.nz*, April 23, 2013.
URL: www.stuff.co.nz/national/8588721/Legalise-multi-partner-marriage-group
3. Jillian Keenan, "Legalize polygamy! No. I am not kidding", *Slate*, April 15, 2013.
URL: www.slate.com/articles/double_x/doublex/2013/04/legalize_polygamy_marriage_equality_for_all.html
4. Martin Zavan, "Identical twins in relationship with same man", *ninemsn*, May 29, 2012.
URL: http://news.ninemsn.com.au/national/2012/10/10/10/58/identical-twins-in-relationship-with-same-man
5. Their website can be found here:
URL: polyaction.nfshost.com/home/
6. "BIG LOVE: Greensparty polyamorists push for equality in Marriage Act", *Vex News*, March 4, 2013.
URL: www.vexnews.com/2013/03/big-love-greensparty-polyamorists-push-for-equality-in-marriage-act/
7. Stephanie Pappas, "New sexual revolution: Polyamory may be good for you", *Scientific American*, February 14, 2013.
URL: www.scientificamerican.com/article.cfm?id=new-sexual-revolution-polyamory
8. Angi Becker Stevens, "My two husbands", *Salon*, August 5, 2013.
URL: www.salon.com/2013/08/05/my_two_husbands/
9. *Ibid.*
10. *Ibid.*
11. Zach Stafford, "'Monogamish': Two is company, but is three really a crowd?", *Huffington Post*, February 27, 2013.
URL: www.huffingtonpost.com/zach-stafford/monogamish-two-is-company_b_2664725.html
12. Heather Clark, "The new modern family? Woman and two men raise son in 'polyamorous' relationship", *Christian News*, February 25, 2013.
URL: christiannews.net/2013/02/25/the-new-modern-family-woman-and-two-men-raise-son-in-polyamorous-relationship/
13. Christopher Bedford, "NYU professor argues against nuclear family, monogamy, anti-polygamy laws", *Daily Caller*, April 30, 2013.
URL: http://dailycaller.com/2013/04/30/nyu-professor-argues-against-nuclear-family-monogamy-anti-polygamy-laws/
14. Jo Fidgen, "How does a polyamorous relationship between four people work?", *BBC News Magazine*, August 19, 2013.
URL: www.bbc.co.uk/news/magazine-23726120
15. *Ibid.*
16. *Ibid.*

References

17. "Multiple partner relationships could become norm, says BBC", *The Christian Institute* (UK), August 20, 2013.
URL: www.christian.org.uk/news/multiple-partner-relationships-could-become-norm-says-bbc/

18. Ibid.

19. Laurie Penny, "Being polyamorous shows there's no 'traditional' way to live", *The Guardian* (UK), August 21, 2013.
URL: www.theguardian.com/commentisfree/2013/aug/20/polyamorous-shows-no-traditional-way-live

20. Ibid.

21. Ibid.

22. *Strained Relations*, pp. 99-105.

23. "Same-sex marriage won't be enough", *Stand To Reason Blog*, July 31, 2012.
URL: http://str.typepad.com/weblog/2012/07/same-sex-marriage-wont-be-enough.html

24. Steven Nelson, "Polyamory advocate: Gay marriage 'blazing the marriage equality trail'", *US News*, June 24, 2013.
URL: www.usnews.com/news/articles/2013/06/24/polyamorous-advocate-gay-marriage-blazing-the-marriage-equality-trail

25. Ibid.

26. McKay Coppins, "Polygamists celebrate Supreme Court's marriage rulings", *BuzzFeed Politics*, June 26, 2013.
URL: www.buzzfeed.com/mckaycoppins/polygamists-celebrate-supreme-courts-marriage-rulings

27. Eric Owens, "Leftist law professor says gay marriage likely to lead to legalized incest, polygamy", *Daily Caller*, July 19, 2013.
URL: http://dailycaller.com/2013/07/19/leftist-law-professor-admits-gay-marriage-likely-to-lead-to-legalized-incest-polygamy/#ixzz2cURICXPP

28. W.W. Houston, "Polygamy now!", *The Economist*, June 28, 2013.
URL: www.economist.com/blogs/democracyinamerica/2013/06/slippery-slopes

29. Houston, *Ibid*.

30. *Strained Relations*, pp. 28-31.

31. Rob Williams, "Stop 'persecution of old men' by lowering age of consent to 13 says top human rights barrister", *The Independent*, May 9, 2013.
URL: www.independent.co.uk/news/uk/crime/stop-persecution-of-old-men-by-lowering-age-of-consent-to-13-says-top-human-rights-barrister-8608794.html

32. Ibid.

33. Jack Minor, "Some homosexual activist groups a 'dream' to pedophiles", *Northern Colorado Gazette*, March 30, 2011.
URL: www.greeleygazette.com/press/?p=8934

34. Jeremy Kryn, "'Evil': Attendees at prominent pro-pedophilia conference horrified by sessions", *LifeSiteNews*, August 23, 2011.
URL: www.lifesitenews.com/news/evil-attendees-at-prominent-pro-pedophilia-conference-horrified-by-sessions

35. Ibid.

36. Alan Zarembo, "Many researchers taking a different view of pedophilia", *Los Angeles Times*, January 14, 2013.
URL: http://articles.latimes.com/2013/jan/14/local/la-me-pedophiles-20130115

37. "Pedophilia is a sexual orientation under CA Bill[?]", *Rethink Society*, February 7, 2013.
URL: www.rethinksociety.com/government/pedophilia-is-a-sexual-orientation-under-ca-bill/

[38] Robert Stacy McCain, "Liberals now arguing for a lesbian's right to have sex with a 14-year-old girl", *The Other McCain*, May 22, 2013.
URL: http://theothermccain.com/2013/05/22/photo-teen-lesbian-14-illegal-sex-kaitlyn-hunt-video/

[39] Robert Stacy McCain, "#FreeKate? movement to normalize pedophilia finds its poster girl", *The American Spectator*, May 23, 2013.
URL: http://spectator.org/blog/2013/05/23/freekate-movement-to-normalize

[40] Robert Stacy McCain, "The #FreeKate narrative melts down: Lies exposed in Florida teen sex case", *The American Spectator*, May 25, 2013.
URL: http://spectator.org/blog/2013/05/25/lesbian-teen-kaitlyn-hunt

[41] The only reference here is simply the website address:
URL: http://supporthonesty.net/

[42] Danny Shea, "Jeremy Irons on gay marriage: 'Could a father not marry his son?'", *Huffington Post*, April 4, 2013.
URL: www.huffingtonpost.com/2013/04/03/jeremy-irons-on-gay-marri_n_3009495.html

[43] Duane Lester, "Columbia political science professor equates his incestuous relationship with daughter to homosexual sex", *LibertyNews*, April 4, 2013.
URL: www.libertynews.com/2013/04/columbia-political-science-professor-equates-his-incestuous-relationship-with-daughter-to-homosexuals/

[44] Ibid.

[45] "Incest charges throw the ick factor right in our privileged faces", *Gender Across Borders*, December 15, 2010.
URL: www.genderacrossborders.com/2010/12/15/incest-charges-throw-the-ick-factor-right-in-our-privileged-faces/

[46] Victoria Wellman, "'Love who you want': The Notebook director says he's fine with incest and compares it to being gay", *Daily Mail* (UK), September 10, 2012.
URL: www.dailymail.co.uk/news/article-2201296/Nick-Cassavetes-says-hes-fine-incest-compares-gay.html#ixzz2SbJjWuuy

[47] Allan Hall, "Switzerland considers repealing incest laws", *The Telegraph* (UK), December 13, 2010.
URL: www.telegraph.co.uk/news/worldnews/europe/switzerland/8198917/Switzerland-considers-repealing-incest-laws.html

[48] Thomas Rogers, "Gay porn's most shocking taboo", *Salon*, May 21, 2010.
URL: www.salon.com/2010/05/21/twincest/

[49] Their site is here:
URL: www.geneticsexualattraction.org/

[50] Thomas Francis, "Those who practice bestiality say they're part of the next sexual rights movement", *Broward Palm Beach NewTime News*, August 20, 2009.
URL: www.browardpalmbeach.com/2009-08-20/news/those-who-practice-bestiality-say-they-re-part-of-the-next-gay-rights-movement/

[51] Ibid.

[52] Katherine Timpf, "Yale hosts workshop teaching sensitivity to bestiality", *Campus Reform*, May 5, 2013.
URL: www.campusreform.org/blog/?ID=4646

[53] Ibid.

[54] Ibid.

[55] Peter Singer, "Heavy petting", *Nerve*, 2001.
URL: www.utilitarian.net/singer/by/2001----.htm

References

56 Ibid.
57 You can see this amazing four minutes of "ethics" here:
URL: www.youtube.com/watch?v=w-cwNg1amRk
58 "Animal brothels legal in Denmark", *Ice News*, May 20, 2008.
URL: www.icenews.is/2008/05/20/animal-brothels-legal-in-denmark/
59 "Bestiality brothels spur call for animal sex ban", *The Local*, February 3, 2012.
URL: www.thelocal.de/society/20120203-40531.html
60 Matt Blake, "Bestiality brothels are 'spreading through Germany' warns campaigner as abusers turn to sex with animals as 'lifestyle choice'", *Daily Mail* (UK), July 1, 2013.
URL: www.dailymail.co.uk/news/article-2352779/Bestiality-brothels-spreading-Germany-campaigner-claims-abusers-sex-animals-lifestyle-choice.html
61 "Zoophiles protest against German bestiality ban", *The Local*, February 13, 2013.
URL: www.thelocal.de/society/20130201-47711.html#.UYdi8qKmg7n
62 Ibid.
63 Ibid.
64 "Swedish man accused of sex with sheep", *The Local*, May 20, 2011.
URL: www.thelocal.se/33882/20110520/
65 Matthew Cullinan Hoffman, "Homosexuals march in Madrid cheering bestiality and demanding 'affective-sexual diversity' in school", *LifeSiteNews*, July 14, 2009.
URL: www.lifesitenews.com/news/homosexuals-march-in-madrid-cheering-bestiality-and-demanding-affective-sex
66 Andrew Taylor, "Donkey sex gets thumbs-up from censors", *Sydney Morning Herald*, September 14, 2012.
URL: www.smh.com.au/entertainment/movies/donkey-sex-gets-thumbsup-from-censors-20120914-25x24.html#ixzz2SaesG62L
67 "Couple arranged sex with dog", *News.com.au*, February 17, 2012.
URL: www.news.com.au/breaking-news/couple-arranged-sex-with-dog/story-e6frfkp9-1226274062179#ixzz2SagMQB8F
68 Hilary Hanson, "Florida bestiality law: Oral sex loophole may only cover some forms of contact", *Huffington Post*, May 23, 2012.
URL: www.huffingtonpost.com/2012/06/23/florida-bestiality-law-oral-sex-loophole_n_1621001.html
69 Simon McCormack, "Malcolm Brenner chronicles his sexual relationship with dolphin in 'Wet Goddess'", *Huffington Post*, September 23, 2011.
URL: www.huffingtonpost.com/2011/09/23/malcolm-brenner-dolphin_n_974764.html
70 "Indiana woman wants to marry her pet dog – Tries to rally support from gay rights' activists", *Divided States*, May 10, 2012.
URL: www.dividedstates.com/indiana-woman-wants-marry-her-pet-dog-tries-to-rally-support-from-gay-rights-activists/
71 Peter LaBarbera, "'Gay rights' icon Frank Kameny says bestiality OK 'as long as the animal doesn't mind'", *Americans For Truth*, May 31, 2008.
URL: http://americansfortruth.com/2008/05/31/gay-icon-kameny-says-bestiality-ok-as-long-as-the-animal-doesnt-mind/
72 "Bernardi pulls out of UK Conversative summit", *The Australian*, September 22, 2012.
URL: www.theaustralian.com.au/national-affairs/bernardi-pulls-out-of-uk-summit/story-fn59niix-1226479350411
73 Their website is here:
URL: www.equalityforall.net/en/

[74] "Puppy love: man marries his dog", *The Chronicle*, December 1, 2010. URL: www.thechronicle.com.au/news/man-marrys-dog-city-first-toowoomba/710538/

[75] "German man 'marries' his dying cat", *BBC News*, May 3, 2010. URL: http://news.bbc.co.uk/2/hi/8658327.stm

[76] Andrea Zimmerman, "Woman marries her dog (seriously)", *HuffPost*, July 8, 2009. URL: www.lemondrop.com/2009/07/08/woman-marries-her-dog-seriously/

[77] Bill Muehlenberg, *Strained Relations: The Challenge of Homosexuality*. Melbourne: Freedom Publishing, 2011, pp. 110-111.

[78] Jude Newsome, "13 people who married inanimate objects", *Ranker*. URL: www.ranker.com/list/13-people-who-married-inanimate-objects/jude-newsome

[79] Sara Malm, "Rock-solid love: Australian woman marries a bridge in France – and even gets the mayor's blessing", *Daily Mail* (UK), July 5, 2013. URL: www.dailymail.co.uk/news/article-2356774/Australian-woman-Jodi-Rose-marries-bridge-France--gets-mayors-blessing.html#ixzz2mTzJZS4g

[80] Julie Beck, "Married to a doll: Why one man advocates synthetic love", *The Atlantic*, September 6, 2013. URL: www.theatlantic.com/health/archive/2013/09/married-to-a-doll-why-one-man-advocates-synthetic-love/279361/

[81] Mark Steyn, *After America*. Washington, DC: Regnery, 2011, pp. 233-234.

Chapter 4. Deconstructing the Family

[1] William Gairdner, *The War Against the Family*. Toronto: Stoddart, 1992.

[2] George Grant, *The Family Under Siege*. Minneapolis: Bethany House, 1994.

[3] Rita Kramer, *In Defense of the Family*. New York: Basic Books, 1983.

[4] Patricia Morgan, *Farewell to the Family?* London: IEA Health and Welfare Unit, 1995.

[5] David Popenoe, *War Over the Family*. New Brunswick, NJ: Transaction Publishers, 2005.

[6] Bryce Christensen, *Utopia Against the Family*. San Francisco: Ignatius Press, 1990.

[7] Christopher Lasch, *Haven in a Heartless World: The Family Besieged*. New York: W.W. Norton Co., 1977.

[8] Philip Abbott, *The Family on Trial*. University Park, Pennsylvania: Pennsylvania State University Press, 1981.

[9] William Bennett, *The Broken Hearth*. New York: Doubleday, 2001.

[10] Sylvia Ann Hewlett and Cornel West, *The War Against Parents*. New York: Houghton Mifflin, 1998.

[11] Susan Roylance, ed., *The Traditional Family in Peril*. South Jordan, Utah: United Families International, 1996.

[12] Brigitte and Peter L. Berger, *The War Over the Family*. Garden City, New York: Anchor Press/Doubleday, 1983.

[13] Stephen Baskerville, *Taken Into Custody: The War Against Fathers, Marriage, and the Family*. Nashville: Cumberland House, 2007.

[14] Maggie Gallagher, *The Abolition of Marriage*. Washington: Regnery, 1996.

[15] Bryce Christensen, ed., *The Retreat from Marriage*. Lanham, Maryland: University Press of America, 1990.

References

[16] James Q. Wilson, *The Marriage Problem: How Our Culture Has Weakened Families*. New York: Harper Collins, 2002, p. 24.

[17] Douglas Farrow, *Nation of Bastards: Essays on the End of Marriage*. Toronto: BPS Books, 2007.

[18] Dana Mack, *The Assault on Parenthood*. San Francisco: Encounter Books, 1997.

[19] Connie Marshner, *Can Motherhood Survive?* Brentwood, Tennessee: Wolgemuth & Hyatt, 1990.

[20] David Blankenhorn, *Fatherless America*. New York: Basic Books, 1995.

[21] David Popenoe, *Life Without Father*. New York: The Free Press, 1996.

[22] Mary Eberstadt, *Home-Alone America*. New York: Sentinel, 2004.

[23] Christina Hoff Sommers, *The War Against Boys*. New York: Simon & Schuster, 2000.

[24] Allan Carlson and Paul Mero, *The Natural Family: A Manifesto*. Dallas: Spence Publishing, 2007, p. 6.

[25] Abbott, *Ibid.*, p. 4.

[26] James Q. Wilson, "The family values debate", *Commentary* (New York), April 1993.

[27] John Witte, *From Sacrament to Contract: Marriage, Religion and Law in the Western Tradition*. Louisville, Kentucky, 1997, p. 315.

[28] *Ibid*, p. 215.

[29] Robert Nisbet, *The Twilight of Authority*. Oxford University Press, 1975, 1981, p. 260.

[30] Robert Nisbet, *Conservatism*. University of Minnesota Press, 1986, p. 104.

[31] For some excellent general discussions of the many aspects to the family crisis, see Allan Carlson's *Family Questions: Reflections on the American Social Crisis*. New Brunswick, New Jersey: Transaction Books, 1988; and George Gilder, *Men and Marriage*. Gretna, Louisiana: Pelican Publishing, 1986.

[32] See for example the many volumes by Peter Berger on the processes of modernisation and secularism.

[33] See for example, Carl Anderson and William Gribbin, eds., *The Wealth of Families*. Washington, D.C.: The American Family Institute, 1982. Alan Tapper, *The Family in the Welfare State*. Sydney: Allen & Unwin, 1990.

[34] See: Peter Collier and David Horowitz, *Destructive Generation: Second Thoughts about the 60s*. New York: Simon and Schuster, 1989; and Myron Magnet, *The Dream and the Nightmare: The Sixties' Legacy to the Underclass*. New York: William Morrow, 1993.

[35] See: Michael Levin, *Feminism and Freedom*. New Brunswick, New Jersey: Transaction Books, 1987; Nicholas Davidson, *The Failure of Feminism*. Buffalo, New York: Prometheus Books, 1988; Christina Hoff Sommers, *Who Stole Feminism? How Women Have Betrayed Women*. New York: Touchstone Books, 1994; and Kirsten Birkett, *The Essence of Feminism*. Sydney: Matthias Media, 2001.

[36] See: Thomas Schmidt, *Straight & Narrow: Compassion & Clarity in the Homosexuality Debate*. Downers Grove, Illinois: InterVarsity Press, 1995; Jeffrey Satinover, *Homosexuality and the Politics of Truth*. Grand Rapids: Baker Books, 1996; and Stephen Green, *The Sexual Dead-End*. London: Broadview Books, 1992.

[37] See: Maggie Gallagher, *Enemies of Eros: How the Sexual Revolution is Killing Family, Marriage and Sex and What We Can Do About It*. Chicago: Bonus Books, 1989; Patrick Dixon, *The Rising Price of Love: The True Cost of the Sexual Revolution*. London: Hodder & Stoughton, 1995; Tom Minnery, ed., *Pornography: A Human Tragedy*. Wheaton, Illinois: Tyndale House, 1986.

[38] See: Barbara Dafoe Whitehead, *The Divorce Culture*. New York: Alfred A. Knopf, 1997; Judith Wallerstein, Julia Lewis and Sandra Blakeslee, *The Unexpected Legacy of Divorce*. New York: Hyperion, 2000; Barry Maley, *Marriage, Divorce and Family Justice*. Sydney: Centre for

Independent Studies, 1993; and Robert Whelan, ed., *Just a Piece of Paper?: Divorce Reform and the Undermining of Marriage*. London: Institute of Economic Affairs, 1995.

[39] See: David Blankenhorn, *Fatherless America: Confronting Our Most Urgent Social Problem*. New York: Basic Books, 1995.

[40] See: Maggie Gallagher, *The Abolition of Marriage*. Washington: Regnery Publishing, 1996; Bryce Christensen, ed., *The Retreat From Marriage: Causes and Consequences*. New York: University Press of America, 1990.

[41] By "natural family" or "traditional family" I mean in a simple sense, mum, dad and the kids. In a more considered definition, I mean that the natural family comprises any group of people related by blood, marriage or adoption.

[42] Moira Eastman, "Myths of marriage and family", in David Popenoe, Jean Bethke Elshtain, and David Blankenhorn, eds., *Promises to Keep*. Rowman and Littlefield Publishers, 1996, p. 38.

[43] Julie Marcus, "The heritage of the Australian family", a paper delivered on October 12, 1994 to the Charles Sturt University inaugural lecture series.

[44] *Ibid*.

[45] Susan Mitchell, "Let love determine who's part of a clan", *The Australian*, June 5, 2000, p. 13.

[46] Quoted in Anne Crawford, "The Australian nuclear family could be extinct by the end of the century. True", *The Age* (Melbourne), August 7, 2000, *Today*, p. 3.

[47] Kristen Walker, "1950s family values vs human rights: In vitro fertilisation, donor insemination and sexuality in Victoria", *Public Law Review*, v. 11, Dec. 2000, pp. 292-307, at p. 307.

[48] Fiona Stewart, "Beware the back-to-the-kitchen brigade", *The Age* (Melbourne), April 6, 2002, p. 11.

[49] Carle Zimmerman, *Family and Civilization*. New York: Harper and Brothers, 1947.

[50] Peter Berger, *The War Over the Family*. New York: Anchor Press, 1983, p. 87.

[51] Aristotle, *Nicomachean Ethics*, VIII, 12.

[52] Bronislaw Malinowski, *Sex and Repression in Savage Society*. London: Routledge & Kegan Paul, 1927.

[53] Robert Lowie, *Primitive Society*, London, 1929, pp. 59, 63.

[54] George Peter Murdock, *Social Structure*. New York: The Free Press, 1949, pp. 2-3.

[55] Peter Laslett and Richard Wall, eds., *Household and Family in Past Time*. Cambridge University Press, 1972.

[56] *Ibid.*, p. 40.

[57] Peter Laslett, *Family Life and Illicit Love in Earlier Generations*. Cambridge University Press, 1977, p. 13.

[58] Cited in *Cultural Conservatism*. Free Congress Research and Education Foundation, 1987, p. 32.

[59] James Q. Wilson, *The Marriage Problem: How our Culture has Weakened Families*. New York: HarperCollins, 2002, p. 24.

[60] *Ibid.*, p. 66.

[61] Ferdinand Mount, *The Subversive Family*. London: Jonathan Cape, 1982, p. 153.

[62] Michael Levin, *Feminism and Freedom*. New Brunswick, New Jersey: Transaction Books, 1987, pp. 283-284.

[63] Peter Wood, "Sex and consequences", *The American Conservative*, July 28, 2003, pp. 8-12, p. 8.

[64] Pitirim Sorokin, *Social and Cultural Dynamics*. American Book Company, 1957, p. 445.

References

[65] J.D. Unwin, "Monogamy as a condition of social energy", *The Hibbert Journal*, vol. 25, 1927, pp. 662, 663.

[66] Lewis Terman, *Psychological Factors in Marital Happiness*. New York: McGraw-Hill, 1938, p. 1.

[67] Helen Fisher, *Anatomy of Love: The Natural History of Monogamy, Adultery, and Divorce*. New York: W.W. Norton, 1992, p. 65.

[68] Kingsley Davis, "The meaning and significance of marriage in contemporary society", in Kingsley Davis, ed., *Contemporary Marriage: Perspectives on a Changing Institution*. New York: Russell Sage Foundation, 1985, p. 5.

[69] *Ibid*.

[70] *Ibid*., p. 19.

[71] Mount, *Ibid*., p. 49.

[72] Karl Zinsmeister, "Marriage matters", *The American Enterprise*, vol. 7, no. 3, May-June 1996, pp. 4-6, p. 6.

[73] David Murray, "Poor suffering bastards: An anthropologist looks at illegitimacy", *Policy Review*, Spring 1994, p. 9.

[74] James Q. Wilson, *The Moral Sense*. New York: The Free Press, 1993, p. 158.

[75] Wilson, *Marriage Problem*, p. 54.

[76] David Blankenhorn, *The Future of Marriage*. New York: Encounter Books, 2007, pp. 159-160.

[77] Morgan, *op. cit*., p. 152.

[78] Zinsmeister, *Ibid*., p. 6.

[79] Lynne Marie Kohm, "Marriage by design", in Lynn Wardle, et. al., eds., *Marriage and Same-Sex Unions: A Debate*. Westport, Conn.: Praeger, 2003, pp. 81-90, p. 82.

[80] William Duncan, "Imposing the same-sex marriage template on state constitutional law: the implications for marriage, constitutional theory, and democracy", in Lynn Wardle, et. al., eds., *Marriage and Same-Sex Unions: A Debate*. Westport, Conn.: Praeger, 2003, pp. 297-308, p. 301.

[81] Charles Reid, "Marriage in the Western legal tradition: A product of natural law or a creature of the state?", in A. Scott Loveless and Thomas Holman, eds., *The Family in the New Millennium*, vol. 2, *Marriage and Human Dignity*. Westport, Connecticut: Praeger, 2007, pp. 3-20, p. 15.

[82] Jennifer Roback Morse, "Unilateral divorce", in Robert George and Jean Bethke Elshtain, eds., *The Meaning of Marriage*. Dallas: Spence Publishing, 2006, pp. 74-99, pp. 75-76.

[83] John Witte, "The tradition of traditional marriage", in Lynn Wardle, et. al., eds., *Marriage and Same-Sex Unions: A Debate*. Westport, Conn.: Praeger, 2003, pp. 47-59, p. 48.

[84] *Ibid*., p. 57.

[85] C. Owen Lovejoy, "The origin of man", *Science*, 211, No. 4480, 1981, pp. 341-350.

[86] Matt Ridley, *The Origins of Virtue*. London: Penguin Books, 1997, p. 92.

[87] Wood, p. 12.

[88] Malinowski, *Ibid*., p. 213.

[89] Popenoe, *War Over the Family*, p. 208.

[90] Margaret Mead, *Male and Female*, New York: Dell, 1949, 1968, p. 188.

[91] Wilson, *Moral Sense*, p. 249.

[92] David Popenoe, *Life Without Father*. New York: The Free Press, 1996, pp. 3-4.

[93] Bronislaw Malinowski, *Sex, Culture and Myth*. New York: Harcourt, Brace & World, 1962, pp. 62-63.

94. Mead, *Ibid.*, p. 200.
95. Mead, *Ibid.*, p. 168.
96. George Gilder, *Men and Marriage*. Gretna, Louisiana: Pelican Publishing, 1986, p. 39.
97. *Ibid.*
98. David Popenoe, in Katherine Anderson, Don Browning and Brian Boyer, eds., *Marriage: Just a Piece of Paper?* Grand Rapids: Eerdmans, 2002, p. 182.
99. Popenoe, *War Over the Family*, p. 119.
100. Bill Muehlenberg, "The case for marriage", *The Australian Family*, vol. 14, no. 4, December 1993, pp. 3-11.
101. Blankenhorn, *The Future of Marriage*, *Ibid.*, p. 83.
102. Stephen Post, *More Lasting Unions: Christianity, the Family, and Society*. Grand Rapids: Eerdmans, 2000, p. 24.
103. Matt Ridley, *The Red Queen: Sex and the Evolution of Human Nature*. London: Penguin Books, 1994, p. 171.
104. Levin, *Ibid.*, p. 284.
105. Ridley, *The Red Queen*, pp. 203-204.
106. Amitai Etzioni, *The Spirit of Community*. London: Fontana Press, 1983, 1985, p. 59.
107. Karl Zinsmeister, "Villages are lousy at raising pre-school children", *The American Enterprise*, vol. 7, no. 3, May-June 1996, pp. 52-54, p. 54.
108. Sam Kiley, "Uproar over kibbutz sex crime claims", *The Australian*, January 23, 2001, p. 8.
109. Black's Law Dictionary.
110. The Universal Declaration of Human Rights, 1948, Article 16, no. 3.
111. The Universal Declaration of Human Rights, 1948, Article 16, no. 1.
112. Marcus, *Ibid.*
113. Wilson, "Values", *Ibid.*
114. Simon Leys, "Teetering on the brink of barbarity", *The Age* (Melbourne), July 4, 1995.
115. Jonathan Sacks, *The Home We Build Together*. London: Continuum, 2007, p. 213.

Chapter 5. The Importance of Both Fathers and Mothers

1. Warwick Marsh and Bill Muehlenberg, eds., *21 Reasons Why Gender Matters*. Unanderra, NSW: Fatherhood Foundation, 2007.
2. *Ibid*, p. 2.
3. David Popenoe, *War Over the Family*. New Brunswick, NJ: Transaction Publishers, 2005, p. 117.
4. Wade Horn and Tom Sylvester, *Fathers Facts*. Gaithersburg: National Fatherhood Initiative, 2002, p. 15.
5. Armand Nicholi, "The impact of parental absence on childhood development: An overview of the literature." *Journal of Family and Culture*, v. 1, n. 3, Autumn 1985.
6. David Blankenhorn, *Fatherless America*. New York: Basic Books, 1995, p. 1.
7. Wade Horn, "Fathers and welfare reform", *Public Interest*, no. 129, Fall 1997, pp. 38-49, p. 49.

References

8. Bryan Rodgers, "Social and psychological wellbeing of children from divorced families: Australian research findings", *Australian Psychologist*, vol. 31, no. 3, November 1995, pp. 174-182.

9. Daniel Lees, *Going Further with Fathers*. Auckland: Maxim Institute, 2007, p. 3.

10. Bronislaw Malinowksi, *Sex, Culture, and Myth*. New York: Harcourt, Brace & World, 1962, p. 63.

11. U.S. Bureau of the Census, 1991.

12. DeNavas-Walt, C., Proctor, B. D., and Lee, C. H., "Income, poverty, and health insurance coverage in the United States: 2005", *The Current Population Survey*, Vol. 2006, pp. 60-231.

13. Kate Funder, et. al., *Settling Down – Pathways of Parents After Divorce*. Melbourne, Australian Institute of Family Studies, 1993.

14. Bob Birrell and Virginia Rapson, "More single parents equals more poverty", *News Weekly*, October 18, 1997, p. 8.

15. "Divorce shrinks income", *Herald Sun* (Melbourne), April 6, 2005, p. 29.

16. Kenneth Aarskaug Wiik, Renske Keizer, and Trude Lappegard, "Relationship quality in marital and cohabiting unions across Europe", *Journal of Marriage and Family*, June 2012, vol. 74, pp. 389–98.

17. Sara McLanahan and Gary Sandefur, *Growing up with a Single Parent*. Harvard University Press, 1994.

18. Cited in Nicholas Davidson, "Life without father: America's greatest social catastrophe." *Policy Review*, Winter 1990.

19. Erin Pougnet, et. al., "Fathers' influence on children's cognitive and behavioural functioning: A longitudinal study of Canadian families." *Canadian Journal of Behavioural Science*. 2011, vol. 43, no. 3, pp. 173-82.

20. Sotirios Sarantakos, "Children in three contexts", *Children Australia*, vol. 21, no. 3, 1996, pp. 23-31.

21. Caroline Milburn, "Fathers key to success", *The Age* (Melbourne), October 5, 2002, p. 11.

22. Robert Sampson and Byron Groves, "Community structure and crime: Testing social-disorganization theory." *American Journal of Sociology* 94, Jan. 1989.

23. Andy Bloxham, "Children from broken homes 'nine times more likely to commit crimes'", *The Telegraph*, (UK), November 4, 2010.

24. Douglas Smith and Roger Jarjoura, "Social structure and criminal victimization." *Journal of Research in Crime and Delinquency* 25, Feb. 1988.

25. Alan Tapper, "Welfare and juvenile crime" in Mike Nahan and Tony Rutherford, eds., *Reform and Recovery*. Institute of Public Affairs, 1993.

26. Beth Vanfossen et al., "Neighborhood context and the development of aggression in boys and girls", *Journal of Community Psychology,* April 2010, vol. 38. No.3, pp. 329-49.

27. Cited in Bryce Christensen, *When Families Fail ... The Social Costs*. University Press of America, 1991.

28. Cited in Nicholas Davidson, "Life without father: America's greatest social catastrophe." *Policy Review*, Winter 1990.

29. Vanessa Hemovich and William D. Crano, "Family structure and adolescent drug use: An exploration of single-parent families", *Substance Use & Misuse,* December 2009, vol. 44, no. 14, pp. 2099-2113.

30. David Fergusson, et. al., "Parental separation, adolescent psychopathology, and problem behaviors", *Journal of the American Academy of Child and Adolescent Psychiatry* 33, 1944, pp. 1122-1131.

31. Muhammad Hoque and Shanaz Ghuman, "Do parents still matter regarding adolescents' alcohol drinking? Experience from South Africa", *International Journal of Environmental Research and Public Health*. January 2012, vol. 9 no. 1, pp. 110–122.

32. Patricia Draper and Henry Harpending, "Father absence and reproductive strategy: an evolutionary perspective", *Journal of Anthropological Research*, 38(3), 1982, pp. 255-273, p, 258.

33. Irwin Garfinkel and Sara S. McLanahan, *Single Mothers and Their Children: A New American Dilemma*. Washington: Urban Institute, 1986, pp. 30-31.

34. Heather Antecol, Kelly Bedard and Eric Helland, "Does single parenthood increase the probability of teenage promiscuity, drug use, and crime? Evidence from divorce law changes", UC Santa Barbara economics paper, August 2001.

35. Cited in "Early menarche", *Catalyst*, ABC TV, October 2, 2003.

36. Kathleen Kiernan, cited in "The bargain breaks", *The Economist*, December 26, 1992 – January 8, 1993.

37. Cited in Nicholas Davidson, "Life without father: America's greatest social catastrophe." *Policy Review*, Winter 1990.

38. Ibid.

39. Nadia Garnefski and Rene Diekstra, "Adolescents from one parent, stepparent and intact families; emotional problems and suicide attempts", *Journal of Adolescence* 20, 1997, pp. 201-208.

40. Gunilla R. Weitoft et. al., "Mortality, severe morbidity, and injury in children living with single parents in Sweden: a population-based study", *The Lancet*, 9354, January 25, 2003, pp. 289-295.

41. Marcia Carlson, "Family structure, father involvement, and adolescent behavioral outcomes", *Journal of Marriage and Family*, Vol. 68, Number 1, February 2006, pp. 137-154.

42. Amanda M. White and Constance T. Gager, "Idle hands and empty pockets?" *Youth & Society*, 2007, vol. 39, pp.75-111.

43. Carol Nader, "Children with sole parent 'less active'", *The Age* (Melbourne), September 2, 2004, p. 8.

44. Geoff Maslen, "Parent link in obesity problem", *The Age* (Melbourne), September 6, 2011.

45. H. K. Kim et al., "Children's mental health and family functioning in Rhode Island", *Pediatrics* 119 Supplement 1, 2007, pp. S23–28.

46. "The 2012 cost of family breakdown index – £44 billion and counting", Relationships Foundation, February 5, 2012.
URL: www.relationshipsfoundation.org/web/News/News.aspx?News=135

47. Steve Doughty, "Family break-ups 'cost taxpayers £50bn a year'", *Daily Mail* (UK), March 18, 2013.
URL: www.dailymail.co.uk/news/article-2295040/Family-break-ups-cost-taxpayers-50bn-year-foot-subsidised-housing-crime-health-social-care-disrupted-education--cost-rising.html#ixzz2SlyITvhY

48. Bruce Robinson, private research paper by author of *Fathering in the Fast Lane*, Sydney: Finch Publishing, 2001.

49. Kevin Andrews, "The family, marriage and divorce", *The Australian Family* 13(4), December 1992.

50. Caroline Milburn, "Industry told family splits cost $1b a year", *The Age* (Melbourne), August 2, 1990.

51. Tim Pegler, "Homeless link to families", *The Age* (Melbourne), October 29, 1997, p. 9.

References

52 Catherine Malkin and Michael Lamb, "Child maltreatment: a test of sociobiological theory", *Journal of Comparative Family Studies* 25, 1994, pp. 121-130.

53 Wilcox, W. Bradford and Jeffrey Dew, "Protectors or perpetrators? Fathers, mothers, and child abuse and neglect", Center for Marriage and Families, Research Brief No. 7, January 2008, pp. 1, 4.

54 Keikki Sariola and Antti Uetela, "The prevalence and context of incest abuse in Finland", *Child Abuse and Neglect*, vol. 20, no. 9, 1996, pp. 843-850.

55 S. Yampolskaya, P. Greenbaum, and I. Berson, "Profiles of child maltreatment perpetrators and risk for fatal assault: A latent class analysis", *Journal of Family Violence*, 2009, vol. 24, no. 5, pp. 337-348.

56 Michael Pirrie, "Child abuse law alert." *Herald Sun* (Melbourne), August 28, 1993.

57 Australian Institute of Health and Welfare, *Child Protection Australia 2002-03*. Canberra 2004, p. 22.

58 Jeremy Sammut, "Don't mention the M-word", *The Drum*, January 31, 2013.

59 See for example my two research papers, "The Benefits of Marriage" (Melbourne, 2004), and "The Case for the Two-Parent Family" (Melbourne 2004).

60 Wendy Manning and Kathleen Lamb, "Adolescent well-being in cohabiting, married, and single-parent families", *Journal of Marriage and Family*, vol. 65, no. 4, November 2003, pp. the 876-893, at p. 890.

61 Yongmin Sun, "The well-being of adolescents in households with no biological parents", *Journal of Marriage and Family*, vol. 65, no. 4, November 2003, pp. 894-909, at p. 894.

62 *Ibid.*, p. 905.

63 Urie Bronfenbrenner, "Discovering what families do", in David Blankenhorn, Steven Bayme and Jean Bethke Elshtain, eds. *Rebuilding the Nest*, pp. 27-38, p. 34.

64 Rebecca O'Neill, "Experiments in living: The fatherless family", *Civitas* (London), September 2002, p. 14.

65 Stephen Baskerville, *Taken Into Custody: The War Against Fathers, Marriage, and the Family*. Nashville: Cumberland House, 2007.

66 Wade Horn, in Katherine Anderson, Don Browning and Brian Boyer, eds, *Marriage: Just a Piece of Paper?* Grand Rapids: Eerdmans, 2002, p. 295.

67 Steve Biddulph, "A creche can't love them", *Herald Sun* (Melbourne), April 7, 1994.

68 Anne Manne, "Electing a new child", *Quadrant*, January-February 1996, pp. 8-19.

69 National Research Council, *Who Cares for America's Children? Child Care Policies for the 1990s*, cited in Richard Gill, "Day care or parental care?", *The Public Interest* 105, Fall 1991, pp. 3-16.

70 Robert Lee Hotz, "Parental care vital to child development", *The Australian Financial Review*, November 28, 1997, *Review Life*, p. 14.

71 Cited in Hotz, *ibid.*

72 John Bowlby, *Attachment and Loss*. New York: Basic Books, 1969.

73 John Bowlby, *Maternal Care and Mental Health*. New York: Schocken Books, 1950.

74 Selma Fraiberg, *Every Child's Birthright: In Defense of Mothering*. New York: Bantam Books, 1977.

75 Robert Karen, *Becoming Attached*. New York: Warner Books, 1994.

76 Jay Belsky, "The 'effects' of infant day care reconsidered", *Early Childhood Research Quarterly* 3, 1988, pp. 235-272.

77 Jay Belsky and David Eggebeen, "Early and extensive maternal employment and young children's socioemotional development: Children of the national longitudinal survey of youth", *Journal of Marriage and the Family* 53, November 1991, pp. 1083-1110.

78 Ronald Haskins, "Public school aggression among children with varying day-care experience", *Child Development* 56, 1985, pp. 689-703.

79 Mary Ainsworth, et. al., *Patterns of Attachment*. Hillsdale, New Jersey: Erlbaum, 1978.

80 Bowlby, *ibid*.

81 Michael Schwartz, "Do we want government to be our baby-sitter?", in Phyllis Schlafly, ed., *Who Will Rock the Cradle?* Washington: Eagle Forum, 1988, pp. 269-288.

82 Steve Biddulph, in the foreword to Peter Cook, *Mothering Denied: How Our Culture Harms Women, Infants, and Society*. Revised edition, 2009.
URL: www.members.optusnet.com.au/pcook62/090424MDA4.pdf

83 Armand Nicholi, "The fractured family: following it into the future", *Christianity Today*, May 25, 1979, p. 11.

84 Anne Borge and Edward Melhuish, "A longitudinal study of childhood behaviour problems, maternal employment, and day care in a rural Norwegian community", *International Journal of Behavioral Development* 18, 1995, pp. 23-42.

85 Cited in Suzanne Fields, "Heart Start preceded Head Start", *Los Angeles Times*, September 28, 1992.

86 Sasha Baskett, "Working mums study", *Herald Sun* (Melbourne), May 18, 2000, p. 11.

87 Kylie Hanson, "Childcare link to teen gangs", *Herald Sun* (Melbourne), July 17, 1995.

88 Reported in Shankar Vedantam, "Child-care link to aggressive behavior", *The Age* (Melbourne), April 20, 2001, p. 4.

89 Susan Gilbert and Caroline Milburn, "Length of time in care can affect children's anxiety, studies show", *The Age* (Melbourne), July 17, 2003, p. 3.

90 Paula Beauchamp, "Tantrum troubles", *Herald Sun* (Melbourne), October 6, 2003, p. 9.

91 Stephen Lunn, "A year of childcare 'disrupts'", *The Australian*, March 27, 2007, p. 3.

92 Cited in Karl Zinsmeister, "Brave new world: How day-care harms children", *Policy Review*, Spring 1988, pp. 40-48.

93 Brenda Hunter, *Home By Choice*. Portland, Oregon: Multnomah, 1991.

94 Fraiberg, *ibid*.

95 Connie Marshner, *Can Motherhood Survive?* Brentwood, Tennessee: Wolgamuth and Hyatt, 1990.

96 Adapted from this site:
URL: www.cfcidaho.org/why-children-need-male-and-female-parent

97 Kyle D. Pruett, *Fatherneed: Why Father Care is as Essential as Mother Care for Your Child*. New York: The Free Press, 2000, pp. 17-34.

98 "Shuttle diplomacy", *Psychology Today*, July/August 1993, p. 15.

99 As cited in Kyle D. Pruett, *The Nurturing Father*. New York: Warner Books, 1987, p. 49.

100 Scott Coltrane, "Father-child relationships and the status of women: A cross-cultural study", *American Journal of Sociology*, vol. 93, 1988, p. 1088.

101 Barbara Dafoe Whitehead, "Dan Quayle was right", *Atlantic Monthly*, April 1993, p. 19.

Made in the
USA
Lexington, KY